E. W. L. (Edward William Lewis) Davies, Henry Hope Crealocke

Wolf - Hunting and Wild Sport in Lower Brittany

E. W. L. (Edward William Lewis) Davies, Henry Hope Crealocke

Wolf - Hunting and Wild Sport in Lower Brittany

ISBN/EAN: 9783742898715

Manufactured in Europe, USA, Canada, Australia, Japa

Cover: Foto ©ninafisch / pixelio.de

Manufactured and distributed by brebook publishing software (www.brebook.com)

E. W. L. (Edward William Lewis) Davies, Henry Hope Crealocke

Wolf - Hunting and Wild Sport in Lower Brittany

LIST OF ILLUSTRATIONS.

THE DEATH-STRUGGLE . . . . . . FRONTISPIECE.

"A stifled sound of mortal fray, mingled with sob, growling and yells, followed; it was the death-struggle of the gaunt, long-toothed beast, overpowered by many foes."

A RIDE FOR DEAR LIFE . . . . *To face page* 24.

"My old hunting-whip now served me in good stead; . . . . . . I stood up in my stirrups, and with all my force brought the heavy thong down over the head and eyes of the leading wolf."

MARS . . . . *To face page* 49.

"He came to a fixed point, his head erect, his tail level with his back, and his whole attitude worthy of Phidias' chisel."

A SAVAGE RUSH . . . . . . *To face page* 97.

"She again came at me with a savage rush. I had just time . . . . . to spring up and catch the friendly bough overhead; then drawing up my legs, she shot under me."

INTRODUCTION.

THE scene of the following papers, contributed in the first place to "Baily's Magazine," is chiefly confined to the region of Cornouaille, in and around the Black Mountains of Lower Brittany, where the Author resided for two winters, and enjoyed the wild sport obtainable in the surrounding forests.

The main features of the narrative may be relied on; but at the same time he wishes it to be distinctly understood, *in limine*, that, owing to the want of sufficient records kept at the time, he has been compelled to depend in some measure for its production both on memory and fancy, twenty years having elapsed since he paid his last visit to that interesting country.

The *dramatis personæ*, too, do not all bear their real patronymics; and where these have been given, as in the case of M. de St. Prix and others, chiefly old companions of the chase at home and abroad, the Author ventures to hope the liberty he has so taken will be considered a venial one by those gentlemen.

In proof that, as yet, the progress of civilisation has not done much to diminish the *feræ naturæ* of Lower Brittany, so far at least as the Wolf is concerned, General Wm. Eden and his family, who were travelling in Finisterre this last autumn (1874), have kindly informed the Author that they saw, with no little astonishment, five full-grown wolves and two foxes exhibited in a cart and dragged triumphantly through the streets of Quimper, all having been killed at a "*grande chasse*" in that immediate neighbourhood.

This successful bag surpasses even that of the sporting Lord Maire, introduced into a French play some years ago. He enters the stage in red coat and full hunting costume, puts down his gun (an old single-barrel), and exclaims, "*J'ai eu une chasse superbe; j'ai tué mes six renards!*"

This, of course, was an imaginary exploit; but the

foregoing authentic account, given by General Eden, encourages the belief that a good and sufficient stock of rough game may still be found in the Brittany forests, to attract the future hunter and gladden the Louvetier's heart.

WOLF-HUNTING,
AND
WILD SPORT IN BRITTANY.

CHAPTER I.

> "Vive la chasse !
> Elle surpasse
> Tous les plaisirs
> Qui charment nos loisirs."
>
> TELLIER'S *Chansonnier du Chasseur.*

THE hunting record of two winters—one of unusual severity—passed in the Black Mountains of Brittany, among the wolves, boars, and foxes of that forest land, may haply be interesting to many who love wild sport, but scarcely know to what extent it may be enjoyed in a country within so short a distance of our own metropolis, and not even a twenty hours' journey from the Hampshire coast. The rivers of Norway, once teeming with salmon, have been fished bare by Anglo-Saxon rods; while the prairies of the Far West and the ravines of the Rocky Mountains have been ransacked by hunters armed with Lancaster guns and Eley's ammunition; but, if wild sport was the object, a fair share

B

of it might certainly be obtained at a far less cost of time, trouble, and expense among the rough game of Lower Brittany.

Before entering, however, into details of the chasse, let me endeavour to present the reader with a sketch of Carhaix and the surrounding district, not a cover of which, within a certain distance of the town, but holds a fox, a wolf, or a tusky boar; and in some of them, such as those of Laz, Kœnig, and Kilvern, each and all of those beasts, besides deer and smaller game, may always be found. And yet this country, so near home, is far less known by Englishmen than the jungles of Oudh or the wilds of Namaqua Land.

Within two leagues of the trackless forests which cover the Black Mountains of Brittany, and at a point where the confines of the three departments of Morbihan, Côtes-du-Nord, and Finisterre are defined, stands the old Celtic city of Carhaix. A noble cathedral of Gothic architecture, the work of English hands in the sixteeth century, crowns the summit of the hill; two hospices, the one devoted to the spiritual, the other to the material wants of the public, especially those of invalid soldiers, occupy a conspicuous position with their lofty and whitewashed walls; and, like other Breton towns, it has its Hôtel de Ville, Gendarmerie, and a respectable French hôtel. A handsome bronze statue, the *chef d'œuvre* of Marochetti, is erected in the Champ de Bataille, in honour of La Tour d'Auvergne, the premier grenadier of France, and a native of Carhaix, who died gallantly on the battlefield of Oberhausen in the year 1800. But the traveller must go farther back than the present century to appreciate the merits of Carhaix. Surrounded by woods, and, till lately, approached only by a precipitous and rugged route, it stands on a high and bold eminence overlooking the country far and wide, and by its isolation seems to have bidden a successful defiance to the inroads of commerce and civilisation. It is essentially a town of past ages: just what it might have been, and probably was, fourteen hundred years ago, when the Romans expelled our Celto-Breton ancestors at the point of the sword, and maintained in its stronghold the head-quarters of their army.

The inhabitants of the more accessible towns of Brittany imagine Carhaix and its environs to be a region of wolves and savages, wild, fierce, and irreclaimable; but, after a long and agreeable sojourn, passed in daily association with the peasantry, I discovered nothing in them to warrant such a fancy; but found them, on the other hand, inoffensive, indolent, and scrupulously honest, although in a state of squalor and poverty that beggars description. It is a fact that the wandering Jew, who pervades all climates, seeks no resting-place here; here, poverty is everywhere too apparent, and scares him from the threshold with its threadbare mien; the waters of the Pactolus are wanting here to tempt his thirsting soul; and he turns aside from granite rocks and sterile wastes, from a soil that blooms with the bracken, the broom, and the furze, from a people that are literally clad in sackcloth and ashes, to wander on in search of other lands more productive and less poverty-stricken, and consequently more congenial to his tastes and desires than old Armorica.

It is equally remarkable that gipsies are totally unknown in this district; the educated Bretons alone, who call them Bohemians, being aware of their Ishmaelitish existence in other countries. Their absence may be fairly attributed to one of two causes: either to the persecution they have long endured from an ordonnance of the States of Orleans, which enjoined that "all impostors and vagabonds, styled Bohemians, should quit the kingdom under pain of the galleys;" or, more probably, I think, to the impossibility of defending their unhoused beasts from the attacks of wolves, which, sometimes in pairs and sometimes in packs, according to the severity of the weather, are a scourge to the whole country. Is it a wonder, then, that between gendarmes by day and wolves by night the gipsy shuns the danger? Our own laws are not favourable to the vagrants, but they find means to evade them in England, and would doubtless do so in Finisterre, if the gaunt wolves, hungry and devastating, and coming as they do in the gloom and darkness of night, did not strike terror to their souls.

For many a league round the city of Carhaix the poorer peasants occupy but one wretched cabin in company, if they are lucky enough to have them, with their pig and cow. A child of the tender age of five or six years is deemed, and is, I am convinced, a sufficient protection to the flock by day; for it was by no means an uncommon thing for me, in my hunting excursions, suddenly to come upon a mere infant in charge of a little black sheep or dwarf cow, in the deepest recesses of a forest or wild broom field, and at the next moment to start and reassure myself on seeing the fresh and unmistakable print of a huge wolf's foot impressed on the clay before me. So long as daylight lasts the child is safe, and so is the flock, for the cowardly villain will not venture to approach them; but the moment the sun sets he skulks from his lair, and at once becomes a daring and destructive enemy; the very houses of the peasantry are not then secure from his attack.

The family of a peasant, consisting of his wife and frequently several children, live huddled together in one dark cabin in a state of indescribable filth and misery. The cabin is built with mud or stone and thatched with broom; a small aperture is left in the upper part of the door to admit air and light; while, the fire being kindled, the smoke oozes out as it can through all parts of the roof, and the whole cabin resembles at a distance a huge charcoal heap in an active state of combustion. In nooks of the wall, as high up as the building will admit, rude berths are constructed, which serve the purpose of beds, the means of access to which, from their lofty position and square contracted entrance, rather resemble the contrivance of a jackdaw's brain than that of a human being. Still, the high perch and the narrow aperture have their advantages, though at first sight the stranger would be puzzled to know how; but let him cast his eye upon the floor of the house, and he will see that the pig, the black sheep, and the little black cow wallow in a mire of Augean filth, if not of magnitude. On inquiry, too, he will find that, ever and anon, the wolf not only knocks at the door, but walks in; that, if he cannot gain admittance by fair means he will by foul; he scratches a hole in the broom roof, and, bailiff-like, descends upon his victims. This is no imaginary danger; the thing has occurred over and over again to the Sabôttiers of Dualt and Huel-goed, vast forests in the neighbourhood of Carhaix. The *garde-du-forêt* of the former, a fine intelligent Breton, pointed out to me a spot in which he said a "wolf tragedy" had occurred within the last two years.

Before, however, I narrate the story, which I will endeavour to do in the garde's own words, I will presume on the reader's indulgence, and describe as concisely as I can the Forest of Dualt. As its name implies in the Breton and Welsh language "black rock," it is, indeed, one pile of granite tors, far wilder and more imposing than those of Dartmoor, rising one above the other in endless variety; huge solitary slabs standing, like giants on guard, in an upright and menacing attitude; while others form cromlechs and dolmens, under which a she-wolf might lay up her young, or a Druid deposit the last relics of his race. As we sat together on a block of sparkling granite, the garde, François Postollec, called my attention to a Sabôttier's cabin built upon the edge of a clump of beech-trees, and surrounded, like Robinson Crusoe's hut, with a strong stake fence.

"Ah, well, poor Antoine needs those barriers," said he, "for the wolves have robbed him already, and they'll rob him again this winter, I fear, in spite of his palisade."

"What!" cried I, "are the wolves so daring as to attack a man's dwelling-place?"

"Attack it!" said he; "a hungry wolf, like a wicked man, has no conscience when the night favours him. It was only last January that they carried off or killed every live animal he possessed. A heavy snow-storm had fallen on the mountains, and for several nights in succession a pack of five or six wolves kept sentry at Antoine's hut, pacing round it, and uttering the most dismal howls. Antoine and his wife, however, were determined to save their little stock; they lighted a good fire, and sat up by turns to keep it burning; but at length, on a dark and tempestuous night, when the wind was whistling and the hail beating against their door, exhausted by watching, they both dropped asleep, and the wood fire soon became extinguished. At that instant a desperate rush was heard in the roof; and before Antoine could arm himself with a pike, five gaunt wolves dashed in upon the floor one after the other, and, seizing his three sheep, tore and devoured them in his presence. A little dog, too, which they valued above all, was snapped up and swallowed at a gulp. Antoine is a brave man, but his heart beat audibly as, from his bed, he stretched out his hands to strike a light; the flint and steel were true, the resin-candle was quickly ignited, and, almost as rapidly as they had entered, the villains sprung over an old armoire, and disappeared through the roof. They come and go like a hurricane," added he, "and, like it, leave desolation behind them."

Wolves in England are a mere tradition of the Heptarchy; but in this mountain tract of Brittany they still abound; nor, until the country is reclaimed from its present condition of heath and woods, will it be possible to dislodge them from the fastnesses in which they now skulk and which they claim as their own. But the beast of the present day is a cowardly one, compared with that of former times. During the War of the League, a period of desolation and brigandage throughout that region, we are told by the old chronicler, in fearfully vivid language, that the wolves got the upper hand of men, and absolutely hunted them into the very towns. The belief in the Loup-garou or demon-wolf is still a prevailing superstition among the Breton peasantry; and many a tale is told over their wood embers of the human suffering and bloodshed caused by that ferocious brute. Times, however, have changed for the better in that respect. Man, instead of being hunted himself, now hunts the wolf in that country with considerable success. His grand, old-fashioned, wire-haired hounds, trained to the scent, rouse him from his lair; and the hunter, well-mounted and armed with a carbine or smooth-bore at his saddle-bow, heads him at down-wind points of the chase, and drops him with a ball.

It is only during a long-continued season of snow that the wolf, pinched by hunger, hardens his heart, and becomes at once both a daring and destructive brute. At such a time it has been found necessary to light fires nightly at all the road entrances into Carhaix, Callac, Gourin, Rostrenan, and other small towns in that vicinity, in order to save the cattle and even the dogs from the rapacity of the hungry wolves. Two or three wolves will tear and eat up the latter, no matter of what size, as rapidly as a pack of foxhounds will dispatch a wild fox.

It was a wet, stormy morning in November, an hour at least before daybreak, when the Count de St. Prix rung out a blast on his horn in the streets of Carhaix that made the window-frames of the old town rattle in their sockets; and scarcely had the echoes of its last-prolonged note died on the ear, when a wild response from other horns in the distance repeated the glad summons, and invited all, who were disposed to come, away to the chase. St. Prix, on whom the rulers of France had long conferred the honourable office of Louvetier or wolf-hunter for Lower Brittany —in this case the right man in the right place—had arrived at the Hotel La Tour d'Auvergne on the previous night; and, as I had been introduced to him by my old friend the Baron de

Keryfan, we soon fraternized together as fellow-worshippers of Diana—men of kindred feeling and like sympathy.

From him I gleaned that a wolf infesting the covers of Kergloff had of late become unusually destructive to the poor peasant's cattle, and had, even in daylight, snatched up many a country cur before the very face of its owner. Consequently such strong representations had been made by the Mayor of the Commune to him, as Louvetier, that, notwithstanding his experience told him at once it was a she-wolf, with a litter hard by, he deemed it expedient to bring his hounds to the spot, and make a show at least of hunting, and, if possible, of driving the destructive beast from that district. To kill her, however, he had no intention; indeed, his solicitude for a she-wolf is quite equal, if it does not surpass, that of the most zealous fox-preserver, who, when he sees hounds running short in April, is on tenter-hooks for the safety of what he has reason to believe is a little vixen.

But in this district St. Prix need not be so particular; the wolves preserve themselves, and will continue to do so without man's favour, so long as the vast granite tors and interminable forests that now bristle over the backbone of Brittany can give them so wide a range and so safe a retreat.

I had just finished my last touch of chin-tonsure, when Keryfan, fully equipped for the chase, that is to say, picturesquely attired in a goat-skin jacket, leggings of the same, and a huge French horn slung over his back, burst into my room, chanting a hunting song, and looking from head to foot far more like Robinson Crusoe than a Breton gentleman.

"Ah," said he, taunting me good-humouredly, "you will not see the rendezvous this day if you sacrifice so much time to the Graces."

"Cleanliness is next to godliness," I remonstrated; "let me finish my wash, and I will be with you in ten minutes. In the meantime, order a cup of coffee for me, do; and ask Marseillier to fill my holsters with bread, brandy, and cigars."

"I've stock enough for a dozen in mine," said Keryfan, who, however wild in his passion for the chase, never neglected the commissariat department either for himself or friends.

Another long twang from St. Prix's horn under my bed-room window, and the impatient snort of his famous old Irish mare, brought my toilet somewhat abruptly to a close; and descending to the porte-cochère, where three or four mounted chasseurs had assembled, I was not a little shocked to find that I had been detaining the whole party, St. Prix deeming it his duty, as a matter of etiquette, to wait for a stranger especially invited, and whom he intended himself to conduct to the rendezvous.

The hounds had been sent on the night before to M. Trevenec's château, standing on the outskirts of Kergloff; so we picked along merrily to the meet, Keryfan and St. Prix incessantly smoking cigars, which, in spite of a strong wind and heavy rain, they kept alight by common lucifer matches adroitly ignited on their saddle-bows, and conveyed in the hollow of one hand to the fragrant weed—a feat of legerdemain that, at the pace we were going, Woudin himself would have been puzzled to execute.

The ceremonious greeting, the bowing, the hat-lifting, and even the cheek salutation that ensued between my companions and the Breton gentlemen already assembled at the cover side, was a sight I shall never forget—a scene it was worthy of Louis Quatorze's court: I thought it would never end. Getting alongside of Keryfan soon afterwards, I ventured, knowing my man full well, to chaff him on the subject.

"You must not think I envy you, Keryfan, the hug you received from that weather-beaten old gentleman. Why, he's as wiry as a Scotch terrier, and hirsute as Esau himself."

"C'est mon oncle, Frank," he responded, with perfect good-humour, by way of explanation.

But I firmly believe he was no more his uncle than his aunt—not he. There was a great deal too much ceremony between them for so near a relationship.

Sixteen couple of hounds, wire-haired, but not rough, standing four or five-and-twenty inches high, with plenty of bone for their bulk, were held in couples on a plot of greensward hard by; while two keen-eyed peasants, acting as piqueurs, had each a single hound in a long leash—the limiers of the chase. One of the men, clad from head to foot in a brown goat-skin suit, gave a cheering account of the game before us.

"I have tracked in," he said, "at least three, if not four, full-grown wolves; one, by his long claws, is an old wolf; the rest I think are cubs."

"And I," said the other, "have gone the circuit of Kergloff twice, and will swear not a wolf has left the cover this day."

"Bravo!" cried St. Prix; "let go the limiers, and, Keryfan, do you and your friend get down-wind with all speed; and, hark ye, if the old wolf breaks, let her go, and stop the hounds, or she'll carry them to Llanderneau. We have a good day's work before us, that's certain."

In one minute the limiers were throwing their tongues vigorously and freely; and, at a signal from St. Prix's horn, the whole pack were at once uncoupled and clapped into cover. I have heard "Jack Russell's" hounds find their fox in the rocky depths of Hawkridge Wood; and Mr. Trelawny's pack view theirs among the cliffs of Skerraton, waking a thousand echoes with their frantic tongues; but never have I listened to such a crash as that which now greeted my ears, and sent the blood whizzing through my veins. Fancy sixteen couple of deep-mouthed hounds uniting in one grand peal of music, and sending forth such a salvo that, if the oaks of the forest were "listening oaks," as Horace describes them,* they must have quivered to their heart's core. Then the fanfare of horns might have been heard in High Olympus, and must have struck mortal terror into every wolf within a league's distance. A pair of ravens made themselves scarce at once; while the green wood-peckers, the magpies, and the jays positively screeched with fear. It was the din of war— a sylvan war, to be sure, but a bloody one for the wolves, as the sequel will soon show.

For one hour the hounds ran as if glued to their game; and ever and anon a roebuck, on the wings of terror, bounded into the open, less dreading the face of man than the storm in its rear; but as yet not a wolf had appeared beyond the cover's edge. Talk of a fox's craftiness, I believe a wolf to be infinitely more wary, more wily, and more ingenious than the other in the presence of danger. Here were sixteen couple of high-couraged hounds tearing the earth up in pursuit of a wolf, and failing to force him beyond the precincts of his cover, the first line of his defence.

At length away breaks the old one—she could stand it no longer—and happily at a point where Keryfan was posted; so he dropped his rifle, took off his hunting cap, and gave the old jade a rattling view holloa as she lopped speedily forward into the open plain. St. Prix, had he the power, would have knighted him on the spot. Then the hounds were turned, and, almost in their first swing, they hit on the line of another wolf that had evidently accompanied its dam to the very edge of the cover, but dared not break away. Again, they were hard at him; and soon it became my turn to catch a view of the gaunt beast. I had ridden about a hundred yards into the cover, and, posting myself in an open space under a huge beech-tree, I listened with breathless delight to the cry, which I knew, from the hounds' tongues being turned towards me, was getting nearer and nearer every

---

* "Auritas quercus;" elegantly translated by Conington as "the listening oaks."

moment. I could hear my heart beat as the dry wood cracked under the tread of the brute, now within twenty yards of my horse's head; but whether he caught a glimpse of me, or merely from habit avoided the open space, he turned abruptly to the left, and, at that instant, the balle-mariée of a peasant crashed through both shoulders, and he rolled over like a rabbit head-foremost into the scrub.

Then there was a grand "mort" sounded by the horns, in which the hounds, after worrying the wolf, joined in wild strain their pæans of triumph over the fallen foe. The brute was a full-grown one; and nothing surprised me more than the disproportion between him and the biggest hound in point of bone and power; the arm just below the elbow was nearly double the size of the other, while his canine teeth, when extracted, measured more than two inches in length, and were so strong and keen that a horse would stand but a poor chance when seized in the throat by such weapons.

CHAPTER II.

THE worry was soon over; and then commenced the business of securing the wolf across a horse's back and despatching him to the Mayor of the Commune, who keeps a kind of death-register, and by his certificate enables the Louvetier to draw the Government reward—thirty francs for a male, and fifty for a she-wolf: happily, as St. Prix whispered to me, in this case it was the smaller sum. But it was no trifling task compelling the horse, though nothing better than a half-starved mountain pony, to submit to the burden; the dread of his natural enemy, though lying inanimate at his feet, no power could overcome. He seemed frantic with fear, snorted, plunged, kicked, and finally threw himself on the ground. In that position half-a-dozen Bretons were on him at once; and, strapping the gaunt beast athwart his back, they soon kicked him on his legs again; he then walked quietly off with the odious burden.

It was now just twelve o'clock; "plenty of time," as St. Prix said, "to kill another wolf." His blood was up for sport; and I could see by the way he scrutinised the condition of his hounds that he was quite satisfied they at least were ready for any further work they might be called upon to do. So he gave the word, "To the Monument of Botderû." This, I soon found, was the favourite rendezvous, the prime meet of the wolf-hunters in the Forest of Conveau, a wild and desolate spot, far removed from human habitation, and at the far end of the chain of covers in which we had killed our wolf. The country, so far as the eye could reach, was one vast forest of rock, scrub, and heather; the last waist-deep, and affording a rare cover for the wolves, foxes, and deer that frequent it.

A narrow path, hollowed out by the sabots of the charcoal-burners, soon brought us to the appointed spot; and here a handsome granite pillar, surmounted by a cross and tastefully enclosed by a belt of planted oak and Austrian pine, the only indication of man's hand for miles around, decorated the lonely scene. The monument had been erected to the memory of a famous chasseur, and bore on one of its four sides the following inscription :

"A la Memoire du Comte du Botderû, Pair de France,
le Nimrod de nos Forêts."

On the opposite side was inscribed, "Rendezvous de Chasse," while the two other corresponding tablets of the square monument bore the shields and arms of the Botderû family.

St. Prix, who knows the habits of a wolf as well as the Duke of Beaufort and Henry Deacon know those of a fox—and without this knowledge the hope of pursuing the wild animal with success is ever a vain one—had rightly conjectured that, if there were more wolves than one in company with the old beast, they would at once be scared from the quarter in which they were roused and would travel in an opposite direction, to the extreme end of the chain of covers. So, lifting his hounds quietly to the highest point of the ridge, he clapped them into cover, and with a wave of the hand and a stirring cheer every hound dashed from his horse's heels into the heart of the woodland range.

When old Will Butler, formerly the famous huntsman of the Badsworth pack, wanted blood for his puppies in the cub-hunting season, and this without over-working and thereby damping their ardour, he was wont to find his litter at break of day; and, after a short scurry, long enough to scatter the cubs and set them "a-travelling," he blew his horn at the first lull and stopped his hounds. He then pottered about for an hour or more in the green pastures, as if he were looking for mushrooms, but quietly eating his frugal breakfast as he gossipped about his "entry."

"You see, sir," he would say, "those cubs have been a-going hard ever since we moved them, but they won't leave the cover; and when we fresh find them at t'other side they will be more than half-beat, and we all the better for our rest."

These tactics were almost invariably successful; Will killed his cub without over-straining his puppies, and often a brace of cubs before the dew was off the grass.

This was precisely St. Prix's move on the present occasion; five minutes had certainly not elapsed before the hounds were once more in full chase, the cry from the rocks above bursting on the ear like a peal of heavy bells from a church tower. Again St. Prix's horn sounded the signal "La vue;" and instantly afterwards, "Les animaux en compagnie;" by which we all knew a brace of wolves were on foot together. But they did not long remain together; the hounds were so hard at them that two lines of scent was the speedy result. The pack, as it happened, were pretty evenly divided, and although one detachment held to the ridge and long heather above, and the other cracked away through the deep cover below, both maintained a parallel course for a distance of nearly five miles, going straight back again for the cover in which the wolves were first found.

So good was the pace, too, that the best-mounted chasseurs utterly failed to head the chase and get a glimpse at the wolves as they crossed the few open glades that intervened between the covers; all of which were as well known to Keryfan and others as the avenues of the Bois de Boulogne. St. Prix alone carried no fusil; his weapon, a long old-fashioned couteau-de-chasse, hung in a leather scabbard over his left hip; a reserve he had often found useful in close quarters with stag and boar at bay, and which now neither impeded his movements nor induced him to quit his place in the management of his hounds.

Crack, crack! went a roaring smooth-bore not a hundred yards in front, but below me in the cover; and at the same time the heavy slugs from a braconnier's piece came whistling through the air, cutting the bushes right and left within a yard or two of my horse's head, but luckily missing both of us; he had killed the wolf, however, and the music of one pack ceased at once. They were close upon their game, and would probably have pulled it down in a few minutes if the braconnier had not interfered. It was a fine full-grown young wolf; but I could see St. Prix was not a little disconcerted at the termination of its existence by the peasant's gun. He had reckoned with good reason on fairly running into him, and wished especially to show me that his powerful hounds, unaided by the fusil, were of themselves able to accomplish the feat.

But St. Prix's vexation was transient as a passing cloud: the other pack had turned when the double shot was fired by the braconnier, and were, as my dear old friend "Jack Russell" would say, swearing hard words at the villain before them. In less than five minutes St. Prix had thrown in at their head the seven or eight couple that followed his horse, and again the old forest rung with the grand music of the united pack.

Short turns, indicative of short wind, speedily followed, and as the cover consisted chiefly of thick, matted underwood, the hounds had it all to themselves, without a chance of losing their laurels by an untoward shot. Suddenly the cry ceased; and a stifled sound of mortal fray, mingled with sob, growling, and yells, followed; it was the death-struggle of the gaunt, long-toothed beast, overpowered by many foes St. Prix's delight was unbounded as two piqueurs, taking the wolf by the hind legs, dragged him into an open space; no mean effort of strength, by-the-bye, inasmuch as two couple of hounds, at least, were hanging on to the wolf's throat with the grip of a blacksmith's vice.

A finer woodland run and a more satisfactory finish it would be difficult to conceive; the hounds did their work nobly, and St. Prix handled them as if he had made, as he has done, the habits of the wolf and the instinct of the hound the study of his life. Congratulations poured in upon him thickly; and well might he be proud of the day's success. But, alas! there was another side to the happy picture on which he was feasting his soul: two or three of his leading hounds had been seriously injured in the last struggle; one, bitten across the loins, trailed his hind legs after him, a paralyzed and piteous object to behold; the other limped along with her fore-leg broken at the elbow; the wolf's teeth had crushed the bone, as a boy's would an Oliver biscuit; the shattered bits absolutely rattled as the poor hound hobbled forward to lick her master's hand and claim the sympathy she so well deserved.

"Ah, Ravisante," he said, despondingly, "is this thy sad fate at last? Far rather would I have lost any hound in my pack than thee, my old companion and true ally."

It is no figure of speech to say that St. Prix's eyes were brimming with tears as he turned away from the painful sight. Keryfan then stepped forward, and conferring with him a minute or so, a piqueur was ordered to lead away gently the two disabled hounds; and, before the last wolf was secured to the back of the terrified horse, destined to bear him to the Mairie, two distant shots were heard in the cover below—the death-boom of those gallant hounds.

It has been already remarked that these hounds were big, powerful animals, wire-haired, deep-tongued, carrying a grand head, and supported by plenty of bone; yet, with these old-fashioned characteristics, and the total absence of any fox-hound blood in their veins, I don't think I ever saw a harder-driving lot in chase in my life. Above all, when, as will always happen in cover-runs, a portion of the pack was ever and anon thrown out, it was delightful to witness the struggle among them to fresh-catch the scent, and the freedom from all *towling* propensity among the tail hounds.

Shall I be regarded as a Goth and a Vandal, if, in spite of the worship paid to kennel-pedigree, long as that of "Bourbon or Nassau," I venture to believe that the present gaudy English foxhound would be **vastly** improved for all hunting purposes, and that too without **extinguishing** one spark of his dash and ardour, if his **mixed blood** were again refreshed by the old standard-hound blood, the *sang pur* of Lower Brittany? I say "mixed blood," because unquestionably the present foxhound is the result of a cross originally contrived between the smooth terrier and the old-fashioned hound of this land in former days.

Were any master independent enough to resort to this ancient stock-hound and invigorate his pack with the original, genuine hound blood, it is the conviction of many experienced houndsmen that better runs in all weathers would be obtained by such mettle. We should then once more have hounds similar in fashion to the **old Beaufort** badger-pies, carrying high crowns and feathered sterns—noble **hounds, that,** no matter how wild the weather, would hunt a **fox to** death inevitable so long as he stood above ground **before them;** or, if the scent served, would kill him in an **hour under any** circumstances. There are no such hounds in England **now as** there were in the time of the sixth Duke. Even their colour—that **long-**surviving **relic of the old type**—is all but lost—bred out and banished **by the black and tan, the** more fashionable hue of modern **days.**

But, as "every dog will **have** his day"—even Queen Elizabeth's pugs being again reproduced, and Dandie Dinmonts *réchauffée'd* in every form save that of the true Davidson—we may yet live to see the present gaudy hound renewed and improved by the pure blood of some original, better-nosed, and less flashy race. That more real sport, and a far finer display of hound's work,

"On dusty road or tainted green,"

would be the sure result of such a revival, is the opinion, I repeat, of many who, after a life of experience with hounds, have given their judgment on this subject.

"Three wolves in one day; and the old dam driven into the Forest of Coedmawr," said Keryfan, exultingly, to me. "A slaughter that would have satisfied Edgar; but one that, if I mistake not, St. Prix would be sorry to indulge in too often."

"That I should quite expect," I replied. "Your country may abound with wolves; but a too frequent recurrence of such a day would doubtless soon thin it, and many a cover would be drawn blank before the end of the season."

"True enough," said St. Prix, joining in the conversation. "The forests are so extensive, and the wolf so suspicious of danger, so shifty, and so erratic in his habits, especially after this month, that an old one found to-day in Finisterre would to-morrow be killing his mutton on the banks of the Loire; so we need have a good head of game, or our sport would soon wane in this wild country. It is now exactly five years ago since we last killed three wolves on the same day; and, oddly enough, we then lost a valuable hound called "Warrior," which was so mutilated in the fray that we were compelled to destroy him on the spot. He was a broken-haired Welsh hound, given me by an English gentleman, and was the only exotic I ever owned that took as readily as our own native hounds do to the scent of the wolf and the wild boar. A better hound never entered a cover."

Then, knowing St. Prix to be a thorough houndsman, I

inquired what foreign hounds he had tried in wolf-hunting, and what age they were when he had made the experiment.

"Your English foxhounds," he replied, "young drafts of which I obtained from some of your best kennels; but, admirably suited as they may be for the style of work required from them in a comparatively open country like yours, they don't suit Brittany. In the first place, they don't take to the scent as if the wolf was their natural prey; and, in the next, they want more tongue to let us know where they are in these interminable forests. Here we have no avenues, like those of St. Germain or Fontainebleau—no royal road to hounds in chase; so, with an old wolf that will run straight on end for fifteen or twenty leagues, holding to strong cover so long as he can find it, your chance of living with hounds would be a very poor one if you had not plenty of music to indicate the line. Again, young foxhounds are so given to riot that the difficulty of getting at them with a whip in our deep covers is all but insuperable; and, consequently, more tractable and less wilful hounds suit our purpose far better."

These, I owned, were indisputable reasons for the preference; and as St. Prix is justly proud of his own grand hounds, there is little fear that, Legitimist as he is, he will ever consent to mix the hybrid blood of our English foxhound with that of his own pure and genuine race.

During the past night, and occasionally throughout the day, heavy rain had been falling on the eastern ridge of the Black Mountains; and the brooks, as we crossed them on our homeward route, had swollen from mere rivulets into fierce and dangerous torrents. The hounds, in many cases, were swept headlong before them, and after a cruel buffeting managed to land some fifty or sixty yards below the ford at which they endeavoured to cross, and where the horses were just able to hold their own and scramble through. At length we arrived at a meadow completely inundated by a broad stream, that foamed and tossed through the middle of it like the tail of a mill-race; the sheet of water, as it filled the valley from the skirts of one wood to the other, was at least a hundred yards wide, and stretched away for miles, as far as the eye could reach, to the westward. One strong plank, resting upon trestles high reared above the flood, was the sole structure by which foot-passengers were enabled to cross from one side to the other; and in doing this they had to wade knee-deep across the meadows ere they reached the bridge. But how on earth were the horses, beaten and jaded as they were by a long day's work, to meet the difficulty? The bridge, if they could have travelled on it, was inaccessible to them, from the rude ladder by which it was mounted, and the stream far too violent for any rider to keep his seat and steer his horse in safety to the other side. St. Prix, however, was fully prepared for the emergency, and shouting to a piqueur, he demanded a rope, which, to the length of eight or ten fathoms, that official speedily procured from a peasant's hut close by—a coil reserved there for this very purpose.

The bridle being removed from his own mare, and one end of the rope secured as a halter to her head, he mounted the bridge, and the sensible, well-schooled animal feeling her way into the flood, he guided her across with as much ease as a skilful fisherman would have guided a salmon to a shelving bank, and there he landed her in safety. In like manner some ten or a dozen horses were thus handled; and by nightfall we reached Carhaix and the Hotel La Tour d'Auvergne without further adventure.

CHAPTER III.

The old town of Carhaix kept wild wassail that night: the three wolves, mounted aloft on the same miserable beasts that had borne them so unwillingly from the battle-field, were paraded in triumph through its crowded streets; nor did Caractacus of yore, led by the conquering legions of Claudius through the city of Rome, inspire the inhabitants with greater joy than was felt by the primitive people of Carhaix at the sight of their fallen foe. Men, women, and children turned out *en masse* to catch a view of the gaunt brutes, the progenitors of which had kept them from youth to old age in a perpetual state of alarm and terror, and, in spite of every precaution, had throttled their horses, devoured their sheep, and even snatched up their favourite dogs before their very eyes! No wonder the old town rang with applause at the noble conquest achieved by St. Prix; no wonder they greeted him with *vivas* as a conqueror returning from a victory, in which every soul of that city was so deeply interested!

The chief medical man of the town, M. Bernard, a good sportsman and a most intelligent man, who had accompanied the French army in its expedition against the Kabyles, and had slain the lion and the panther in their native wilds, confessed to me that he had often been in far greater danger among wolves than in the fiercest fights with those more powerful animals. "The latter," he said, "you encounter single-handed; but an old wolf, with his family at his back, brings fearful odds against a horse and his rider. If beset at any time, as I have frequently been when on a professional visit to some poor peasant's cottage in the heart of the forests, don't forget that your best weapon is a box of lucifer matches: these, when ignited on your saddle-bow, will scatter them at every flash like dust before the wind. I can remember, some four winters ago, I was roused at midnight, in bitter weather, to give immediate attendance to a peasant's wife living in the forest of Huel-goed: the case was an urgent one, and delay would have been fatal; so in ten minutes I was dressed, mounted, and off to the poor sufferer's aid.

"I had scarcely ridden half a league from the town, before I became aware, by the snorting of my mare, that a wolf was paying rather more attention to both of us than the mare at least seemed to think agreeable. One wolf, however, did not disturb me; for, as yet, but one had shown himself, springing ever and anon on the hedge-bank within six feet of my head, and instantly disappearing behind the fence as I cracked a fusee on my saddle-bow. I spurred my mare into a quicker canter, and hoped by the pace to choke off the pursuer; but, so far from this being the case, I soon found, as we sped by a broad gap in the fence, that not only was he holding his own, head and head with the mare, but that four other wolves were close on his quarters, joining hard in the chase. In another second two of the brutes again bounded on the hedge-bank; and, growing bolder as the chase grew hotter, kept stride and stride with us so closely that I could absolutely smell the breath of the brutes as it tainted the night air. The Brittany lanes, as you well know, are simply tunnels hollowed out of the land, and flanked on either side by high, broad banks, from the top of which the wolves with ravenous eyes were now looking down upon us, measuring my strength and the mare's probable endurance. Had she fallen or even stumbled in her gait, the pack would have been on us with one bound; but, luckily, the little mare was safe as Notre Dame; and I took care to keep the lucifers going, flashing them in their faces, and frightening the skulking brutes, ever as I did so, into the adjoining field.

"For two long leagues," continued the doctor, "did we travel on in this perilous fashion; till at length I began to fear the mare would drop from exhaustion. She had been going, from the first, fetlock-deep in clay, and was now so terrified by the wolves that any unusual impediment would, I felt sure, bring her headlong to the ground. My lucifers, too, were running short; and as I had a good half-league farther to ride, I economised my stock by only flashing single matches, and that, too, when more than one wolf traversed the bank in such dangerous proximity. My old hunting-whip now served me in good stead: hitherto I had carried it between my thigh and the saddle, but drawing it forth, I stood up in my stirrups, and with all my force brought the heavy thong down over the head and eyes of the leading wolf. The success of this manœuvre was instantaneous; not another wolf dared show again till I reached in safety the peasant's hut, into which I rode the little mare with a thankful heart. No fox ever gained his earth more opportunely, for another ten minutes must have been fatal at least to the mare.

"The cowardly brutes, however, though baffled, were not beaten. There they still were, watching the hut and prowling around it with dismal yells, denoting their disappointment. So I deemed it prudent to carry a mass of burning embers just outside the door and to feed that until daybreak; and this alone, I am quite confident, kept them off the broom-roof and saved my little mare from certain destruction."

When the doctor had finished his story, I inquired how the poor peasant had fared on his return from Carhaix, unarmed as he was, and unfurnished probably even with a box of matches.

A RIDE FOR DEAR LIFE

"Oh, he would be safe enough," said the doctor; "it was the mare was the attraction; and only in case of our being down together would my life have been in danger. In Brittany at least, no matter what their numbers nor what their need, they never attack a human being, great or small, by day or night. Man's dominion, given him by the Creator, is paramount here."

I was fortunate enough that night to sit next to the Count de Kergoorlas at dinner; and hearing he was a master of wolf-hounds in Upper Brittany, I gleaned from him some interesting information with respect to the style of hound he considered best adapted for his particular sport.

"A big, bold, broken-haired hound is what I keep for the work; and occasionally I invigorate the race," said he, "with a strain of wolf-blood."

"And how, pray," I inquired, "do you manage that?"

"Nothing is more simple. The dog and the wolf being congeners they breed readily together; nor does the law affecting mules affect the hybrid race, as the offspring of the first cross reproduce their litters with the same facility. I keep a dog-wolf brought up by hand; and he, suckled in infancy by a hound dam, lives in perfect concord with any hounds I think fit to enclose with him in his kennel; while a day or two reconciles a strange hound to his company."

"And do you find the first cross," I asked, "as manageable in chase as your ordinary hounds?"

"Far from it," he replied; "insomuch that I only keep that produce to breed from. They usually run mute or all but mute, and are so self-willed in chase and so fierce in kennel, that I merely use them as stud hounds, and enter the second cross. These, the grand-offspring of the wolf, become rare wolf-hounds, fierce, fine-nosed, desperate in chase, and never tiring during the longest day. But, to be candid, they have one great fault: they are too shy of their tongue; nor can this defect be bred out for several generations, although tonguey hounds are especially chosen for the purpose of every cross. The old nature of the wolf appears and reappears, and no device of human ingenuity can pitchfork it away."

I have since learned in my own country, from that keen and experienced sportsman, Mr. Waldron Hill, who brought over several couples of these hybrid hounds from the Department of Eure, and whose object it was to enter them as otter-hounds, that they had at least one other fault, which he found utterly ineradicable, in fact, the old wolf coming out again in them. They *would* kill sheep; and, as he justly remarked, that to hunt the sheep was a far more expensive amusement than hunting the otter, he hanged the whole of them. In the Count's country, however, this vice would not be observable, as there flocks of sheep are not found depastured abroad and roaming at will on a thousand hills, as in this more favoured land.

For the next two days, after the triple kill at Conveau, St. Prix deemed it advisable to give his hounds perfect rest; so, in order to employ the time more profitably than in frequenting Madame Laurent's café and billiard rooms, St. Prix, Kergoorlas, Keryfan, and myself formed a shooting party, and arranged to sally forth in search of woodcocks to the Pencoet and Ty-meur covers, all within two leagues and a half of the town of Carhaix, on the following morning.

In spite of Admiral O'Grady's advice at whist, "never to look back too much into futurity," I am tempted to make a backward cast with respect to the wolf-hunting, as before detailed. The sport, as I have already said, was good as it could well be; the hounds admirably suited for the work, and the "field" as ardent and practical a set of men as I ever wish to meet at a cover-side. It was, however, at first impossible for me to reconcile the system of riding to a glorious pack of hounds, armed as each man was with a double "smooth-bore," with the simpler style of chase adopted in our own country. It is quite true the wolf differs from the fox in the magnitude of the mischief he is capable of perpetrating, when plundering or pursued: the one is a pettifogging pickpocket, worrying old women and gamekeepers only, while the other is a brigand on a big scale, doing murder in bands, and bringing heavy loss and dismay to whole communities. The fox is hunted for sport alone; the wolf for the public weal; though, it must be admitted, St. Prix and his friends manage to include with that a vast amount of sport into the bargain.

A Breton chasseur would as soon think of riding to hounds without his saddle as without his gun; with him it is a "vade mecum," whether he pursues the hare or the roe-deer, the wolf or the grisly boar.

Not long ago, that prince of men, Lord Palmerston, was entertaining a dinner-party at Cambridge House, and amused his guests with an anecdote characteristic of this Breton and French practice. "Last season," said he, "a well-known French diplomatist did me the honour to pay me a fortnight's visit at Broadlands; and before he left, having enjoyed two or three days' fox-hunting in the neighbourhood, he expressed a wish to have his portrait taken as an English chasseur, and consulted me as to the artist he should employ for the work.

"'Frank Grant,' said I, 'is your man; he understands horses; and, from always being in good company, his portraits look like those of gentlemen and ladies.'

"So Frank Grant was invited to Broadlands, when the following conversation ensued between them:—

"'And how,' inquired that eminent artist, 'do you wish to be painted?'

"'Je me ferai peindre en chasseur Anglais; le fusil à l'epaule; à ma droite mon fidèle chien; à ma gauche un renard mort,' answered the Diplomat, with the utmost gravity.

"I expected," said Lord Palmerston, "at least to see a twitch of mirth on Grant's countenance; but he was too well bred for that; he quietly remarked that the hound and fox would do admirably, but that the gun would be unsuitable for the picture."*

When the Count de Kergoorlas' drag drove to the door of the Hôtel La Tour d'Auvergne the clock struck seven, and at that early hour in a November morning every one was astir in the house, and even in the streets of Carhaix. Whatever may be thought of French morals in general, those of rising early in the morning are, unquestionably, habitual to them; and that, too, not among the ouvriers only, and those on whom the labour of life falls heaviest, but among the higher classes of the community. It was barely dawn; grey, cold, and comfortless; and yet there sat Kergoorlas on his box, looking as cheerful and as happy as if he were going to drive a party of pretty girls to a summer fête in the forest of St. Germain.

"Mount, mount," said he, "the horses are longing for the road; and the braconniers of Carhaix will catch the first flight of woodcocks if we delay our departure much longer."

I was happy to feel that, on this occasion, I was not the delinquent; St. Prix had been gone an hour to his kennel, in order to examine the hounds after their work of yesterday, and had not yet returned. As I approached the drag, I ran my eye hastily over the team that stood, to all appearance, in no hurry for a start; though, to judge by the way in which four Breton peasants held each horse by the head, there was evidently some misgiving in Kergoorlas' mind as to the steadiness of the whole lot. A few minutes later St. Prix joined us, and, on mounting

* The above story is substantially correct; but, since its first publication, the author has been kindly informed by Lord Aberdare, to whom Lord Palmerston related it, that the French Anglomane was M. Charles de Mornay, and Lord Alvanley the man whom he consulted as to the painter; moreover, that the circumstance occurred soon after the restoration of 1815, when Sir Francis Grant had not long escaped from his petticoats.

to the vacant seat on the box, Kergoorlas, with a lively crack of his whip, ordered the peasants to " let them go ;" and immediately such a scene as I never witnessed before, and hope never to witness again, ensued on that granite road ; the near wheeler, on hearing the whip cracked, made a plunge forward, broke the rope traces, and came head and legs in and on the near leader's flanks ; an intrusion that instantly set both leaders a kicking so viciously, that it appeared to me a miracle how the forelegs and skulls of the wheelers remained unsmashed by the assault. However, Kergoorlas, who sat on his box with the most perfect *sang-froid*, as if he had been accustomed to such antics from his cradle, held on by the reins, and plied the whip vigorously ; and notwithstanding the near-wheeler, now held by the pole-chain alone, continued his frantic plunges in the air, he got the whole team into forward action, and steadied his coach through narrow streets and by protruding shop-windows with a precision never to be forgotten.

" The speed of the Tantivy trot," in former days, was that of a donkey's gallop compared with the pace at which our team descended the hill from Carhaix to the Roman Bridge below ; and nothing but the iron arm and steady nerve of the Count de Kergoorlas, backed up by the *mécanique* hard-turned upon both hind wheels, saved our imperilled bones. The " yawing " of the coach, high slung upon its wheels—not a patent-safety one of modern invention—as it reeled over the narrow road, bounded on one side by a quarry, and on the other by a precipice, the near-wheeler still plunging and kicking his shoes off, would have staggered many a man of the O.B.C., and inevitably brought him to grief ; but Kergoorlas never for one moment seemed to lose his presence of mind, proving himself indeed to be

"A daring pilot in extremity."

Beyond the bridge, crossed at a gallop, but crossed safely,

Kergoorlas got the first pull at his team, and brought them up in steadier form at the foot of the following hill. New trace-ropes were then substituted for the broken ones, and the remainder of the journey to Ty-meur passed off most pleasantly.

CHAPTER IV.

The covers of Ty-meur, in Finisterre, are, perhaps, as favourable for woodcocks and woodcock-shooting as any in Lower Brittany. Its alder-beds and oak-copses, abounding with holly, are fringed with narrow water-meadows; and if, here and there, an occasional black bog, devoid of all growth, compels the chasseur to wade knee-deep in its mire, it affords rare feeding for cock and snipe, as well as open ground, to catch them when they rise in the adjoining covers. In many respects there is a great similarity between the glades of Finisterre and the coombes of Devon; and were it not for the occasional appearance of a Breton peasant dressed in antique and quaint costume, or of a tethered black and white cow, indicating by its diminutive stature the poverty of the land, a Devonshire man in Lower Brittany might fancy himself wandering among the hollow vales and hanging woods of his own unrivalled county. The broad banks enclosing mere strips of pasture, and unnegotiable by any horse less favoured than Pegasus, the vegetation of the valleys, the sparkling brooks alive with trout, and doing the duty of irrigation in every meadow, are precisely what he sees at home: but the moment he ascends to the hill-tops or table-land, where it can be said to exist, the country in general is an uncultivated wilderness, overgrown with timber, broom, furze, and heather; less wild, perhaps, than the Forest of Dartmoor, but serrated, as it is, with vast "clitters" of rock and granite tors. No finer cover in the world for the plunderers that frequent it, the fox, the wolf, and the tusky boar.

But our business, at present, is with the woodcock; and as, during the late full moon, a cold easterly wind, with a point of north in it, had prevailed, large flights were known to have arrived in the neighbourhood, the best covers of which were unquestionably those of Ty-meur and the adjoining district; so we fully anticipated a fine day's sport. The proprietor of the estate being a wealthy banker, resident at Brest, we were received at the grand old château by a Breton garde-du-bois, left in charge of it and the woods, and apparently the whole property. A greater ruffian I certainly never encountered in Brittany, where the peasantry are usually a quiet, well-conducted set of men; but this fellow, at nine o'clock a.m., was so drunk and so dangerous, that he several times fell head foremost, loaded gun and all, into the midst of our dogs, and, on recovering his feet, used the grossest language my ears ever listened to.

I am not strait-laced, nor a very nervous subject, but candidly own the prospect of being accompanied by this garde-du-bois filled my mind with apprehension and disgust: the chance of being potted like a partridge was not a pleasant one, but the brutality of his conduct was far less endurable. Our party of four guns being divided into two lots, Kergoorlas and St. Prix going in one direction, and Keryfan and myself in another, the Breton garde-du-bois constituted himself my guide—for metallic reasons, of course, as every Englishman is believed to be a travelling Crœsus; but, as he affirmed, for the purpose of showing the stranger the most favoured cock-ground in the Ty-meur covers. My mortification at this arrangement I can scarcely describe; but, although I did my best to conceal it, St. Prix saw at a glance what my feelings were in the matter.

"See you," said he, calling me on one side, "yonder knoll in the fir trees? Close below it is a small wayside auberge; you have only to take that beast within sight of the mistletoe-bush hanging over its door, and you'll dispose of him for the rest of the day."

Thanking him for the hint, I resolved to profit by it, and cut the incumbrance adrift with the least possible delay; so I signalled to Keryfan, and whistling at the same time to my spaniels, two brace of which I had brought with me from England, we entered a long hollow oak and holly cover, and, beating as we went, made our way straight for the knoll; a course that, apparently, seemed to be quite in unison with the views of the garde-du-bois. Before we arrived at that point, however, the spaniels had flushed some fifteen or twenty cocks, out of which we only managed to bag six; indeed, the chance of our getting even so many was greatly against the guns, as the garde had brought with him a brace of wild setters, utterly unbroken, and regardless of all control. These, leading the spaniels to riot, ranged madly through the cover about a hundred yards ahead of us. In vain their master swore, kicked them with his heavy sabots, and at length fired after and into them, until they howled with agony; and in vain Keryfan and myself remonstrated loudly, and begged him to couple them up, and take them back to their kennel, as they were only spoiling the sport of the day; to which he ever replied, with an appeal to the sacred mother, "Curse the mongrels; they'll be quiet enough shortly, and then they'll find more cocks than all your spaniels would in a week."

Keryfan at length nudged my elbow and said, "It's no use, Frank, we are only wasting our words; let us get on to the auberge as fast as we can; that is our best chance now."

"Yes," I replied, "or our spaniels will be ruined as well as the sport; but it's my firm conviction the fellow is more knave than fool, and has brought out these dogs on purpose to save his

D

woodcocks for another day. He is evidently not so drunk as he pretends to be."

A few more cocks, which, ever and anon, passed overhead in wild flight backwards, fell to our guns before we reached the auberge, into which the garde led the way, swearing he was so thirsty he should become a corpse if he did not sustain his sinking nature with something to drink. Without calling for his liquor, however, he cast himself at full length among the dry heather that lay in the chimney corner; and, taking off his huge sabots, both ends of which were shod with iron, he threw them savagely at a pig's head that was quietly stretched on the opposite side of the hearth, enjoying the heat of the smouldering embers with perfect felicity. A piercing scream from the pig, whose head quivered as if at least one eye had been knocked out, instantly roused the indignant wrath of the aubergiste, who, seizing a cudgel by the small end, as the Bretons usually carry it, sprang like a tiger on the garde-du-bois, snatched away his fowling-piece, and then dealt him two or three tremendous whacks over his shoulders that must have left their mark there for many a day. In a moment the garde was upon his legs, closing with his adversary; but, like Roderic Dhu without his targe, he was powerless without his sabots, a Breton's chief weapons of offence in every such struggle; the aubergiste kicking him in the shins and twisting him by the collar, as a Cornishman "at play" would do, threw him once more prostrate to the ground; as fair a back-fall as a "stickler" ever witnessed. Had they been rival Irish peasants meeting at Donnybrook, their pugnacious ferocity could scarcely have been stronger; for no sooner was the garde floored than, like Antæus, he sprang again to his legs, and, this time, made a dash into the aubergiste, and gripped him fiercely by the throat.

Murder must have been the result speedily, if Keryfan and I had not now interposed. We dragged them asunder with great difficulty; and it was not till I had tossed down a five-franc piece, and ordered the aubergiste to produce a bottle of "Bordeaux" (I might as well have asked for Jove's nectar), that the sense of self-interest diverted his wrath; while, at the same time, the demand for wine excited the thirsty appetite of the sorely-bruised garde-du-bois. But wine alone, such as it was, did not satisfy the latter. He called loudly for a chopine of cider, with a goutte of eau-de-vie to qualify and warm that harsher liquor; and six successive chopines of the mixture did he gulp down in the space of a few minutes. He then settled down again in the chimney corner, as if he intended making a night of it with the less disgusting beast, now no longer molested, in the opposite corner.

Keryfan signalled to me, and said, in an undertone, "Frank, we shall have no more trouble with this fellow; in ten minutes he will be as drunk as Bacchus, and then we'll make a fresh start of it."

Quite true; in less time than that he was lying on his back, snoring aloud, like Polyphemus in his Trinacrian cave.

"Now, then," said Keryfan to the aubergiste, "take care to close the door as we leave the house; for if those dogs of his follow us, I'll shoot both of them in the first cover."

The man, in a subdued whisper, expressed his readiness to do as he was directed; but intimated his conviction that the garde, on waking up and finding the gentlemen gone, would comport himself like an unchained wolf.

A few steps brought us to the edge of Penmaen Wood; a few more, and we were threading our way through the oak and alder-bushes of this extensive cover, the spaniels working busily in a narrow circle around us, and flushing a cock frequently under our very guns. Twice Keryfan bagged his right and left shots; but, on this occasion, I did not get the same chance.

It is human nature, perhaps, to be prejudiced in favour of one's own race; and to believe, as almost every Englishman does in the matter of field sports, that his practical knowledge thereof is unequalled by the inhabitants of any other country. However true this may be as a general rule, I am bound to say that I have met with many exceptions to it among my Breton friends. The Baron Keryfan, for instance, is not only a good shot and a fine horseman, but thoroughly understands how to draw a cover, where to look for his game, and, whatever that game may be, so to handle his hounds in pursuit, that he can usually render a successful account of his day's sport. The Count Charles de St. Prix, too, although not much of a shot, knows the habits of a red-deer, and how to hunt him, as well as Mr. Fenwick-Bissett, or the " Prime Minister" Russell, two men who, beyond all others in the west country, have studied this grand game and given the wild dun-deer his due value as a beast of venery, rather than a mere target for a rifle ball. Across country, and such a country as Brittany is, St. Prix fears no rival; and to an old wolf breaking cover and facing the open, the Louvetier is as fatal an enemy as Anstruther Thompson ever was to flying fox in the Bicester Vale. Others, too, might be named in Brittany; such as MM. de Celler, Kerjeguz, Tregwernez, than whom it would be difficult to find in any country better shots or keener craftsmen.

There is one point, however, in woodcock-shooting, and that a very essential one, in which even the foremost of Breton fowlers signally fail; and that is, in their mode of beating a large cover with advantage. A Breton, for instance, will invariably post himself in some open spot, while his dogs are ranging through the cover; and, if a cock flies in his direction, he probably gets a shot at him; but, for every chance he thus gets, he loses many better, by not following his dogs up and taking whatever snap-shots he can obtain at every cock, as he is flushed, in thick or thin cover. By this means a moderate shot, whose spaniels are under fair command, and who can walk well up to them through cover, will make a far better bag in a day's shooting than the most accomplished marksman who posts himself in an open space or outside a cover, waiting until the cocks come to him to be shot. Old Cleave, a famous cock-shot and keeper in Cornwall, used to say, " I like to see a man and his dogs go out of sight, and head-over-ears in cover, and then I know they mean business."

This practice enabled Keryfan and myself—for he had acquired it during his frequent visits to England—invariably to kill a far greater number of cocks than any Breton chasseurs with whom we shot during two seasons in Brittany : indeed the advantage on our side was usually as much as six to one cocks bagged, although, in the open, we were in no respect better shots at snipe, red-legs, or running game.

Our heads were now pointing in the direction of Carhaix ; and as, by falling back to rejoin our friends Kergoorlas and St. Prix, whose distant and random firing we could barely hear, we feared the drunken garde-du-bois might burden us again with his company, Keryfan dispatched his Breton servant to Ty-meur to let the grooms know we did not intend to return thither, but to shoot our way home to Carhaix. At the same time the opportunity was taken of conveying to the drag the contents of our carnassière, now filled to its very edge with fifteen couple of woodcock, three couple of snipe, a brace of teal, a mallard, and a wood-pigeon— exactly forty head.

The covers through which we now ranged in the direction of Pencoet being so matted with heather, we scarcely flushed a single woodcock before we reached the fir-plantations of M. Gourdin—a French proprietor, who has reclaimed a large extent of barren land, planted it with Scotch and larch fir-trees, and built a solitary chateau in the midst of his wild and umbrageous domain. Every moonlight night of his life he can hear the wolves howling in the covers around him, responding to each other's cries, or chiding the planet that would throw its pale light on their dark orgies ; a music dismal enough, but in full harmony with the solitude of the surrounding scene. Here, if we except these predatory neighbours, to which he is always paying tribute, but without gaining their good-will, M. Gourdin is literally "monarch of all he surveys," and, although a man of wealth, and a bachelor to boot, prefers the solitude of the forest to the charms and amenities of a more social life.

Not two hundred yards from his chateau, in a dry hollow, unplanted with fir-trees and wholly occupied by heather of a gigantic growth, lies a patch of ground about four acres in extent, which Keryfan pointed out to me as St. Prix's favourite "draw," when he hunted this district. In the midland counties of England, proprietors are wont to plume themselves on the perfection of their fox gorse-covers; and certainly, if art, judgment, and expenditure could ensure a "certain find" and a good run, they are fairly entitled to such results. But here was a cover of nature which no art could equal; a homestead for wolves; dark, dry, quiet, and dense as an Indian jungle; with deep woodlands on all sides, into which, when disturbed by hounds, a wolf could break at any point unviewed by mortal eyes.

Our spaniels, with hackle up and terrified looks, regarded the cover with infinite suspicion, and no coaxing nor encouragement would induce them to show a nose within its dangerous precincts. Hollow, arched runs, indeed, in the otherwise solid mass of heather, indicated too clearly on its edge how frequently they were used by wolves in their passage in and out from the surrounding woods; and doubtless, by the manner of the spaniels, the scent of the wild beast was even now strong on the heather.

"Sensible dogs are they," said M. Gourdin, who had just joined us, "not to enter that cover. Not a month ago, a she-wolf and her litter fell upon my faithful old Hector, when chained at my very door-post. I had gone to Concarneau to see the wonderful piscicultural establishment for sea-fish, which M. Coste, a member of the Academy of Sciences, has managed with so much ability for more than twenty years at that place. Will you believe it, my only injunction—to unchain Hector and take him within doors at night—was utterly forgotten by my Breton servant? and the consequence was, not a vestige of him could be found in the morning, save his fine old head, which was dragged so tightly into his brass collar that it alone remained to tell the tale of the night's feast. The Breton confessed to hearing the fight; and had the cowardly rascal cracked a whip or lighted a match, the old dog's life would have been saved to a certainty; but while he listened from his bed to the gorging and growling 'o'er carcase and limb,' and 'they were too busy to think of him,' his heart failed him, and he suffered the hungry brutes to hold high carnival over my poor faithful dog."

I was greatly interested by this story, as, on my previous visit to Brittany and these covers, I had especially admired Hector, the grandest specimen of a Wallachian mastiff I had ever seen. He was at least thirty inches high; and, single-handed, no wolf would have conquered him: fettered as he was, though, his big bone and powerful frame were no match for the many Philistines that fell upon him in that luckless night. Between M. Gourdin, the Frenchman, and the Breton peasantry of his neighbourhood there was no love lost; his occupation of land, and the legal redress he always resorted to when his rights were infringed, created a bitter jealousy and vindictive feelings akin to those, alas! too well known in our sister isle. His covers were fenced round, and no longer available for the firewood hitherto obtained from them without let or obstruction. Besides his master, Hector, by day, was the chief guard of the whole domain; and woe be to the wretched sackcloth-clad peasant who ventured to gather a bundle of sticks within the enclosed ground. The dog heard him a mile off, and pinned him to a certainty, holding him by his sackcloth collar till his cries brought the proprietor to his rescue : then followed the procès-verbal, leaving a worse grip than even the mastiff's teeth. In Ireland M. Gourdin's life would not have been worth a week's purchase ; nor will it be a matter of surprise if, as was believed at Carhaix, the Breton servant designedly omitted to shut up Hector, but exposed him to the almost certain fate of being devoured by the wolves that infested the adjoining cover—a cruel revenge, but one that might reasonably be expected from a peasantry not half civilised and desperately tenacious of privileges rightly or wrongly maintained from time immemorial.

The Breton peasant naturally hates the rich French proprietor, not only because, armed with the terrible power of the law, he puts it in force whenever an act of depredation occurs, but because, speaking a totally distinct language, and differing from him in physique and natural character quite as much as a veritable Milesian differs from an Englishman, he regards him as an intruder on the soil—an alien and a tyrannical neighbour. It is a fact that, throughout Lower Brittany, the Celtic language is universally spoken by the Breton population, and that—with the exception of a few Frenchified words, necessarily adopted to describe new articles introduced from France—the language is still in many respects much as it was a thousand years ago, or even in the fourth century, when, in the reign of the tyrant Maximus, the first great exodus occurred from this country to the ancient Armorica.

The isolation of Lower Brittany, no less than the prejudices of its people, has doubtless contributed to this unusual result ; for unusual it certainly is, if what Sir Charles Lyell says be true, that "no language seems ever to last for a thousand years." That the languages of modern Europe—especially those of England, France, Germany, and Italy—have undergone during that period a complete transmutation, is an unquestionable fact : for instance, "no English scholar," a philologist might say, "who has not specially given himself up to the study of Anglo-Saxon can interpret the documents in which the chronicles and laws of England were written in the days of King Alfred ; so that we may be sure that none of the English of the nineteenth century could converse with the subjects of that monarch if these last could now be restored to life." Indeed, so rapid has been the change in the English language, that even Spenser's " Faëry Queen," written in the year 1590, can scarcely now be enjoyed except by the erudite ; while Chaucer and Barbour, poets of the fourteenth century, require a skilled linguist to read and understand the obsolete style of those authors.

In France "there is a treaty of peace still extant, a thousand years old, between Charles the Bald and King Louis of Germany (dated A.D. 841), in which the German king takes an oath in what was the French tongue of that day, while the French king swears in the German of that era ; and neither of these oaths would now convey a distinct meaning to any but the learned in these two countries." Again, in Italy the Latin of the Augustan age was utterly unknown, even in Rome, by the uneducated people, before the end of the eighth century ; while " the modern Italian cannot be traced back much beyond the time of Dante, or some six centuries before our time."

Yet, in spite of all these proofs of change in the four languages mentioned, that of Lower Brittany has certainly not suffered in a like degree. A Breton ballad of the sixth century, entitled "Gerent, Mab Erbin," published by the Comte de la Villemarqué, and compared by him with the Welsh version, as given in " Le livre rouge de Herghest," a folio volume containing the works of 'Llywarc'h Hen and Taliesin,* is quite intelligible to both Bretons

---

* This curious old work is to be found in the library of Jesus College, Oxford.

and Welshmen of the present day. So, indeed, are the songs in general which M. de la Villemarqué has collected in that most interesting work of his, "The Poems of the Breton Bards of the Sixth Century." That gentleman, when he visited the principality of Wales about thirty years ago, established the fact, since corroborated by many others, that a Breton scholar with a knowledge of English and a Welshman understanding French, can carry on a conversation in the Breton language with little difficulty to either—all the old words being the same, although when written the spelling of them may be very different.

"But," I hear an impatient enquiry, "what on earth has all this to do with wolf-hunting and wild sport in Britanny? *Cui bono* the knowledge that the Breton language has or has not outlived the period of existence assigned to all languages by Sir Charles Lyell?" The answer to which is simply this: That, by the old Breton peasantry, the connection between Great Britain and Lower Brittany is still cherished with a sentiment of respect and pride; that an Englishman is regarded with far more favour than their very dissimilar and uncongenial French neighbours; and that if a Welshman speaking his native tongue visit that primitive people, he will be received by them with especial favour and kindness, and welcomed as a brother possessing the same old Celtic blood in his veins as that of which they are equally proud.

This community of blood and language is a key to the Breton's heart; and if, in addition, the sojourner in quest of sport carry a well-stocked tobacco-pouch, and is liberal therewith, he may hunt, shoot, or fish, where his inclination lead him, throughout the length and breadth of Lower Brittany. I speak from experience, having passed two pleasant seasons among the people, and traversed, in pursuit of game, its wildest nooks. I never once was looked upon as an intruder, but, on the contrary, received the right hand of fellowship wherever I roamed from the peasant proprietors of that rugged land. True, the aforesaid requirements were fulfilled; I spoke Breton, and half-ruined myself by my expenditure in French "caporal."

Our further sport in M. Gourdin's plantations is scarcely worth recording; suffice it to say, Keryfan and myself, when the day's bag was counted, had killed nearly three times as many woodcocks as Kergoorlas and St. Prix; both of whom, although shooting equally well, if not better than ourselves in the open, never attempted to enter a close cover nor follow their dogs throughout the day.

CHAPTER V.

The principal towns of Lower Brittany, such as St. Brieux, Morlaix, Brest, and L'Orient, are in no respect deficient in the accommodation required for the comfort of travellers sojourning in that country; but, as a general rule, the smaller towns, especially those out of the beaten track, are sorry quarters even for men able and willing to undergo considerable discomfort in quest of sport; for ladies they are simply unbearable. At Carhaix, as I have said before, there is, fortunately, a very fair provincial hotel, La Tour d'Auvergne, the host of which, M. Marseillier, having once been *chef-de-cuisine* on board King Louis-Philippe's yacht, has seen more of the world than hosts in general; and, still proud of his white cap, doing duty at his charcoal stove, chatting, singing, frying omelettes, and concocting the most delicate and savoury dishes, he does all a man can do to make his guests comfortable, and his house popular. Madame, too, is a rare manager, looking sharply after the housemaids, famous for her snow-white linen, and particular, as regards the sleeping apartments, as any woman in Brittany.

But Marseillier's qualifications as a cook and a landlord are not his only good points; he is also devoted to the chase; and if, perchance, a foreigner, wishing to see a little wild sport in that country, take up his quarters at the Hotel la Tour d'Auvergne (and nowhere within reach of the Black Mountains could he be better located), Marseillier, whether he had a houseful of guests or not, would shoulder his "Faucheux" and show him the favourite rocky ground of the red-leg, the best dingles for cock, and the deep covers around, in which the fox, the wolf, or the boar would always be a sure find. The very first day I shot in the neighbourhood of Carhaix I won Marseillier's heart by disclaiming any share in the honour of killing a hare, which had jumped up between us in a field adjoining the town, and which we had both fired at simultaneously. He was a very poor marksman, and his delight on receiving my assurance that the hare fell to his gun was unbounded; away he went, promising to be back in two minutes, straight for the hotel, where, as I afterwards learned, he pleasantly described his superior skill, and instantly set to work to prepare the hare for a ragôut intended for our dinner that very day; so it was close upon two hours before he joined me again.

One word about his hare-ragôut, in the concoction of which few were his equals, and none surpassed him: it was somewhat similar to our English jugged hare, but far superior in its delicate flavour and rich gravy. However, he professed to have learned the secret of making it from the chef on board H.M. the Queen of England's yacht, when, as Queen of the Ocean, Her Majesty paid that memorable visit to Louis-Philippe, and so delighted the French monarch with her affability and queenly dignity. Old Neptune, however, is a god who does not respect earthly powers, be they never so exalted or never so puissant; and it so happened that, on that occasion, he rolled and heaved in a most independent and restless fashion 'neath the keels of the royal yachts; and, as Marseillier always relates the story with great humour, it was his especial duty to mix hot brandy-and-water for the Queen of England, who, owning the power of the great god, was in imminent danger of paying the same tribute to him as the weakest of her subjects; but, happily, was saved from doing so by a potent mixture of French eau-de-vie and Marseillier's care.

After our day's diversion in the covers of Ty-meur—a day that especially gladdened Marseillier's heart, for he it was who chiefly profited by the bag—both Keryfan and myself hoped St. Prix would bring out his pack and draw M. Gourdin's plantations and heather-brake, so short a distance from Carhaix, and a sure find at all times. But *dis aliter visum;* and so did the Louvetier. "The hounds," he said, "required more than one day's rest after their unusually hard work; and it would never do to bring a slack pack into such large covers, bristling with furze, and matted with heather from one end of them to the other."

Accordingly, as an idle hand comes to no good, we, the four gunners of the previous day, made immediate arrangements for a day at Locrist—a heather and buckwheat district, in which, if Marseillier was authentic, the partridges, red-leg and grey, swarmed *en masse.* So, at break of day, just as

> "The feathered songster chanticleer
> Had wound his bugle horn,
> And told the early villager
> The coming of the morn,"

Kergoorlas' coach rattled over the rough paving-stones of the old town, and brought many a pretty *bonnet-de-nuit* to the open windows, as it cracked along towards the modest "place" in front of the La Tour d'Auvergne. It was a cold, shivery morning, the ice in the shallow puddles crackling 'neath the horses' feet, and the grass and fallen leaves sparkling with hoar-frost. The sun was affecting to shine; but, in point of heat, its effort was a mockery, so keen was the north wind and so raw the damp exhalation arising from the foliage, withering on all sides around us. About a league from Carhaix, I was in the act of fastening up the last button of my great-coat, when my eye caught sight of an object, the recollection of which even now brings a shudder to my bones. It was the figure of a man, naked to the waist; he was leaning against a rough upright stone that marked the kilometres of the road, and was engaged in vigorously rubbing his back and shoulders against it; and then, to cool the irritation produced as well by this process as by the parasitical company of which he was endeavouring to rid himself, he rolled fiercely in the crisp, wet grass, to allay the feverish pain that seemed to madden him. Had his skin been less thick than that of a badger, he must have torn it into strips against the surface of that rugged stone, as again and again he rose from the ground and applied himself with renewed vigour to the disgusting labour in which he was engaged. As Kergoorlas, hearing my exclamation of horror, slackened his horses' pace, we all recognised the man who in Carhaix was well known as "Le Grand Loup," a huge, sturdy vagrant who never had done an hour's work in his life, but subsisted on plunder and the misplaced charity of strangers, who, seeing him in the garb of Lazarus, lying from morning to night at the doorpost of the hotel, soliciting alms or tobacco from all who entered, only encouraged by their gifts the idleness and vagrancy he had so long practised, and which was so prevalent in that country. Keryfan tossed him a few sous, telling him to buy a piece of soap, and that its application to his skin would do him far more service than all the *menhir* of Carnac.

As he rolled from the grass and clutched at the coin in the dirty road, he poured forth a string of blessings, long as that of an Italian mendicant monk, and probably quite as beneficial; then, looking up with the expression of a hungry wolf, he said: "Ay, but the soap won't fill my empty stomach; that is my first want." Keryfan's sympathy was touched again, and so unmistakably earnest was the vagrant's appeal, that a loaf and sausage were at once pitched into his upraised hands.

Locrist lies in a valley, and is charmingly situated at the confluence of a small stream with the Carhaix river, the fine overhanging woods rendering it one of the most picturesque spots in that neighbourhood. The little hamlet, however, boasts but of one mill and a couple of poor cottages; so that accommodation there was none, much less "good entertainment for man and horse," in any of those buildings. It was found necessary, therefore, to send on the team and coach to Callac, a small town near the Forest of Dualt, about two leagues beyond Locrist, and on the eastern road between that place and Guingamp.

Our arrangements for the beat were soon made: St. Prix and Kergoorlas, who were bent on having their revenge, taking the hill on the right bank of the brook; while Keryfan and I worked the rough ground on the opposite side of the valley. By this plan we mutually derived immense advantage, as we were able not only to mark for each other, but to save our legs from the labour of following the coveys that continually, in their first flight, crossed and recrossed the deep ravine that lay between us. The red-legged birds were especially addicted to this manœuvre. When sprung on one side, they almost invariably crossed to the other; and then, taking advantage of some intervening knoll—just as a fox would place a line of hillocks or the screen of some undulating ground between him and the eyes that would tally him—they recrossed the valley, and perhaps dropped into a strong piece of gorse within a field or two of the spot on which they were just found. But, by drawing both sides of the valley simultaneously, we completely out-manœuvred their tactics; and this, too, without shouting or disturbing the ground otherwise than by the report of our guns and the legitimate work of our dogs. When birds were marked down, a hat waved in the direction served as the simple but effective semaphore to indicate their exact whereabouts. Then, not a word passed between us, so that the running propensity of the red-leg received no stimulus from our babbling tongues.

No country in the world can surpass this rough ground of

MARS.

Brittany in point of scent. It carries in its long grass and heather both a foot and a side scent; while the humid air is highly favourable to its long duration on the soil or vegetation with which the game has come into contact. It is no exaggeration to say that I have seen a Brittany pointer, when down wind, find a covey of birds, feeding on green wheat, at least five hundred yards up-wind from the spot at which he first winded them. On the present occasion it was a grand treat to witness the way in which a fine old-fashioned dog, called Mars, found his birds at certainly that, if not a greater distance. With nose high in air (the Brittany pointers never rake), he stepped along, straight as a crow would fly, across a large field, stood a moment on the bank, drew rapidly across the next, again stood on the bank, crossed a third and a fourth field; and at length, on the top of the fifth bank, came to a fixed point, his head erect, his tail level with his back, and his whole attitude worthy of Phidias' chisel. A covey of redlegs were lying close hid in the buckwheat stubble not twenty yards from his nose. Keryfan got a brace; but, as I was somewhat blown by the exertion of following the dog, my foot slipped at the fence, and before I could recover myself the birds were out of range.

I was not, however, doomed to disappointment; for in less than two minutes Kergoorlas' hat was waving steadily downwards; and we soon learned from the signal that the covey had dropped in a thick hanging cover in the vale below us. Thither we quickly sped, and had only just time to mount the bank commanding the wood, when Mars and Dian began to draw, and almost immediately came to a steady point within a few yards of the fence. Both dogs had been trained to break point when encouraged to do so, and Keryfan's one word was quite sufficient to send them headforemost into the dense mass of gorse, bramble, and scrub wherein the birds had taken refuge. At once there was a whirr, and again Keryfan knocked down a brace, while I only managed to floor my second bird.

There was a good deal of high, branchy timber, chiefly oak, too, with the leaf still on, standing in the cover; and, as Keryfan announced a brace down to his barrels, I could not resist a few words of applause. "Bravo, Baron!" I exclaimed; "I never saw man and dogs do better work."

"Hold hard, Frank," said he, "wait till they're gathered. Both my birds, if I mistake not, are runners; and if so, the dogs' hardest work is yet before them. Red-legs, in such a cover as this, are far more difficult to stop on foot than they are on wing."

He had scarcely finished speaking, when Dian, with her short, stumpy tail eloquently expressing her satisfaction, sprang on the bank, bearing aloft my dead bird, its head and legs dangling from her jaws, but not a feather crushed by her tender mouth. She dropped it gently into Keryfan's hand.

Again, away she flew at her master's command, as if she was well aware, too, there was more game still to be recovered. I could hear Mars in hot pursuit, as the dry sticks crackled in his track; but Dian knew her business far too well to interfere in his work. She had her own to do, and seemed to understand it instinctively—the result, doubtless, of careful training and high sagacity. Battues and beaters are abominations! "Procul, O procul este, profani!" Give me one hour with such dogs as Keryfan's, and pleasantly will my memory dwell on it to the day of my death.

In a little more than two minutes both dogs appeared on the bank, each with a red-leg alive in his mouth. As before, Dian trotted directly up to Keryfan, and literally put her bird into his hand; but Mars was not so complaisant. He, proud of his capture, and carrying his head high, marched round and round his master, indicating, with all the signs of which he was capable, his extreme delight in the successful chase. Never did I see better work, nor a prettier sight. Well might Keryfan be proud of such a brace of dogs, and fairly might he be pardoned for believing they were faultless in their work as any man's dogs in Brittany.

A year only afterwards Mars and Dian became my property. Keryfan had sustained a shock which made him renounce the gun for the rest of his life. His confidential servant, Pastor, keeper, *piqueur*, henchman, and friend to him, had his head blown to pieces by a blundering Englishman, who, in shooting at a covey of birds, missed them, and killed the man. Knowing well my appreciation of his two dogs, he wrote me the following letter after that sad event.

"DEAR FRANK,

"You will be grieved to hear the bad news this letter conveys. Yesterday poor Pastor was killed in the field. He was out shooting with a novice, who, bungling with his triggers, shot him instead of his bird. I am greatly distressed by the accident, for, as you know, Pastor was my right hand in all things, an honest man, and a friend I could ill spare in these times.

"I have made up my mind never to shoot again. So if Mars and Dian will be of any use to you, pray accept them from

"Your old friend,

"KERYFAN."

There is one especial feature in which the Brittany pointers far excel all I have met with in other countries; they will face the strongest gorse cover without hesitation, and draw it for birds, as a foxhound would draw it for a fox. They certainly are not so fine in the skin as the Spanish or English pointers; but, although they do not carry long-haired jackets and feathered sterns like setters or spaniels, their coats are thick and close-set, and well adapted to the rough country in which they do their work. They have probably some admixture of hound blood in their veins; their long, pendant ears, high crowns, and the almost universal habit of throwing tongue when in hard pursuit of a hare, would indicate affinity with the hound race; and if thus descended, their courage in drawing gorse and thick cover is readily explained.

It may be a natural, and is decidedly a patriotic feeling, to believe that no nation in the world understands the breeding and management of dogs so well as we do.

> Hounds, and their various breed,
> And no less various use.

Yet the poor, uneducated peasant of Lower Brittany, the *braconnier* who gets his livelihood by the chase, shooting seven days in every week, and shooting *partout*, breaks a pointer for his own use immeasurably superior in many respects to the highly-trained dogs so often met with in our turnip fields and grouse moors. The former will break fence, it is true, and will foot a hare like a very hound; but this he has been taught and encouraged to do —it is a qualification essential to the bag. On the other hand, he will, as has already been stated, face the thorniest brake, never rake in drawing for his birds, and, above all, will retrieve his wounded game by land or water perfectly. Without these accomplishments, especially the first and last, he would be valueless to the *braconnier* in that land. However, *suum cuique* is doubtless the fair conclusion: certain it is that the thin-skinned, highly-bred, and highly-broken English pointer is found to be utterly useless in Lower Brittany; while probably the coarser-bred dog of that country would be unequal to the quick stubble work and fine style required in this.

There is a sad disfigurement practised on Brittany pointers, which, considering the gorsy nature of the covers they draw, has doubtless its advantage; but, on the other hand, it detracts largely from the good looks, and even the dignity of the dog in action; the tail, that indicator of all a dog's thoughts, that silent tongue that explains all he means, is chopped off in puppy-hood, and a mere stump is left, scarcely longer than that of a Salisbury sheep-dog. Shame on the *braconnier*, for his utter disregard of the pointer's beauty and graceful movement! Better might he have rounded his ears, as we do those of the fox-hound, than mutilate the tail in such barbarous fashion. The former operation would be far more serviceable, and, at the same time, less disfiguring to the appearance of the dog. What a sorry object a stump-tailed pointer would cut side by side with those grand animals exhibited in that class at our National Dog Shows! And yet, over and through the rough cover-land of Brittany, the latter, as I have abundantly tested, will bear no comparison with his coarser congener. He is worth a parish pound-full of the other for the scrub work required of a pointer in that country.

But to the sport. It was our turn now to hoist the hat; the five birds escaping had dropped in a *genêt*, a plot of broom, on the opposite side of the valley; but before Kergoorlas and St. Prix could reach the spot a sturdy peasant, accoutred in a brown, shaggy goat-skin jacket, shambled up from the valley below, whence he had doubtless been watching our operations, and, with the aid of his stump-tail dog, kicked the birds singly up, and actually bagged four out of five of them before our friends gained the enclosure. This is a land of freedom and equality—at least so say the modern French songs; and certainly if a poor peasant *braconnier* could take this liberty, as he did with impunity, there must be some ground of truth in their burden. He had just knocked over his fourth bird as Kergoorlas and St. Prix topped the fence close to him; and, so far from being either surprised or even conscious of doing what he had not a perfect right to do, he lifted up his broad-brimmed hat, and at once commenced chaffing St. Prix, whom he evidently knew, with coming too late to share the sport he had just been enjoying. "But come," said he, with infinite coolness, "you shall not be disappointed; there are redleg and grey partridges *en masse* in this valley, and if you follow me you'll burn all your powder and fill your *carnassière* before midday."

St. Prix, one of the proudest of the old Breton *noblesse*, whose mother was maid-of-honour to Marie Antoinette, and he a Legitimist to the backbone, could ill brook the peasant's familiarity. "Follow you," he said, deliberately; "no; we neither require your leadership nor your company. You go your ways and we'll go ours."

In no wise discomfited by this rebuff, the man, who was really a good-natured fellow, said pleasantly, "Well, M. de St. Prix, if you won't take a good offer, I'll quit you, certainly; but mind, if you require my service in any way, I shall be within easy reach of you for the rest of the day." So saying, he lifted his hat, whistled to his dog, and disappeared over the adjoining fence.

These, as we afterwards learned, were his usual tactics, depending on the labour of others to fill his bag, and "living," as he was wont to say, "like the lion, on the prey hunted down for him by the jackals that came into the Locrist valley." On future occasions, whenever I went shooting alone into that neighbourhood, I generally found that my first right and left shots brought the lion out; and being always well provided with tobacco, I had no difficulty in securing his good services, and getting him to show me the *remise* of every covey sprung on the adjoining hills. That is the name given to the cover, whatever it be, into which the game, when disturbed on feed, immediately flies for concealment; and as the whole face of the land, barring a patch of oat or buckwheat stubble here and there, is one mass of gorse, broom, heather, and brushwood, a single chasseur, without a knowledge of the *remise*, and without a marker, might as well bide away; he sees a covey once, and never sees it again. He might far better hope to recover a blackcock in the ravines of Benvoirlich, than a red-leg under such circumstances.

Kledan, or Kledan Kam—for, owing to a lame leg, the *braconnier* was thus surnamed—had arrived at this knowledge by a plan clever enough and peculiarly his own. Being physically unable to work hard for his game, it was his habit, in default of less natural jackalls, to send his wife and dog to scour the surrounding hills and feeding ground; while he, mounted on some knoll that commanded the whole valley, took the bearings of every covey disturbed by them, and thus ascertained the *remise*, far or near, to which it winged its flight. Hence, as a guide to the game, he was more effective than a dozen dogs would have been in that district; and if, at the end of a day, a franc piece and a brace of birds were added to the two ounces of tobacco which at least in a few hours he converted into smoke and ashes, poor Kledan was made unspeakably happy. We gradually became great allies; insomuch, that if I failed to pay the valley of Locrist a weekly visit, he would loudly complain of my long absence; and when, at length, the time came for my departure, a stranger would have supposed Kledan was about to lose the dearest friend he had upon earth. "But for my wife and dog," he said, despondingly (he always bracketed them together, and it often puzzled me to know which of the twain he loved the best); "but for my wife and dog, I would cross the sea to-morrow, and be your *garde-chasse* in England for the rest of my days. But they would soon want bread if they lost me; and that chains me to Locrist."

Poor Kledan! little did he know what a fish out of water he would have been as an English gamekeeper: the night-watching would scarcely have suited him so well as killing red-legs and playing the lion over the jackalls that visited his native valley. His thorough independence, too, would have astonished a stranger at the cover-side. I turned my back on him soon afterwards with infinite regret ; but my memory often reproduces him before my mind's eye, a fresh, earnest, and manly Breton peasant as that country ever produced.

About twenty brace of birds, red-leg and grey, six woodcocks, and a hare or two, had fallen to our guns on both sides of the valley, when an incident occurred that somewhat marred our sport, and set St. Prix in a blaze for the rest of the day. Kergoorlas' favourite pointer, in jumping off a bank, pitched exactly on the bridge of a huge wolf-trap, which, instantly springing, caught him with its iron jaws by both forelegs. They were broken on the spot; and a merciful shot from his master's gun, there being no alternative, released the poor brute at once from further suffering. We all grieved for the dog; but St. Prix's trouble, as the Louvetier of that district, arose chiefly from the trap: not even Sir Watkin, nor Russell, nor Meynell, of old, could have been more jealous for the fair life of a fox than he was for that of a wolf; his vexation, then, in discovering that foul play was practised in this, his favourite hunting-ground, burst forth at intervals for the next day or two, like the fiery eruptions of a disturbed volcano. Kledan, who suddenly dropped over the fence and joined us at this juncture, naturally aroused St. Prix's suspicion; and bitter were the invectives he levelled at the *braconnier's* head. He, however, stoutly denied all knowledge of the trap; and, to show his sincerity, at once volunteered to carry it and throw it into the deepest pit of the river below; a proposal St. Prix derisively scoffed at, saying to the *braconnier*, "You may do that if you please; but you'll fish it up again before the sun rises to-morrow morning."

"I never have trapped, and never tried to trap a wolf in my life," said Kledan, fiercely; "but there's no knowing what I may do for the future, when, on my oath, you refuse to believe my word."

St. Prix had fairly exasperated him, and, I believe, did him great injustice; for, as I afterwards discovered, Kledan feared no man, and would speak the truth in the face of death itself. How this altercation would have terminated, it is useless now to conjecture; but, just at the moment it bid fair to culminate into violent action between St. Prix and the *braconnier*, a peasant opportunely appeared in the field, hastening towards us, and bearing by his manner some tidings of import to some of the party. He walked straight up to the Louvetier, and, lifting his hat respectfully, entreated his immediate help at Trefranc. "For," said he, "the wolves are eating us up there. Two days ago they killed my cow by daylight; and last evening they seized my horse by the gullet, and would have killed him in half a minute, if I had not rushed to his rescue and scared the brutes away: as it is, they have stripped his skin down from the throat to the chest. So pray, monsieur, don't delay."

St. Prix at once slipped a five-franc piece into his hand, and gladdened the poor fellow's heart further by saying: "To-morrow morning my hounds shall be at Trefranc Rocks at eight o'clock; and if the loup-garou is roused, let him look to his skin."

CHAPTER VI.

"The wolf-hounds at Trefranc Rocks to-morrow at 8." No sooner had that fixture been announced, than away sped the grateful peasant, fast as his heavy sabots would carry him, to communicate the glad news to the surrounding hamlets. Up hill and down dale, over many a mile of rough country did he speed, like Malise bearing the fiery cross when Vich-Alpine summoned his mountain clans to the muster-place at Lanric Mead. Not a hamlet nor a hut within many leagues of that centre but knew the rendezvous, and responded to the peasant's cry of "War and death to the wolf;" not a glen that sent not its hardy tenant forth to destroy the skulking robber, that, first or last, had plundered each and all of them in turn, and brought want and misery to so many hearths.

Any one wishing to see the Celtic population of Lower Brittany in its rude simplicity—natural, wild, and unchanged as it is by the varnish of modern civilisation—should go to a wolf-hunt: the peasant's blood is then up, and, both in garb and action, he fairly represents the appearance and character of our ancient forefathers, as described by Tacitus and other later authors. Clad so far as his waist in a shaggy goat-skin mantle, his nether limbs encased in the coarsest sackcloth, quaintly fashioned in the form of spacious "bragues" or tight fitting to the legs, his feet stockingless, but protected by huge beechen sabots well stuffed with straw, and his long curly locks, which apparently have never been violated either by scissors or comb, falling wildly over his back and shoulders, he presents the appearance of a veritable Ancient Breton, such as that individual might be supposed to have been before the period of the Saxon Heptarchy. Then see him in chase, his weapon a club or a pike, if he is not rich enough to possess a gun, and his game the wolf! He is then "the noble savage" all over; his passion is roused, and the hunting instinct natural to man blazes out in him uncontrollably, and converts at once the peaceable Breton peasant into the similitude of a wild Huron or a Crow-foot Indian.

His cries of "A'hr bleiz, a'hr bleiz!" when the wolf is afoot are almost unearthly, his object being, doubtless, to cheer the hounds and terrify the wolf; but that he should be more successful in the latter than the former result may be gathered from the tone of execration, very bitter and very unmusical, that accompanies every shout. He grinds it out, as it were, through his teeth; and the sound of "A'hr bleiz, a'hr bleiz!" ringing through the woods is enough to terrify the stoutest wolf; and if a stranger hear the yell, it will remain impressed on his memory for many a future day.

Not commonly, however, does the Louvetier communicate the meet of the wolf-hounds to the peasantry at large; it is only when a wolf or a litter of wolves become exceptionally bold and destructive, that he proclaims the war-note aloud, and the whole country is gathered together, far and near, to avenge the havoc and check its farther progress. On such occasions, as may be supposed, the beauty of the chase is sadly marred by the hubbub and confusion accompanying the hounds on every side; the danger, too, from the whistling slugs and wild use of their musketry by the peasantry is often serious; and St. Prix, like many a master of hounds in this country, is sometimes sorely tried by his motley and unruly crowd.

It was a glorious hunting morning the day they met at Trefranc. No gossamer glittered on the grass, no "spangles decked the thorn;" but the soft west wind blew freshly over the heath, the clouds were high, and all betokened steady weather and good scent.

"If it's not more than one old dog-wolf that has done all this mischief," said St. Prix, as we approached the clump of beech trees that towered over the little hamlet of Trefranc, "he'll find some difficulty in clearing the cover with a whole skin."

His experienced eye had detected, at the distance of half a league, a perfect cordon of peasants surrounding those points of the cover at which wolves pointing for Dualt were accustomed to break in times past.

"It will be a fiery ordeal for him, at all events," said Keryfan, noting the crowd; "I devoutly hope the wolf's will be the only skin to suffer on the occasion. For myself, I'll take precious care to give those muskets a wide berth, as I should sorely object to a slug wound from such weapons. To be potted by a peasant in mistake for a wolf would indeed be an inglorious finale."

"Quite right, too," said St. Prix; "follow the hounds closely, and the chances are you will be clear of all danger from the flying shot. The wolf usually keeps well ahead of them; and where he breaks there will break the storm of leaden hail."

This bit of advice was of course intended for me; as, with the exception of St. Prix himself, no men in Brittany had seen so many wolves killed as Keryfan and Kergoorlas; whereas this was my first experience of an open peasants' day. The Louvetier had scarcely done speaking when Louis Trevarreg, the trustiest of his piqueurs, advanced rapidly from the cover-side, leading old Tonnerre, the famous limier in a leash, and, lifting his hat respectfully, Louis informed us he had tracked in a couple of old wolves where they had crossed the brook in the northern valley; that Tonnerre had nearly dragged his arm off in his eagerness to follow the trail; and that, on laying on the pack, he ventured to say they would rouse them in less than half an hour.

"I knew there must be more than one wolf at Trefranc," said St. Prix, "to have done so much mischief. The cowardly brutes "rarely commit wholesale murder single-handed."

The pack, consisting this day of not more than twelve couple, just two-thirds of the lot usually hunted on less dangerous occasions, sat quietly on their haunches on a plot of short heather within a hundred yards of us, but down wind of the cover we were about to draw. The moment, however, they discovered the Louvetier's voice, vain were the whips and frantic efforts of the piqueurs to prevent their rushing forward to welcome his arrival; and, considering they were all in couples, it was a marvel to me that no accident occurred by their fouling the horse's legs, as they pressed forward tumultuously on every side and even under his very girths. But St. Prix, who had a caress for one and a kind word for another, was delighted at the demonstration, and took no heed whatever, neither did his horse, of the jingling chains and uproarious action evinced by the hounds. On my expressing surprise at the steadiness of his hunter, he said, with a smile, "Ah! Barbe-Bleu knows better, when I am on his back, than to kick at a hound; but, left to himself, and without a hand on his bridle, a more dangerous brute never accompanied a pack." I have often heard the immortal "Jack Russell," the keenest of all hound observers, say, that it is not the man who feeds the hounds, nor the man who hunts them in the field, whom the hounds love best; but the man who opens their kennel door and gives them freedom; here then, methought, was an exception; St. Prix neither fed nor unkennelled his hounds, but led and cheered them to the chase; and yet he, unquestionably, was their chief joy. Not a hound looked at a piqueur from that instant to the end of the day.

"Let go six couple," said St. Prix to the piqueurs, as they rushed up to secure the hounds; "and hold the rest in couple till you hear my horn; then, if it sounds 'Le Loup,' slip them all."

This order was occasioned by St. Prix's knowing the cover of Trefranc to be a favourite one for foxes; and the result soon proved its necessity. We then trotted off with the uncoupled hounds, Louis Trevarreg being our pilot, to the brook-side, where the wolves had left their tracks ere they entered the great cover. When at least a hundred yards from the spot, the hounds, catching wind of the scent, dashed eagerly forward, and, throwing their deep tongues simultaneously, shot like arrows into the cover and disappeared in full cry. I could see a shade of uneasiness on St. Prix's countenance as he listened, still and mute as a statue, to detect, if he could, any change in the hounds' tongues, as they carried the drag merrily over the hill and towards the strongest holding in the valley below. Once or twice he looked round at me and just nodded his head approvingly; as much as to say, "They're all right now, and will soon have him on his legs." Once or twice, too, he put his horn to his lips to give the signal; but, as his fine ear distinguished that, as yet, hot as the drag was, the wolf was still unroused, that cumbrous but useful and picturesque instrument swung back unsounded over his shoulder-blade. I wondered, at the moment, what some of our hard-riding masters of hounds would say, if they were constrained by fashion to carry such horns; and I pictured to myself the fractured bones and contusions they would inevitably sustain by the encumbrance of such heavy metal attached to them when they fell. How St. Prix escaped utter annihilation, as he and his horse rolled over together amid pits, grips, and granite boulders, will be a mystery to me so long as I live! Some angel must have guarded him tenderly.

Bang, bang, bang! from the hill above, and the shrieking sound of slugs hurtling through the air but a few yards above our heads roused me from my momentary abstraction: then, instantly, the shout from many brazen throats of "yr louarn, yr louarn!"—a fox, a fox—resounded on our ears. The hounds heard it at once, and, throwing up their heads, the cry suddenly ceased. St. Prix turned pale with rage, and dashing into the forest, rode straight for the quarter whence the wild yells were continued. No whip in the world, not even Jack Goddard in the golden age of the Heythrop, could have got at his hounds and stopped the mischief more promptly. As he crashed through the bushes, in the very nick of time, and headed the leading hounds, one short blast of his horn gathered the six couple around him like a stroke of magic; and, before they could feel for the scent on which the peasants were hallooing them, he lifted them back at a hand canter, and in a few seconds recovered the line from which they had been so vexatiously diverted. Had they settled on the fox, the wolves, in all probability, would have slipped away and our sport been marred for the day. The peasants, too, would have been greatly annoyed at the result of their own riotous behaviour. A wolf with a good start in his favour, and a distant strong point, like the Forest of Dualt, to gain, is as bad to catch as the wildest fox that ever broke from a Dartmoor tor. However, all's well that ends well; every hound was quickly again at work and the cover cracking with the music. St. Prix's horn, too, was again, ever and anon, lifted spasmodically to his cheek; but it was only drag, and the Louvetier still gave no signal.

The hounds, with their mouths away from us, were now pointing for a precipitous rocky ravine, matted with thorny brushwood and the wild clematis, through which it was all but impossible on horseback to force one's way. Twice I was dragged bodily from the saddle to the ground, while my coat was literally torn to tatters on my back; the clematis, intertwined with the bushes, formed a rope-like rigging as difficult to pass through as the shrouds of a ship; and I longed for a cutlass to hew my way through the provoking growth. St. Prix, however, in his close-fitting hunting-cap and green velveteen attire, still forged ahead, and I could see him between me and the sky-line fighting bravely forward, but, like myself, at some distance astern of the hounds. Notwithstanding the Louvetier's advice to stick to the hounds, Keryfan and Kergoorlas, as I very soon found, had avoided this pass, and traversing a more open part of the cover, had joined the peasants on the opposite hill.

I was just emerging from a network of clematis, by which I had been nearly strangled, when I caught sight of "Barbe-Bleu" jerked back suddenly on his haunches, and St. Prix grasping at his horn; at the same moment, the hounds' heads being turned in my direction, the angrier, sharper tone of their tongues told me at once the wolf was afoot, and they hard at him entering the ravine. Instantly the exciting blast of "Le Loup" rung from the Louvetier's horn, and, responding to the signal, at least half a dozen other horns proclaimed the "find" from distant parts of the cover. Then the "relais," the six couple in hand, were thrown in at front, till what with hounds, horns, and echoes, the old forest of Trefranc fairly rocked with applause. Had Diana been there, that wild sylvan harmony would have driven her mad with delight; and had the goddess seen Keryfan as, now with the hill in his favour, he crashed through the cover, clearing the clematis before him like so many cobwebs, her anti-matrimonial views would have vanished like a summer-cloud, and she must have lost her heart to him for ever. But, if the truth be told, had Venus herself been there, I doubt very much if, under the circumstances, Keryfan would have looked a second time at her; so strong and so pure is the passion for the chase that, when it is kindled, not even "Love is lord of all."

For a whole hour the hounds appeared glued to their game, driving hard every moment of the time, and carrying a grand head whenever the hollow cover enabled them to do so; but as yet not a wolf had been viewed by one of the field, nor was it known for certain whether a brace or a single wolf was in front of the hounds. However, this doubt was soon dispelled. A long, narrow strip of open, short heather lay exactly in the line for which the chase was now pointing, and, as the cover in this direction ran, like a peninsula, far out from its main area, whatever the hounds were running was bound to break at the far end or turn short back, there and then, in the face of them and the mounted field.

Simultaneously, and side by side, a brace of grand old wolves now broke over the heather, striding, with an easy, long gallop, as evenly together as a pair of well-matched leaders in the old Quicksilver mail. Had they suspected, however, that in escaping from Charybdis they would only be falling into the jaws of Scylla's dogs, no power would have forced them to quit the stronghold of Trefranc. There, at least, if not gorged with flesh, they might have baffled the stoutest hounds in Christendom for many a long day; but this was the down-wind point, and, wary and suspicious as they ever are, it was simply beyond the compass of their eyes, ears, or nose to discover that fifty peasants or more stood at short intervals on the edge of that cover, each bearing a deadly weapon expressly for their destruction.

The fusilade at that moment was terrific, but scarcely less deafening than the hue and cry raised by the peasants at sight of their enemy. One wolf fell dead, riddled with slugs, but the other, evidently badly hit, headed back, and either squatting in the brushwood as the hounds flung over him, or shooting past them unviewed, he managed to gain the main cover without further difficulty.

The danger of that fusilade was in reality no joke, even to the chasseurs that followed the hounds. Keryfan, notwithstanding his precaution, received a shot in his bridle arm; but, thanks to a thick jacket and the intervening distance, it was a mere scratch —drew blood and no more. Two of the peasants, however, fared far worse: one carried his leg as if badly wounded in that limb, while the other lay on his side in the heather, groaning aloud in his agony. A crowd had collected around him, eager to help the poor fellow, and equally anxious, each one of them, to shift the imputation of having shot him on any one's shoulders but their own; while all stoutly swore that every slug of their guns would be found in the dead wolf's body. On drawing near to investigate the extent of the injury, I was somewhat startled to find that the wounded man was Kledan Kam, the *braconnier*; but, although the slug had cut an ugly gash in the fleshy part of his lower back, and it bled profusely, the missile had not lodged there; so I cheered his heart speedily with a goutte of brandy and the assurance that he would be all right again in a few days. When the pain had a little abated, and he had recognised me as one of the chasseurs at Locrist on the previous day, his thoughts instantly reverted to the charge of setting a wolf-trap made against him by St. Prix. "I assure you, monsieur," he said, " I am too fond of hunting the wolf with gun and hounds to set a night-trap for him; and Monsieur de St. Prix's refusal to believe my word has wounded me more painfully than this cursed slug, and pray tell him so."

For one hour over the fallen foe a fanfare of horns proclaimed the victory far and wide, while the hounds, sitting on their haunches, and every now and then taking a savage grip at the gaunt brute's throat, bayed a wild response to the joyous notes. It was evidently St. Prix's object to rest his hounds, otherwise he must have paid readier attention to the entreaties of the peasants, and gone at once in pursuit of the other wounded wolf; besides, fearing perhaps the damage his hounds might receive in their encounter with that formidable antagonist, he purposely delayed proceedings, hoping the wolf might bleed to death ere the hounds closed with him in some unapproachable ravine of that great cover. If such were his reasons, he was doubtless right in his dilatory tactics, though I confess I fully shared the impatience loudly expressed by the excited peasants.

The bombardment of the wolves reminded me of a scene which, many years ago, I more than once witnessed on the south coast of Devon. Between the rugged cliffs on the west side of Dartmouth Harbour and Start Point extends a beach of rough sea-sand for a distance of more than two miles; at the back of which, that is, on the land side, a lake of fresh water, called Slapton Lea, runs parallel with the sea, and is divided from it only by that narrow sandy barrier throughout the whole distance. The Lea, bountifully fed from the valleys above by two never-failing trout-streams, abounds with jack, perch, roach, and eels; and in winter swarms of wild-fowl, especially coot, which are bred among the reeds, frequent its waters. The principal owner is Sir Lydston Newman, although a strip of the lake on the eastern side belongs to Mr. Toll; but that portion of it is so overgrown with long reeds and aquatic plants that, serviceable as it is for a breeding-place for the wild-fowl, it is not so convenient for the passage of boats as the western and larger portion, the property of Sir Lydston Newman. Most kind and liberal is the baronet with respect to sport on this water. A grand public "Lea-day" is annually fixed for the bombardment of the wildfowl; and every farmer "outwardly given" to such amusement for many a mile round looks forward to it as the one great holiday for the winter season. But, ye gods! if there are swarms of coot darkening the air, swarms of shot are flying after them from every available quarter; not ordinary gun-shot, but No. 2 slugs and swan drops, and those, too, impelled by fabulous charges of powder from fowling-pieces of antiquated fashion and mighty length. The last time I was present, five boats, each manned with four or five gunners, traversed the lake to and fro abreast, while an army of outsiders flanked the water's edge on each shore, and at every flight of the fowl, utterly regardless of consequences, these last poured their hap-hazard volleys, high or low, into the passing fowl, and not unfrequently into some unlucky boat. Such a cry and commotion as then arose it is utterly impossible to describe. Threats of vengeance were hurled back, and sometimes, if a farmer was hit, a return shot was instantly fired at the offenders, right into the brown of them, promiscuously. Then the occasional bursting of a fowling-piece did more serious damage, and swelled the casualities of the Lea-day into a frightful list.

Matters now are probably better managed; but the scene I have endeavoured to describe is no exaggerated picture of a "grand Lea-day" in former times, when bell-mouthed guns and flint-locks were far more general than detonators, and when French copper-caps not unfrequently burst like shells and flew in splinters into the gunner's face. From that day to the one at Trefranc I had seen nothing like it, nor, in point of casualty, was there a pin to choose between them.

But now to the wounded wolf. The hounds clapped on to the scent, soon settled to it, and, to judge by the crash that followed, it might be supposed he was not a minute ahead of them. "That's his blood they're enjoying," said St. Prix to me, as he listened with intense delight to the rattling peal: "the faster it trickles the better the scent, and, above all, the easier will be the victory to the hounds in the last fight."

"Then it will be soon over," I remarked, hearing the pack

driving desperately. "If badly hit, he can't last long at that pace."

"He is an hour ahead of them," rejoined St. Prix, "and will keep going so long as life lasts."

We now rode to head the chase, safe, at least for a time, from the random shots of the peasants, many of whom still lingered behind, feasting their eyes on the carcase of the fallen wolf, while the remainder straggled on, unposted, in the rear of the hounds; but ever, as we reached the far side of this great cover, the wolf, shirking the edge of it, doubled back for its innermost depths, and again and again threw us out, and baffled St. Prix's hope of being able to help his hounds with his couteau-de-chasse in the last savage struggle. An accident now occurred to Kergoorlas that I greatly marvel did not end more seriously. His horse put his fore legs into a badger's earth, and almost turned a summersault on his rider. The latter, however, as luck would have it, fell on a heap of soft, newly-excavated earth, and, although he smashed his horn flat as an opera-hat, he escaped with only a few bruises.

I was hastening towards him with the view of rendering all the assistance in my power, when I heard the hounds throw up and the cry suddenly cease, and at once all was quiet as the lull after a raging storm. Kergoorlas heard it too, and, casting his horse's snaffle-rein over the stump of a blackthorn, dashed on foot into the cover like a foxhound running for blood. St. Prix's head, about a hundred yards in front of us, was still visible above the scrub; and, with that for our guide, Kergoorlas and I together forced our way as best we could towards the heart of the cover. Before, however, we could reach the very spot, the angry growl of the hounds worrying the wolf fell on our ears. Then came the fighting, tearing, and death-struggle of the powerful brute, and with it the occasional shrieking howl of a hound lamed or maimed for life. It was barely half a minute after our arrival ere St. Prix, having lashed Barbe-Bleu at a safe distance, joined the fray; and no Irishman at Donnybrook ever dashed into a row with more alacrity. In he went into the thick of it, his right hand aloft and his couteau flashing in the sun. One stroke, quick as lightning it need be, struck the wolf to the heart, and he fell a lifeless carcase among the exulting hounds.

After many a fanfare on his and Keryfan's horns, the peasants crowded in from every point; and Hercules returning from the capture of the wild boar of Erymanthus, could never have received a heartier ovation from the inhabitants of that country than St. Prix from the wild Breton peasants of this district. He was their deliverer from the scourge that devastated their little flocks, and brought their grim poverty to its last pinch! and to him they were according their hero worship with a truly grateful heart. Had he performed this feat of public utility in the days of magnificent old Rome, a temple "with costly sculpture decked" would have been reared to his honour, and he promoted to the skies.

CHAPTER VII.

In England the mode of entering young hounds to their game is simple enough. Harriers take to it instinctively, and, getting their early blood with little difficulty, soon become useful workers. Fox-hounds require a longer process, the two months of September and October being scarcely sufficient to steady the puppies from riot and qualify them for the discipline and duty required of them in the following November. Otter-hounds, however, are far less readily entered than either of the former, owing, in the first place, to the scent being, as I hold it to be, an artificial one to hounds; and, in the next, to the many blank days that attend the sport, and to the difficulty of finding, and killing, when found, that wild animal. Consequently, otter-hounds rarely become clever and knowing in their work until they have had long experience, and become, at least, middle-aged hounds. The famous Carlisle hound Swimmer was never better than in his tenth season; and, according to Mr. Carrick, his owner, he did lots of useful work up to his fourteenth year, when the veteran died.

To enter hounds on wolf in the wild forests of Brittany, which, in Finisterre and Morbihan, at least, never lack that game, might be considered a simple process, and one requiring little or no trouble from the piqueurs charged with that service. But the fact is otherwise. Not only is there a vast variety of attractive scent, so tempting to young hounds, in the shape of hare, fox, martin cat, wild boar, and deer of different kinds, always to be met with in the covers frequented by the wolf, but, from the want of "rides" or even footpaths, the covers themselves are, many of them, all but impenetrable, and so rocky that it is quite impossible for a score of piqueurs to check riot when hounds have settled to it in earnest in their deep ravines. Added to which, the scent of a wolf is at first distasteful to hounds; and many a time will a young hound, on crossing the fresh line, put up every bristle on his back, and, with strong symptoms of disgust and alarm, take refuge behind the heel of the nearest piqueur. Nor is this repugnance to the scent evinced by the cowardly or ill-bred hound; the most courageous puppy, famous for its ancestry of high-mettled wolf-hunters, will equally turn tail on its first acquaintance with the distasteful scent. The force of example, however, soon cures this difficulty, and the fire of the pack rapidly kindles a like flame in the well-bred hound. The covers and the "riot" with which they abound are the chief hindrance; nor is this ever sufficiently overcome to render it safe to throw a pack of hounds into cover and draw for the wild beast without the aid of a trained limier and piqueur: the former to mark the line, and by his action to indicate whether the scent is fresh or stale; and the latter with his eye, keen and practised as that of a Red Indian, to detect by slot, spur, or heel, the nature of the game on which the hound is drawing on his game.

The ancient process of entering hounds at wolf is described at length by Jacques du Fouilloux in that quaint work of his entitled "La Vénerie," an authority regarded by the Gallic chasseurs of old with the highest respect, and quoted by them as Beckford is by the houndsmen of this country. It is not remarkable that "The Thoughts" of the latter, sound in reason as the arguments of "Blackstone's Commentaries," and published in the early part of the present century, should still be our chief textbook in all matters relating to hounds, in kennel or chase; but it is very remarkable that Du Fouilloux's instructions, written as they were in the reign of Henry II. of France, that is, about 1550 A.D., more than three hundred years ago, should continue to be the French gentleman's chief guide in the science of venery down to the present day.

The Comte Charles de St. Prix, a thorough houndsman from his earliest years, looked upon Jacques du Fouilloux as a second St. Hubert, and had studied his precepts with so much care and respect, that he was ever ready to quote from "La Vénerie," in support of all questions pertaining to hounds or beasts of chase. After our grand day at Trefranc the conversation on our homeward route turned to the subject of entering hounds at wolf; and, although he detailed to me minutely the method recommended by Du Fouilloux, I could see a twinkle in his eye when I inquired if that was really the practice he adopted in the management of his young hounds, as I said it appeared to me a process of unnecessary trouble.

"Quite true," he replied; "we now find that waiting for the wolf to come to us, lying in ambush, is a tedious affair, and requires more patience than my piqueurs possess. Besides, shooting the brute before we hunt him is so antagonistic to the principle of fair play that I have ventured to differ from that great authority on this important point."

The passage is altogether so quaint and so primitive in its injunctions that I am quite sure a free translation of it will amuse, if not astonish, the modern houndsman of this country. It runs thus:—

"Very necessary is it that princes and grand seigneurs should have hounds bred from a race that love to hunt the wolf, and that they should be well-fed together, so that they may become big, strong, and courageous. And if, peradventure, there should not be hounds already entered to the scent which could train them to their work, it would be advisable to slaughter a carcase and place it near a water-mill, on the other side of its small stream; and there, within the mill, to conceal a cross-bow man, armed with his cross-bow and bolt, to shoot at the wolf when he comes to devour the carcase; then, having wounded him, let him bring his young hounds, not more than a year or so old, and clap them on the blood and trace of the wolf, exciting and encouraging them to the scent with a goodly company of men. Thus, by following the trail of the blood, they will at length come up to the wounded wolf, and, disabled as he is, will bay around him; and if he is dead they will paw him with their feet.

"That being done, it would be well to skin the wolf and cook his flesh, and when it is well cooked to chop it into pieces, and mixing it with good wheaten bread, milk, and cheese, to stuff it into the wolf's skin, in order that it might be impregnated with the odour and taint of the brute. Then sound the horns, open said skin near the throat and mouth, and let the hounds rush in and eat the whole. So ought all the first wolves, when taken, to be thus treated."

The ordinary plan, however, adopted by St. Prix and other masters of wolf-hounds, considering the variety of riot to which young hounds are exposed, and the impenetrable character of the Breton covers, is found to be a safe and successful one. The limier first warms upon the drag, then a few steady old hounds are uncoupled, and when they have settled on the scent, another batch, the next steady to them, are allowed to join the cry; and so on by relays, till at length the puppies are thrown in, and encouraged by shout and horn to take their part in the exciting chase. Nor is this system discontinued when the season has advanced, and the young hounds have been well entered, for the further reason that a Brittany pack is not kept exclusively to one game, but, on the contrary, is expected to hunt deer, boar, wolf, and fox, severally, as the season or occasion demands its use. However, as one hound takes best to this scent, and another to that, their several fancies are soon ascertained; and the relays are formed and thrown in according to the game they are most inclined to pursue.

Notwithstanding the universal belief in Brittany that wolves will not attack a human being, however young or defenceless, a fearful sensation prevailed at Carhaix, a month or so before my arrival, by the sudden disappearance of a peasant girl from the neighbourhood of Huelgoet, one of the wildest forests in the department of Finisterre. The poor little trot, only six years old, had been left by her parents, as is the common practice of that country, to take charge of a small black sheep, which her mere presence was supposed to protect from the attack of wolves frequenting the adjoining forest. The plot of enclosed ground in which she was stationed was so overgrown with old broom that a score of Brittany bullocks might have wandered unseen beneath its topmost twigs, while here and there, from the densest portion of it, appeared sundry ominous track-ways, worn by wolves in their passage to and fro from the neighbouring cover. The parents of the child, well aware of these signs and the proximity of those dangerous robbers, yet never for one moment entertained a doubt either as to her safety or that of her charge; and great indeed was their dismay and agony on finding, ere the sun went down, that no trace of either, beyond a few scattered bunches of wool, could be discovered in that or the adjoining fields. Tracks there were, however, in the soil, deep and recent, of the presence of a huge wolf close to the bank near which the child and sheep were last seen; but beyond the wool no other vestige was left to indicate the too probable fate of both.

Still, the belief of the peasantry in the inviolability of the human person by a wolf remained strong and unshaken; and large parties, aided by the gendarmes of the district, banded themselves together and searched diligently for many days, and even weeks, in the forest of Huelgoet and the broom fields around. Fires, too, were lighted in lone spots and kept burning throughout the night, with the hope of attracting the little wanderer's attention and rescuing her, if alive, from the starvation to which she must otherwise succumb. But all efforts proved unsuccessful, till, at length, hope became extinguished in the hearts of all, save those of the parents. Some peasants, indeed, in their superstition, came to the conclusion that the footprints in the mud were those of the Loup-garou, and that the demon-wolf had carried off the child; others thought that, had no such fate overtaken her, the sight of the wolf had probably scared her from the spot, that she had then wandered into the forest, and died there from hunger and exposure. This opinion, after awhile, seemed to be generally accepted, and further search for the poor child was abandoned by the public as hopeless and unavailing.

The parents, however, parent-like, still clung to the belief that their little Marie was not lost to them for ever; and for many a weary day they threaded the deepest nooks of Huelgoet, returning only at late eve, when the howling of the wolves was the sole sound that fell on their anxious ears, and the pale stars the sole light to guide them on their lonesome path. Nightly, too, they burned a resin-candle in the one small window of their cabin, trusting it might prove a beacon to guide the little wanderer home.

Six weeks or more had elapsed, and hope, with all, was at its lowest ebb, when a charcoal-burner, following his lonely avocation in the heart of the forest, was startled by the apparition of a child timidly approaching his hut; this, of course, was little Marie; but exposure and want of food had almost converted her into a living skeleton: her face begrimed with dirt and blackberry juice, her hair matted with particles of moss and other lichens, making her head look more like a bird's nest than that of a human being;

half clad, too, and wild in manner as any fawn of the forest, no wonder the simple peasant stared again and again before he could be assured it was a real child that crept into the darkest corner of his hut, too timid to speak, and yet pinched by hunger even to death's door.

A moment's thought, however, convinced him that this must be the lost child, respecting whom the gendarmes and others had already paid him sundry visits and, being of a kindly nature, the man, when he had fed her bountifully with his black buckwheat bread and washed her face, lifted her on his broad shoulders and carried her directly home to the cabin of her parents. Marie's eventful history was soon told: she had left the broom field in search of blackberries, and on returning to her charge was just in time to see a huge wolf jump the bank with the little sheep struggling in its jaws; the beast at once entered the forest, and Marie, crying and screaming, and hoping to scare it from its prey, followed on until she soon became lost in its mazes, and found it utterly impossible to retrace her steps or distinguish even the direction of her parents' home. Her sole food had been beech-nuts, blackberries, and a few chesnuts; and, although sleeping nightly in the very presence of wolves, she had never been disturbed for a moment by a sight of the ravenous brutes.

The next morning after the sport at Trefranc we were all seated round the table of the *salle-à-manger*, discussing at the same time the various incidents of the chase and the bountiful *déjeûner* provided by the host, when Marseillier's jolly face, always bearing a happy smile, but now unusually lighted up with some pleasant intelligence, suddenly appeared in the room; and, as he lifted his paper cap and twisted his white apron on one side (for the cutlets and omelettes were still under his delicate manipulation), he marched up to St. Prix's chair and announced the arrival of a deputation from Treganteru.

"They have come," he said, "to complain of the damage

done to their crops by the wild boars in the neighbourhood of Laz and Kœnig, and entreat your aid."

"They shall have it by all means," said St. Prix, heartily; "but show them in, Marseillier, and let us hear what they have to say on the subject."

In a few seconds, accordingly, six veritable Breton peasants, all clad alike in dark, long-haired goat-skin jackets, tight canvas trousers close-buttoned down to the ancle, heavy sabots stuffed with hay instead of hose, and round-crowned, broad-brimmed hats, which, with a cluster of long curly locks, fairly overshadowed their shoulders, entered the room; and, after lifting their hats in salutation, and replacing them at once on their heads, the leader of the party proceeded forthwith to explain the object of their visit.

"We are come," he said in the Breton tongue, "to tell you of the damage done by the wild boars in our mountain land. Not a farm from Gourin to Chateauneuf that has not suffered from their ravages; not a crop that has not paid a heavy tax to those plunderers—whole fields of potatoes have been upturned by their snouts; and standing corn, where not eaten, has been trampled, like so much stubble, into the earth. Then, the chesnuts which, at Kilvern, were wont to supply our families and pigs with so much wholesome food, were totally demolished this autumn; in truth, if something is not done to diminish their number, they will ruin us all before next winter."

The peasant's earnest appeal, as he stood forward with hand uplifted above his head, as if calling on a higher Power to attest the truth of his statement, amounted almost to eloquence, insomuch that his few simple words went like an arrow to the mark; and the Count de St. Prix, in spite of his anxiety to protect, so far as he reasonably could, the *feræ naturæ* of the Brittany forests, especially the rougher portion of them, at once gave his word that no effort of his should be wanting to redress the evil of which the deputation so justly complained.

"Then, Monsieur de St. Prix," said the peasant respectfully, "will you do us the favour to name an early day for bringing your hounds to Kilvern? The *môch meur* (the big pigs) have made that cover their head-quarters; and if you hunt and kill a few of them, the lesser swine will not be so bold in their depredations."

"What say you, Kergoorlas," inquired St. Prix, "will Monday next suit you to bring your hounds to join us at Gourin? We could then give them a week in those covers, and probably supply our friends" (bowing to the deputation) "with plenty of good chesnut-fed bacon for the rest of the winter."

I could see the hitherto solemn faces of the peasants sparkle at the thought of not only killing but eating the plunderers that had grown fat on the produce of their small farms; the idea of retaliation to the extent suggested by St. Prix had probably already occurred to them, and even now seemed to be sharpening their appetites in anticipation of the coming day.

"Certainly," said M. Kergoorlas; "Monday will suit me exactly; "and if your hounds meet at Laz on that day, my pack shall draw Coet-Koenig on Tuesday, and take the alternate days with yours to the end of the week."

And thus it was agreed, to the great satisfaction of the peasants, to make Gourin the head-quarters of the hunt, and to give the boars of Kilvern a rattling such as they had not met with for many a long year.

The deputation then withdrew into an adjoining *salon*, where, by St. Prix's order, they were regaled with food and wine to their hearts' content, Marseillier himself presiding, and by his pleasant manner and marvellous tales of the chase establishing himself for ever as the first of hosts in the peasants' eye. If all the boars' heads promised to him that morning found their way to the Hôtel la Tour d'Auvergne, I can only say his guests would have no cause to grumble at the lack of *charcuterie* in that hostelry for many a day to come.

CHAPTER VIII.

"FRANK," said the Baron de Keryfan to me, immediately after the interview with the Breton peasants, "we shall have hot work next week at Kilvern: the whole country will be there, from Pontivy to Landerneau; and every peasant owning a musket or a blunderbuss will bring his weapon, and use it, too, in the most reckless fashion on that occasion—the slugs at Trefranc were mere hail compared with the weight of metal deemed necessary at Kilvern: the 'balle-mariée,' which is simply a couple of leaden bullets screwed into one, is rammed into every barrel when a pig is the object of the chase; and this, if it hits not its mark, is apt to glance awkwardly from rock or tree, and create serious results."

"A pleasant prospect for men and hounds," I replied. "If that is to be the order of the day, one might as well encounter a band of armed savages as join these wild Bretons when excited by the chase. By St. Hubert! after the pinking you had yesterday, would it not be safer for you to send a messenger for one of those Crusader hauberks that hang in your hall at Pen-meur; it at least would protect your body from mortal injury, and your head and limbs might take their chance."

"You're chaffing me, Frank," said the Baron, good-temperedly; "but, believe me, the storm of random bullets will be no joke when a pig comes to run short in those hollow glens."

"Well, but if the sport is good," said the Count de Kergoorlas, chiming in, "I'll be bound to say we shall none of us give the bullets a second thought. However, it would probably be advisable to warn the Kilvern peasants, ere they leave this house, that the gendarmes will be sure to attend the hunt, and that every gun will be seized, if its owner cannot produce his *permis-de-chasse*."

"That may deter some few of them," said M. de St. Prix; "but the majority of the peasants, whether possessing or not that legal qualification, will care no more for the gendarmes than you do for the Loup-garou, that forest bugbear of our old women and children. However, give them that hint by all means. I only wish my hounds, in times past, had suffered as little from the boars' tusks as the chasseurs from the glancing balls of the Brittany peasants."

"Do your hounds, then, venture to worry him," I inquired, "when the boar is brought to bay?"

"Aye," said St. Prix; "they go in at him as if he were a mere fallow doe; and it's an awful sight to witness the slashing and gashing inflicted on the best and bravest of my hounds ere we are able to give him his *coup-de-grâce*."

"That, of course, you do with your *chasse-couteau;* but is it not a service of some danger to yourself, closing with him at a time when, maddened with rage and driven to a stand-still, he catches his wind and charges furiously on every enemy?"

"It would certainly be so," said the Louvetier, "to a man who does not thoroughly understand the use of his weapon: he must be cool, too, and know where to strike; then, his blow must be quick as a flash of lightning, or it would probably fall in vain; and, if so, let the bungler look to his safety."

The use of the rapier has ever been a favourite study with our continental neighbours; and, as it is a thrusting weapon akin to the *couteau-de-chasse*, it will readily be understood how expertly

G

the latter may be managed by a man long accustomed to the exercise of the other. He may not be a hunter, skilled in all the shifts of a pig or deer when brought to bay, and he may be profoundly ignorant of the vital spot at which his thrust should be aimed; but instruct him on these points, and he will deal his blow with a quickness and precision unknown by the less adroit swordsmen of this country. St. Prix's confidence in his *couteau* made my flesh creep: no matter where the boar was at bay, whether with his back bearing against a huge granite rock, or immersed up to his belly in the bed of a brawling brook, the hounds assailing him in every quarter, and the glare of his wicked eyes infuriated with fire, St. Prix never hesitated a moment in getting at him and plunging his weapon, with the rapidity and precision of a matador, hilt-deep into some vital part—a service of infinite danger, no doubt; for, if the point of his *couteau* were to come into contact with a bone, and death were not almost the instant result of his blow, the penalty of his failure would be a charge to a certainty, and probably a serious gash or two from the animal's tusks. So, a firm hand, eye and nerve, and, above all, skill in the use of his weapon, are essential in the encounter; or the death-wound will not be given with the exact nicety requisite at such a time.

After the departure of the Kilvern peasants from Carhaix, the afternoon of that day was pleasantly passed in a visit to the hounds, quartered as they were in a peasant's cottage hard by the town. Not an article of the scanty furniture had been removed for the occasion; but there, in the chimney-nook still strewed with its wood-embers, under the table and on the table, and in a hollow recess of the wall, hitherto claiming the dignity of the peasant's own bed, lay the swarthy hounds, apparently as comfortably kennelled after their hard work as her Majesty's staghounds might be on their luxurious benches at Ascot Heath. Grievously marked about the head and neck were several of them in that last worry at Trefranc; while a couple or two came limping along on three legs to meet and welcome the Louvetier, as he entered the grimy hovel in which they were confined. One old hound, a grand specimen of the St. Hubert breed, standing 26 inches at the shoulder, and topped by a head and ears such as Snyders never saw, rose leisurely from the bed-recess and exhibited a face covered with scars—a recent ugly one, extending from his cheek-bone to his nose, added dignity, if it did not otherwise improve his look; while countless old seams about his neck and head reminded me of that ancient warrior, Curius Dentatus, whose body bore the marks of a hundred wounds, and all in front. He was well named "Cæsar," for he looked like an emperor and a conqueror from stem to stern.

St. Prix's remedies were simple enough; a bucket of water and a sponge being the sole appliance for all wounds—except, indeed, where the sores had generated proud flesh, when he used blue-stone with an unsparing hand. If a wound, however, was within reach of a hound's tongue, he never troubled it with artificial treatment, well knowing the all-healing power given by nature to that member. Half-a-dozen hounds had submittted very quietly to the sponge and water process—no joke for their sores under the rough hands of Louis Trevarreg—when it became old "Cæsar's" turn to undergo the same ordeal. I could see at a glance, however, that he was a hound not to be handled by a novice; and that even the experienced piqueur would gladly have deferred the operation, if his master had not been present to insist on its performance. "Cæsar," said St. Prix, very distinctly, as he ran the thong through the keeper of his whip and drew the loop tightly round the hound's neck; "Cæsar; ici, mon enfant;" and out stalked the grand old hound, slowly and reluctantly, towards the bucket in front of the door. Two or three deep growls, and a few spasmodic twitches with the end of his stern, indicated but too plainly that he was in no humour to be handled with impunity; so, while St. Prix held him firmly by the head, Louis Trevarreg threw his right leg over the hound's shoulders, and, grasping them with both knees, fixed him as in a vice, and at once proceeded to wash out the wound without further danger. But the storm that had been brewing now burst forth with a roar of thunder from the hound's tongue, and flashes of lightning from his angry eyes; and it was quite work enough for the two powerful men to hold him securely to the end of the operation. The moment, however, the fine old fellow was liberated, he came up to St. Prix, flourishing his stern good-naturedly, as if he meant to apologise for the trouble he had given and the uproar he had made under his hands.

The day following this visit to the kennel was Saturday; and as our party was now reduced to St. Prix, Keryfan, and myself—Kergoorlas having gone to his chateau on the Loire, and the other chasseurs to their respective homes—Keryfan proposed driving us to see the lead-mines of Huelgoet, famed for their hydraulic pump, the handiwork of a M. Juncker, an Alsatian engineer, nearly related to the great naturalist Baron Cuvier. St. Prix at once disclaimed all knowledge of, or interest in mining or machinery; but, as he said, the drive would be a pleasant one, and, barring a billiard-table, there was nothing whatever to do by way of amusement in the dull town of Carhaix, he readily agreed to accompany us; and so, by ten o'clock that morning, we were under weigh, Keryfan handling the ribbons, and the tandem-team stepping along right merrily at the rate of eight or nine miles an hour—no mean pace, considering the hill-and-dale character of that country.

The main roads are always in admirable order, even in Finisterre, being under the management and supervision of the French Government; but, if the traveller on wheels venture to diverge from these, he will soon come to inevitable grief. The by-roads are supposed to be repaired by the several Communes through which they pass; never, however, do I remember seeing a peasant at work on them; so that as a rule, in winter, they have ruts axle-deep, no metal on their surface, and sloughs or spews everywhere. In fact, many of them, if supplied with seed and manure, would grow as good a crop of potatoes as the adjoining fields. I have been in far greater peril riding sure-footed horses through the mire and spews of these lanes by night than in the wildest fox-chase I ever joined; and when I say that, let me add how frequently it has been my happy lot to see some glorious days over Dartmoor with Mr. Trelawny's hounds, and not a few with Mr. Russell over Exmoor, not less the region of bog, rugged ground, and wild foxes, than its sister forest on the southern coast. But even Diamond Lane on Dartmoor, paved as it is by nature with blocks of granite scattered broadcast on its surface, and some of them far bigger than bishop's heads, is safe-going—nay, is a fair coach-road compared with many of those parish tunnels in Lower Brittany.

Before twelve o'clock our team, the leader of which had maintained a continuous short canter throughout almost the whole distance, pulled up at the Lion d'Or, the small inn that welcomed us on arriving at Huelgoet. The landlord was the first to rush to the door, and instantly recognising St. Prix, the Louvetier, and, by virtue of that office, the public benefactor of his country, it is scarcely possible to overstate the amount of attention he paid him and us during our short stay at his hostelry. The man had been a miner himself, and avowed his intention of accompanying us to the mine, and showing us all that was worth seeing within its subterranean precincts. So, starting at once for the works, a distance of more than a mile, we traversed a wild, picturesque gorge, through which a strong mountain stream, unseen by the eye, but very perceptible to the ear, rushed and roared 'neath the colossal boulders that barred its course in vain.

The ponderous machinery, which it was our object to see, has been at work in the bowels of the earth for a great number of years night and day, raising, without noise or irregularity, a vast body of water, four cubic metres per minute, to a height of 750 feet. A column of water, brought in by an aqueduct, and falling from a height of 200 feet, gives the machine the power of 280 horses; and thus, by its incessant labour, the mine is kept dry. We descended by a bucket and rope to a great depth below the surface of the earth, our host, a man of 16 stone, leading the way, and testing, as he affirmed, the safety of the gear for our especial benefit. The test proved ample, and on alighting in the mine we were courteously received by the resident Director; and all the operations of the men at work, all the movements of the mighty machine—a masterpiece of mechanical invention—and the whole process of separating, by mercury, the silver from the lead (for the mines include both these ores amalgamated together), were duly explained to us by that intelligent man. Without pretending to enter more fully into the subject, I can only say our subterranean visit proved to be a most instructive one, and that even St. Prix, on our return to Carhaix, confessed to having passed a most agreeable day, and seen with wonder the power and efficiency of M. Juncker's machine.

The next day being Sunday, the whole town was agog and stirring long before daylight; heavy, iron-shod sabots clattered through the streets, and men were hastening from all quarters to mass, so that, the short service over, they might sally forth to the *chasse* with a sense of having done their duty, and without a scruple of doubt to mar the pleasure of the sport for the rest of the day. The desecration of the Sabbath was certainly far from the minds of those *ouvriers* who, after six days of toil, rested from their labour, and devoted the seventh—their morning sacrifice having been duly offered—to the innocent recreation of body and mind; their creed being, doubtless, that "the Sabbath was made for man, and not man for the Sabbath." You may break, in some countries—Christian so called—every law, human and divine, without a throb of indignation or a word of remonstrance from the bystanders; but if you just whistle a lively tune on a Sabbath day, the woe, woe, of a coming doom is pronounced with pitiless horror on your profane head.

But a short time ago a friend, possessing an extensive moor in Scotland, told me the following anecdote: He was walking, he said, one Sunday morning, near some of his best breeding-ground, in company with a gillie and a wild young setter, the latter ranging a-head and disturbing the grouse in every direction. After sundry growls and angry expressions on the part of the gillie, he turned round abruptly, and said, "Wull ye whustle the dog, Sir Greville?" His master, not exactly catching what he said, and making no immediate response, he exclaimed impatiently, "Wull ye whustle the dog, Sir Greville? for 'tis the Saubbuth day, and I mauna whustle mysel'." And yet this man, who, to save himself and the birds, had no objection to Sir Greville's going to perdition, was the most immoral, dissolute fellow on the whole estate; his Sunday evenings being especially devoted to the whisky bottle and other excesses.

But to return to Carhaix. The hubbub in the town about day-break on a Sunday morning was more than I can adequately describe. Horns sounded the most discordant notes, dogs yelled, and men shouted and *sacristied* across the street, from window to window, arranging their plans for the campaign, and deciding who should, and who should not, accompany them to the chase. Sometimes parties of even fifteen or twenty in number clubbed together, and, with guns, hounds, and dogs of every description, fell upon some ill-fated district, and literally combed it clean of every living thing bigger than a Jenny wren or a cock-mouse.

This, of course, would be a desert land for many a day to come; but, as the *ouvriers'* raid was necessarily confined to a certain foot-distance from the town, it was my usual custom to ride to a point outside and beyond the circle of their operations, and thus beat virgin ground, un-get-atable by these marauders.

In less than half-an-hour after the last dog and chasseur had quitted the town, the deathlike stillness that reigned over Carhaix for the rest of the day was something awful. Not even the usual gathering of women at the well, nor the gossip that accompanied it, was seen or heard for one moment around that attractive spot; and, but for the occasional flitting of a grisette, in gay holiday attire, from one house to another, the absence of all living creatures from the streets was absolutely appalling. On the present occasion, however, the monotony of the day was somewhat enlivened towards the afternoon by the departure of M. de St. Prix's hounds, horses, and men, for Gourin, which, although but a small village, and possessing but scanty accommodation, was selected as the most convenient quarters for the forthcoming campaign.

Lower Brittany, especially that portion of it in the region of the Black Mountains, is the land of storms; indeed, had the ancients fixed upon this country as the kingdom of Æolus, instead of those seven pleasant little islands in the Mediterranean Sea, it would, methinks, have been a happier fiction, and far nearer the truth. Some hours after the party had left for Gourin, I mounted a well-bred cob, that I had lately bought out of the Morlaix mail-cart, at a hundred and twenty francs—just four shillings and twopence less than a five-pound note—and a gamer animal no man ever crossed. I was scarcely off the flag-stones, when a thunder-cloud burst overhead, and poured such a deluge of rain down that, notwithstanding a double-milled great-coat, warranted waterproof, in which I was enveloped, I was soaked to the skin in less than half-an-hour. The wind, too, blew a hurricane; and the lightning, which seemed to play upon the sheets of water that covered the road, so terrified my horse, that twenty times did he stop short, wheel on his haunches, and refuse to advance a yard further. In the interval of the flashes, the darkness around was that of Erebus itself; and, but for my thorough knowledge of the road through the forest of Conveau, the best wolf-cover in the Black Mountains, I should have despaired of finding my way to Gourin on that terrible night. The road is a broad one, however; and the wind, as it blew furiously in my teeth from the moment I quitted Carhaix, kept me well posted as to the direction I was required to keep.

On arriving at the Cheval Blanc, where the chasseurs had their mess, I found a party of ten or twelve gentlemen all seated at table, and the supper nearly at an end; and never shall I forget the hearty welcome I received on making my appearance, in a half-drowned state, at that festive board. My carpet-bag had been left for the diligence, which would not reach Gourin till the following day; so, discovering this fact, two or three of the company instantly rose and rushed off for a complete set of dry clothes for me; and there and then (they would have it) before the huge log-fire of their *salle-a-manger*, I was divested of my wet garments, and speedily reclothed in the dry and comfortable apparel brought me by those kind friends. Need I add that a pleasanter evening I never spent in my life?

CHAPTER IX.

The great cover of Laz, where M. de St. Prix's hounds were appointed to meet at eight o'clock that morning, being at some distance from Gourin, the chasseurs at the Cheval Blanc, some of them, I fear, with very heavy heads, were up and astir long before daylight, and, as the wassail of the previous evening had been maintained to a late hour, the snatches of sleep enjoyed by the last of the revellers must have been short indeed, and disturbed to the uttermost extent. The little square in front of the hotel had been traversed the live-long night by peasants assembling for the hunt, of whom it would be difficult to say whether their tongues or iron-shod sabots made the greater noise; added to which the horses in the stable hard by, wherein nothing in the shape of a stall existed, the most unruly being separated by a bar only from each other, kept up a ceaseless turmoil and contention during the whole night. Then followed the inevitable horns; the performers thereon standing like maniacs at open windows in their shirt-sleeves, too-tooing for their lives "Le point du Jour," and disturbing not only every soul in Gourin, but the affrighted wolves in the neighbouring forest of Conveau.

The misery of that morning, however hopeful the prospect, I shall never forget; and even at this moment the thought of it strikes a chill upon my bones. The wind was at north-east, bitterly cold and stormy, and, blowing in fitful gusts, brought down heavy showers of rain and snow alternately. Still, was not Laz the meet? and were there not twelve couple of strong, roaring hounds, eager to rouse the grisly boar from his lair and pursue him to the death, even now trotting across the little *Place* in front of my window? The very sight of them, as the grey light of morn enabled me to catch just a glimpse of their mottled sides, acted on my spirits like an electric spark. I shouted to "Marie," the stereotyped name of the Breton women, to bring me my stockings, which, with my other *uvida vestimenta*, had been suspended the night before within the chimney nook. Alas! my Highland hose had fallen into the live wood embers, and the mere tops of them, brought in by a young chasseur with a broad grin on his face, alone remained to attest the fact; the rest had been turned into tinder. This was vexatious enough; but the unsuppressed laugh of the youth chafed me to the quick; and, had he not been a bidden guest of St. Prix's, I should have certainly hurled him out of the room without farther ceremony. However, I smothered my wrath as I best could; aud, requesting him to throw the rags on the floor, proceeded to pull on the pair of thin cotton stockings lent me by Keryfan the night before, my own baggage not being expected by the diligence before mid-day. But this was only the prelude to far greater annoyance and discomfort: my hunting-boots, at least the feet of them, were still sopped with wet; and although I emptied a lot of burning wood-cinders and tossed them rapidly to and fro inside the boots (just as a man shakes shot in a bottle he is attempting to clean), and then wiped them out with a pocket handkerchief, my feet in five minutes were wet and cold as a lump of snow.

Few men, however hardy their nature or inured to discomfort, care to put on dirty boots, to say nothing of wet ones, on a hunting morning; but on such a morning as this, ye gods, defend me from a similar fate for the rest of my life! Nothing but young blood and the prospect of a day's sport enabled me to "grin and bear it" on this occasion. Nevertheless, bad as the start was, my own personal discomfort distressed me far less than the scene I witnessed inside the stable. Within sight and within a few yards of the horses a young wolf, three-parts grown, was chained to the opposite manger: a strong iron muzzle secured his jaws together, and his wild, wicked eyes told but too plainly the necessity for such a measure. Every horse in the stable was sweating with terror; not one, as I afterwards found, had dared to lie down: my own brave little cob was trembling like a brook-reed; not a grain of his corn had he touched, nor a mouthful of hay. There the wild brute, I was told, had been chained for a month, and was getting every day more accustomed to horses and less violent in his struggles for liberty. The latter I could well believe, as, judging from his lanky, famished look, he was all but starved to death; and as to his becoming familiar with horses, it is quite certain they would never become reconciled to his company.

The "sacristies" of my friends whose horses had been quartered in that stable were of little avail: the mischief had been done; and we mounted, each of us, our trembling steeds unfed and half-jaded before the work of the day had begun. The light-heartedness of my companions, however, on our way to cover soon made us forget this annoyance; although, from the rocky and roadless mountain ridge over which we passed between Gourin and Laz, freshness and the full possession of his muscular power were very needful to a horse in his transit over this broken ground; and great care was required by the rider to avoid the grips and rock-holes that presented themselves on every side. Still, we were all landed in safety, about eight o'clock, at the cover-side; so far well, but to have attempted more with our already beaten horses would have been an act of sheer brutality. A short consultation ensued; and a suggestion of Keryfan's that we should put up our horses and run with the hounds, as the peasants did, for the rest of the day, was at once agreed to as the only solution for this difficulty: and to it, chilled as I was by my damp clothes and slow riding, I probably owed my escape on that occasion from rheumatic fever or a like ailment.

It so happened that the cover-owner was present, the Comte de Kerjeguz (I hope he will pardon the phonetic liberty I take with his Celtic name), who, overhearing our conversation, was kind enough to offer his stables for our use, and, moreover, to send our horses so far, not a mile off, under the care of his own servants. Accordingly, this being done, our anxieties vanished for the day; every man—and there were six of us in the same predicament—at once joined the hounds on foot: an arrangement, as it afterwards proved, by no means disadvantageous to us, as we were thus enabled better to view the sport and take up our position in rocky and precipitous parts of the cover, which, on horseback, would have been utterly inaccessible.

The pack was a short one, only eight couple out of the twelve having been selected for the dangerous duty anticipated in these covers, the other four—Cæsar being conspicuous amongst them from his great size and badly scarred face—were chiefly wolfers; and, partly on that account, and partly because St. Prix feared the additional risk that a larger body of hounds would run, these were despatched with the horses to M. de Kerjeguz's stables. The result, however, did not confirm the Louvetier's apprehension.

At half-past eight o'clock exactly two couple of hounds were thrown into cover, on the edge of a ravine, into which several well-worn paths, hollowed out by use, and bearing the fresh track of pig on their surface, led directly down to the rocky fastnesses in the glen below. Not a word of encouragement did the hounds need; but, dashing at once into the brushwood, in one second they were out of sight, and, in another, throwing their tongues so vigorously that an inexperienced hand would have concluded the game was afoot and they swinging after it like tenor bells. But St. Prix, at least, knew better; so did the hounds coupled at his heels: with ears puckered forward and deep furrows indenting their faces, indicative of intent thought and earnestness, they stood mute and still as statues, evidently, however, noting every change in the cry, and apparently aware that their time for action had not yet arrived.

Some forty years ago, the well-known Devonshire Squire, George Templer, had a hound called Guardsman that, so long as hounds were drawing or even running the drag with much music—not in those days considered so great a barbarism—never quitted his horse's heels: but, the moment the fox was really up, then went Guardsman to the front, and held his own there against all comers. I have heard Mr. Templer say that the hound was most valuable to him for that very quality; inasmuch, as frequently in the deep covers he hunted, when hounds were all but out of hearing and their notes undistinguishable by him, Guardsman would let him know the very instant the fox was found: like an arrow from the bow he sped forth, and never stayed his course till he had run him to ground or brought the fox's head home in his own jaws. I speak of sport antecedent to the period of the "Let-'em-alones," when a pack of foxes were literally kept in kennel by Mr. Templer and turned out as bagmen before those hounds, and when horsemen, like the Rev. Henry Taylor and John Templer, more like centaurs than men, rode over that rough country as if they were carried by winged dragons, and not by mere horse-flesh such as we see in the present day; men, who so long as honour, manliness, and genial sociality are valued, will long be remembered in the county of Devon with unqualified respect and affection.

But, hark back! I am over the line, and getting somewhat

riotous; the two couple of hounds are doubling their tongues with great animation, and quickly getting farther and farther away from us into the depths of the cover. Luckily, however, they are working up-wind, and the faithful echoes, borne back on the favouring breeze, report progress with the speed and fidelity of an electric wire. St. Prix, seated on Barbe-Bleu, is silent and motionless as the statue of Marcus Aurelius in the court of the Capitol; every peasant has left him and followed the chase, and the hounds too, still in couples at his heels, but for the whip of a piqueur, would have also joined the cry long since. St. Prix beckons to me and almost whispers (for his ear is still fixed on the drag) that the boar, in order to be sure that the coast is clear, invariably retires up-wind to his lair, and almost as invariably traverses back over the foiled ground when he is pressed in the chase; so, pointing to a rocky knoll about forty yards below us in the cover, he recommends me to station myself at that point and await the result.

A sudden change in the cry is now noticeable; the hounds' tongues, hitherto growing every moment more and more indistinct, are now turned towards us, and every note is heard short, sharp, and earnest, as if the strife had begun and the hounds were actually on the haunches of the game. Louis Trefarreg, the chief piqueur, stood by, keeping his eye fixed on St. Prix, and expecting his order to uncouple some more hounds; but the Louvetier, hearing the cry draw nearer and nearer, and suspecting there were more pigs than one afoot, gave no sign as yet; the horn only was held in readiness, and one blast from it would send "the relay" headlong from their leashes.

One, two, three ringing reports from the peasants' guns in the ravine below made my pulse throb audibly; a state of excitement that was not a little increased by my catching an occasional view of at least four or five large pigs close in front of the hounds; the biggest of them, which proved to be an old sow, bringing up the rear, and covering, as best she could, the retreating herd. Their heads, too, as they galloped over the rocky ground on the opposite side of the gully, were pointing directly for the spot on which I stood; and, unless untowardly headed, another minute or two would bring them within easy range of my smooth-bore; and, as both barrels were charged with the *balle-mariée*, I confidently anticipated turning two of them into bacon without the shadow of a miss or difficulty.

St. Prix, who never carried with his hounds any weapon but his *couteau-de-chasse*, had on this expedition, for the sake of the suffering peasant-farmers, requested his friends to bring their guns, and to shoot down every pig, young or old, that gave them the chance of doing so. To myself, as being a novice at the sport, he was kind enough to give a few cautionary hints, one of which, I have no hesitation in saying, was the means of saving me from a dangerous encounter: "Be sure," said he, "when you are choosing your position for a shot at a pig, not to choose it too near a run or foot-path, but some yards wide of it; and secondly, in case you should wound and not kill your game, it is always well to station yourself under the horizontal bough of a large tree, so low that, in emergency, you may spring up, seize it with both hands, and so lift yourself a few feet above the ground. This move will securely place you beyond reach of the boar's tusks, and the animal, thus foiled, will pass instantly on."

The first part of this good advice I had grossly neglected, not having observed that the portion of rocky ground on which I stood was completely denuded of moss, and was, in fact, the well-worn run and highway of the pigs; so, instead of getting a broadside shot as they passed, I had to take them "stem on," or "fore and aft," as I best could—a manifest disadvantage that exposed me to imminent danger, and, but for the impending bough, would probably have brought me to grief. As four of them advanced rapidly in single file, the old sow being about

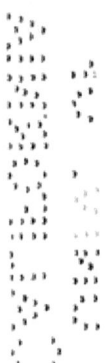

twenty yards astern, and two couple of hounds close on her haunches, I brought my gun to bear on the leading pig, touched the trigger, and over he went, dead and motionless as a bag of sand; the other three dashed on one side, and keeping a huge boulder between me and them, evaded my sight; so my second barrel was reserved for the old brute now close at hand. Seeing the dead pig in her path, and doubtless concluding that I was the cause of the calamity, she charged at once, and with such an impetus that no time was left me to choose my aim, or even to guard against the chance of killing one of the hounds; so I fired in her face, and down she came head-foremost at my feet. But the brute was not dead: my *balle-mariée* had glanced from her forehead, and, merely stunning her for a moment, she struggled on her legs and again came at me with a savage rush. I had just time, however, to back a yard or two, spring up and catch the friendly bough overhead; then, drawing up my legs, she shot under me and passed instantly forward, with the hounds still at her heels.

At that moment St. Prix, viewing the single pig, had thrown in a fresh relay; and these, some two couple or more, forcing the pace, soon brought her to bay under a shelving rock within fifty yards of the cover-edge. Before I could re-load and reach the spot, St. Prix, on foot, was tearing to the scene, his whip in his left hand and his *couteau* gleaming in the right; and, without pausing an instant or looking out for 'vantage-ground, he went straight into the fray, and with one quick, powerful stroke of his weapon, the fierce pig rolled dead at his feet.

"Not a hound scratched!" was his first joyous exclamation, as I hurried forward to lend him, as I hoped, a hand; "but," he continued, "my teeth chattered when I saw you take that last shot: and how old Balafré escaped destruction will be a mystery to me so long as I live."

"Well, it was a close shave and a snap shot, I admit; but

the old brute charged so unexpectedly and so furiously that there was little time for reflection; I could not, however, see the hound when I touched my trigger."

Old Balafré at that moment was giving the most demonstrative proof of his being not only uninjured, but in the highest condition of warlike vigour: with the grip of a vice, only relaxed to catch a fresh hold, his jaws were fastened on the throat of the quivering pig; and, even when the peasants, who were employed to carry off the carcase, attempted to remove it, the hound still clung to his hold with the savagery of a bulldog.

Both pigs were now borne in triumph to an open space in the cover below; whence they could easily be removed on the back of a Brittany pony to those peasants' farms which had suffered most from their depredations. Then sounded the death-note from St. Prix's horn, loud and long, which not only awakened a wild response from the thousand echoes of the glen, but roused at least a dozen other horns into action from different parts of the cover. Nor was the sound an uncertain one to the peasants, who, to the number of one hundred or more, now gathered together round the dead prey, and loudly applauded the success of the chase. Considering the value of the meat to such a population, living chiefly on farinaceous and vegetable diet—and of that possessing but a scanty store—it might have been expected that much jealousy would have been shown in its distribution, and that those who had suffered most from the porcine plunderers would expect the lion's share of the booty; but, if felt, there was certainly no such feeling expressed by a single peasant: no shuffling for the bag; but, on the contrary, the sport alone seemed to satisfy all.

The usual council of war—the most tedious of all meetings as practised by our Gallic neighbours at a cover-side—now ensued; and after a long discussion, in which every one present had something to say, it was determined to clap the hounds on the line of the three pigs already viewed, before a fresh draw was made, especially as they were all full-grown animals, and immediate sport would be the probable result. One or two adventurous spirits had long tales to tell about the size and fierceness of a monster boar that frequented Laz: they knew, they said, his very homestead among the granite rocks, overhanging the waterfall in the vale below; he was black as ink, his bristles were nearly a foot long, and his tusks a fabulous size—every oak-stump on that quarter, on which he used to whet them, gave token of their mighty strength and gashing power. St. Prix's mouth watered as they spoke, and gladly would he have gone at once to search for this monster pig; but discretion prevailed, and the thought of saving his hounds from the neverfailing consequences of attacking a "*solitaire*" turned the scale; so away he trotted, cap in hand, in pursuit of the younger and less dangerous game.

In less than ten minutes from that time, the four couple of hounds that had already distinguished themselves were again swinging away merrily on the line of the three pigs; the peasants, too, had disappeared, posting themselves at different points of the cover; while such of them as possessed not the *permis-de-chasse* were hurrying stealthily back to resume the muskets they had hidden during the short suspension of the chase. That this was a necessary precaution on their part was clearly demonstrated, not only by the presence of three or four gendarmes in cocked-hats and full accoutrements, but by their seizure of one peasant's gun, the owner thereof not being able to produce the legal qualification. This episode in the chase would have unquestionably led to serious results, as the blood of the peasants was fairly roused, and they were ripe for a row or any violence needed to rescue the gun and defy the law. But St. Prix, either informed of the *fracas*, or coming accidentally to the spot, most opportunely interposed, and by whispering a few words to the peasants, like oil on the troubled waters, those words seemed at once to calm their passion and still the storm: the crowd separated again; the peasants returning to the chase, and the gendarmes marching off in triumph with their one captured gun.

In the meantime the hounds were still running hard, though several shots had been fired in the same direction, but apparently without bringing them to a check. At length, after a continuous burst of wild music for more than two hours, the hounds sticking like glue to their game, three rapidly successive shots brought the din of war to a sudden lull; then almost instantly followed a ringing blast from Keryfan's horn, and every chasseur, noble, and peasant, from the cover-head on the Black Mountain down to the rocky stream roaring at its base, knew the import of that joyous note; they knew the strife was over, and the chase brought to a successful end. The three pigs had, one by one, fallen to the peasants' guns; and thus far, at least, was St. Prix made supremely happy by again being able to say, "Not a hound scratched in the fray."

The peasants, too, rejoiced over the slain; but, as before, conducted themselves with the utmost propriety, not a murmur being heard as to the distribution of the meat. The pigs on an average weighed at least two hundredweight apiece; and each being divided into four quarters, half a hundredweight of the best bacon-pork fell to the lot of no less than twenty peasants, making, for the time being, ample compensation to them for the loss of their chestnuts and the damage done to their crops in the last harvest. Nor were the boars' heads promised to Marseillier forgotten; two of the deputation that had visited Carhaix remarking that the hospitable reception they had met with at la Tour d'Auvergne, and the success that followed it, rendered them his debtors for the rest of their lives.

The *chasse*, and the arrangements consequent therefrom, fully occupied St. Prix and the peasants till the hour of three in the afternoon; and then, as the ardour of man and hounds had been somewhat chilled by a heavy snow-storm that blackened the sky and whitened the ground, the Louvetier announced his intention of returning to Gourin without further disturbing the cover—a move that, considering the day's sport and the busy work expected on the morrow with the Count de Kergoorlas's hounds, seemed to give general satisfaction.

CHAPTER X.

HAD it not been for the Baron de Keryfan's kindness to me at Gourin, I scarcely know how I could have endured, even for hunting's sake, the filth and discomfort of that wretched little town. Good company, it is true, will make some amends for such evils; but the misery of being forced into bad company the moment you seek the retirement of your chamber, hoping for rest but finding none, is indescribable. If the minor evils of life make up the great mass of human suffering, these at least to which I allude form no insignificant ingredients in the bolus we are all compelled to swallow, first or last. This is not an agreeable subject to dwell upon; yet I cannot resist the opportunity it gives me, to relate an anecdote I once heard from a country gentleman. He had taken expensive apartments in Park Street during the season of the International Exhibition in 1851, and had brought his family with him to enjoy the wondrously attractive novelties congregated therein. The very first night of his occupation, however, gave him sore proof that a troublesome tenantry were already in full pre-occupation of the beds. So the next morning, summoning the landlady to his presence, he bitterly complained of his disturbed rest, and announced his intention of not remaining another day in the house.

"But you've taken the apartments, sir, for four months," was the indignant reply; "and, as to the beds, unless you brought the fleas yourself, I'll undertake to say you'll not find a single flea in them."

"I fully believe you, madam," said he; "for they are all married, and have very large families."

This brought the conversation at once to a climax; the lady flung out of the room in a rage, and the gentleman quitted the apartments that very day; nor was he troubled farther with respect to the tenancy.

Keryfan's experience of hunting-quarters, from the luxury of Leamington to the bush-life of northern Africa, had warned him to take certain precautions against the exigencies of this Gourin campaign. A corner of his portmanteau, for instance, was fitted up in the most convenient fashion, with small bottles of eau-de-Cologne, spirits of camphor, and a pot of mollifying salve; added to which he had brought with him a mosquito net, the gift of a friendly Bedouin, within the folds of which, saturated as it had been in a decoction of cedar-wood, he was as safe from the attacks of all vermin as the Elector of Saxony boasted himself to be when shut up in the virgin fortress of Königstein, and Napoleon was in vain attempting to batter it from the opposite heights of Lilienstein. Thus protected, Keryfan could laugh at the foe that drove me and others to madness: but, careful as he had been of himself, let me do him the justice to say, that self-comfort in no wise contracted his views with respect to the comfort of those around him. That pot of salve saved me from a thousand pangs; and even the net, which had been laced together through the middle, he divided into two parts; and giving one to me, I passed at once from Hades into Elysium, and became, so far as my pests were concerned, as invulnerable as Achilles after he had been dipped in the Stygian lake.

By the invitation of the Count de Kergoolas, a large additional party of chasseurs had arrived at Gourin from his own country on that side of Upper Brittany contiguous to La Vendée, in former days the classic hunting-ground of the Bourbon kings and the old noblesse of France. The little town was already full to repletion; and it was only by extraordinary shifts and contrivances that night-lodging could be obtained for the numerous guests; for instance, Keryfan, giving up his room to four of Kergoolas's friends, contented himself with a mattress on the floor of mine, while St. Prix, to whom had been allotted the state apartment at the Cheval Blanc, accommodated a like number: the grooms, kennel-men, and even the valets, all to a man, slept in the hay-lofts adjoining their respective stables. Every night several of these men were more or less intoxicated; and as they staggered about with a pipe perpetually alight in their mouths, and often with a smouldering wood-ember, suspended by a small wire tongs to their wrists, from which they borrowed the fire, the wonder was that the whole town was not reduced to a heap of ashes before the end of the week: as it happened, however, the only casualty that occurred befell a small outhouse, in which one of M. de Kergoorlas's piqueurs, with three couple of hounds, was quartered. The man had retired to his domicile in a state of helpless intoxication, and, heedless of the live ember suspended from his wrist, had cast himself upon the heap of straw in company with the hounds. Fortunately the straw was somewhat mouldy and damp, or he and the three couple of hounds would speedily have been reduced to so many heaps of calcined bones. The fire, however, gradually gained ground; and at length burning some of the hounds, they set up such a wail as never was heard in Gourin before. Kergoorlas, either suspecting the mischief or recognising the tongue of his hounds, was the first to reach the hovel; and, bursting open the door, he seized the recumbent piqueur by the leg, dragged him, still in a state of unconsciousness, to a heap of manure hard by, and then, with half-a-dozen peasants, soon extinguished the flames. A hound called Caporal, a red, rough, Brittany tufter, had been considerably singed and blistered; but the rest of them, man and all, had escaped miraculously; while the hunting-cap, that had fallen from the piqueur's head, had been burned to a cinder.

There is a popular old hunting song, in which the music of hounds in full cry is described as a "musical din;" but the expression is not a happy one, and would far better describe the clatter of horns that roused every soul in Gourin, set the hounds baying, and the bowels of every horse in commotion, a long hour before daylight on the morn of the Kœnig hunt. Soon after seven o'clock, while yet the pall of night was hanging in heavy, misty clouds over the little town, but gradually growing into a lighter and less sombre hue, M. de Kergoorlas, with eighteen couple of hounds at his horse's heels, jogged leisurely past the Cheval Blanc. The picture would have been one of infinite beauty to a houndsman's eye, had there been light enough to enjoy it; but so dark, rufous, and grisly-grey in colour was the whole pack, that it was impossible to distinguish the figure of individual hounds as they trotted past the hotel in that murky gloom. Afterwards, however, both in the field and in their several kennels —for they occupied at least three peasants' cottages—ample opportunity was afforded for inspecting the distinctive points of these magnificent hounds.

The race of all French hounds, claiming a pedigree, is usually traced, or rather attributed, to the blood of St. Hubert, a good bishop who hunted the country of the Ardennes about the year 1680, and whose representatives, occupying the monastery of that saint, paid an annual tribute of young hounds to the French kings, addicted to the chase, in the Middle Ages. From the royal patronage bestowed on these hounds, it is reasonable to infer that their blood found its way into every kennel of the land; and, prized as we know it to have been for power of nose and perseverance in chase, great care and attention were doubtless bestowed on the purity of the breed for many generations. Hence, if anywhere a trace of the blood still exists, it may fairly be looked for in the Vendean land, the favourite hunting-ground of royalty, and the country, *par excellence*, of grand packs established for ages. To Lower Brittany, too, the same argument would apply even in a stronger degree; inasmuch as that peninsular land, so isolated from the rest of France, and so unvisited by innovation, once possessing the blood, would be more likely to preserve it pure among its ancient kennels, than a country more frequented by strangers and the changes incidental therefrom.

But M. de Kergoorlas laid no claim to the remote age of St. Hubert for the pedigree of his hounds: he would, however, descant for hours on the success he had achieved in resuscitating the old Vendean race, effete and worn-out by in-breeding and long prejudice, and in producing a hound that for good nose, driving power, and endurance in chase, was far superior to the heavy, soft-skinned, bell-mouthed animal described by du Fouilloux in "La Venerie," and still found in the Vendean country. He had bred them, he was wont to say, by perpetually infusing fresh blood among the pack he inherited, and always going to the stoutest kennels of which he had record. To St. Prix he was especially indebted for many a useful cross; and from his kennel he had derived those grand, brown-grey or fulvous-coloured hounds of which he was so justly proud. The Royal Vendean hounds are described by the French writers as being milk-white in colour, and fine as satin in their coats: but, if this was the case, these characteristics have been long since out-bred and obliterated in M. de Kergoorlas's pack, not a hound of which had a patch of white upon him, nor was there a smooth coat among them. The bold appearance of these hounds was quite remarkable; standing 25 inches at the shoulder, and carrying their long-feathered stems well arched over their backs, with high crowns, long faces, and silky ears, and above all, with good legs and feet below, they looked all over a working lot, and admirably adapted for the rough game and rough country in which they were bred.

Kergoorlas, as we jogged along together towards the meet at Kœnig, took great pains minutely to describe the merits of individual hounds to me ; and seemed to be highly pleased with the favourable remarks I could not help making on their grand and workmanlike appearance.

"In colour," said he, "they are assimilated to that of the boar, the wolf, and the fox, the wild beasts they were bred to pursue : and, if I may venture to say so, in fierceness and fleetness they are a fair match for the stoutest of those animals."

"I doubt it not," I replied ; "for they look strong enough and bold enough to run down a buffalo, and hold him afterwards."

"Not quite that : but it is really wonderful how firmly they will hold a boar, no matter how big or how fierce he may be : they take him fore and aft, under the shoulder and behind the hams ; and when four or five couple have fixed their fangs into his hide, no power of his can shake them off; nor will they relax their grip till I have buried my *couteau* in his heart's core. But sometimes, alas ! a courageous young hound will catch him by the ear ; and then follows the usual sad result—a fearful gash, that too often ends fatally."

Considering that M. de St. Prix on the previous day had only worked four or five couple of hounds at a time, I ventured to ask Kergoorlas if the pack, numbering eighteen couple, was not a dangerously large one for the adventurous work of hunting the boar ?

"St. Prix would think so, unquestionably," was his ready reply ; "but he lives in perpetual dread of accident to his hounds ; and his misery, when one is wounded, is quite painful to witness. Proper caution is of course commendable ; but, to forecast the form of care in the hunting-field must detract largely from the pleasure of the chase. I love a crack of music; and, to secure a full volume, eighteen couple of hounds are not one too many: then, in full cry, it is indeed a glorious treat to listen to them in these rocky glens: it is like a peal of musical thunder rolling around you. So I run all risks, and uncouple every hound I have for the sheer enjoyment of this pleasure."

The weather now gradually improving, and the pleasant chat about hounds in which, at every step among that rugged scenery, my companion and I indulged, rendered our ride to cover that morning a most enjoyable one. Every word that fell from his lips were those of a houndsman, dearly loving the chase; and all the details incidental to the breeding of a pack and its management in the field, into which he entered, indicated a knowledge of woodcraft far in advance of his compatriots, among whom I sojourned in Lower Brittany. Even St. Prix, who had devoted his life to hounds, might have gleaned many a corn of useful information from the field of Kergoorlas's experience, as the latter had moved in a wider circle, and, like Ulysses, had not travelled without observation.

It is not given to all, however, to see and observe. Three or four years ago, two gentlemen of considerable book-knowledge, both having taken high honours at Oxford, started from a city in the West of England on a tour through Spain, Greece, and the islands of the Archipelago, purposing to devote at least two years to the full enjoyment of this expedition. At length, as the time came round for their return, it is impossible to overstate the interest it created among their acquaintance in the aforesaid town. Dinner-parties vied for their company; and people, whose inhospitality had become a proverb, threw open their doors once more to welcome the gifted travellers. The mirage of the desert, however, was not more illusive than the hope of these friends. To every question asked respecting this or that town, with its old-world memories and classical associations, the disappointing answer referred only to the quality of the cooking and the character of the hotels: "A miserable mixture was the Olla-podrida of Andalusia, although Ford lauds it as food fit for the gods; and, as for the Gazpacho, the stomach of a Devonshire reaper would rebel at its intrusion; what else could you expect from rancid oil, vinegar, garlic, and dirty cooks?" Again, "As to Chios (the birth-place of Homer), where at least we hoped to get palatable wine, we found it simply execrable. What Lord Palmerston said to Mr. Gladstone, when the latter produced at his table a bottle of Ionian wine, the fruit of his visit to the Seven Islands, might truly be said of the Chian wine, '$\Alpha\rho\iota\sigma\tau o\nu\ \mu\epsilon\nu\ \upsilon\delta\omega\rho$.'" Such is a veritable specimen of their general answer; the comfort or misery of their daily fare appearing to be the sole impression left upon their memories.

Owing to the serious damage done to their crops, the peasants of the district had taken care to promulgate far and wide the meet of M. de Kergoolas's hounds at Kœnig on that day; consequently, a large gathering of sturdy Celts, yet not a man of them standing more than 5 feet 6 inches high, clad in all the variety of costume peculiar to the Communes ranging from Rostrenen to Scaër and Rosporden, converted the usually quiet cover-side into a scene strangely picturesque and gay. But for the friendly greetings and pleasant badinage perpetually going on, the crowd, armed as it was with muskets of mighty length and antique form, might have been easily mistaken for a band of insurgents bent on some desperate adventure. The weapons, too, had probably most of them belonged to the Chouans, who, in the Royalist insurrection of 1792, maintained that desperate guerilla struggle against the Republican Army with such extraordinary persistence and success, and who were chiefly Vendean and Brittany peasants.

That was a very serious affair when the game was man; but in this case, where the gathering was purely a social one organised for the sake of sport and the capture of a few pigs, well might it be one of happy prospect and joyous anticipation; and verily the peasants made it so, for they chatted and laughed with so much exuberance that, had it not been for the sudden and very unwelcome appearance of two gendarmes in full martial costume, it would have been difficult to understand what arrangements Kergoorlas had made for the chase of the day. The hubbub, however, was hushed in a moment; and it was quite evident that the presence of Mephistophiles and the Demon Huntsman of the Black Forest would have been a far more acceptable addition to the party than that of the two officers now mingling in the crowd. The old loyal spirit is still alive and strong in the breast of the Breton; and if ever another Larochejacquelin comes to the front to maintain the cause of royalty, it is quite certain he will not lack followers among the nobles and peasants of Upper and Lower Brittany. Here they ever have been and ever will be Bourbonists to the backbone; nor will the carnage perpetrated by Marceau, nor the atrocities of the Convention ever be forgiven.

Then, by way of rousing the peasants from the sudden chill caused by the cocked-hats, Kergoorlas addressed them aloud: "Friends," he said, "the boars are plentiful in Kœnig, and the hounds eager for the chase. Let me ask you to repair at once to your several posts in the cover; to be careful where you stand; and, above all, not to fire when the hounds are in conflict with a boar. The chase will now commence."

Not more instantaneously was Roderick Dhu's wave of the hand obeyed by his hardy clansmen than the signal given by Kergoolas to his Breton "field."

> "Each warrior vanished where he stood,
> In broom or bracken, heath or wood;

> Sunk brand and spear, and bended bow,
> In osiers pale and copses low;
> It seemed as if their mother Earth
> Had swallowed up her warlike birth."

The disappearance of the peasants was almost immediately followed by that of their natural enemy the gendarmes, who, having been successful on the previous day in capturing a musket, made a show at least of doing their duty on the present occasion, and pursued the peasants' track with the pertinacity of two sleuth-hounds. Already had the piqueurs, at break of day, ascertained with the Lymers that several boars had entered the cover, and that one of unusual size had gone singly to his lair in a pile of rocks overhanging the river. This, in Louis Trefarreg's opinion, was the great boar of Laz, the terror of the peasantry for miles around. The ferocious brute had probably, he thought, taken alarm at the din of war that had disturbed his "ancient solitary reign" in that cover, and had shifted his quarters to this stronghold in Kœnig; and, if so, the piqueur predicted serious danger to men and hounds in forcing him to break away from this granite fortress. However, M. de Kergoolas did not hesitate a moment, but, treating the vaticination as emanating from an over-careful servant, rather than an experienced hunter, he ordered his men to uncouple a lot of old hounds, and to clap them at once on the track of the boar.

I had again, with M. de Kerjeguz's kind permission, sent my horse to his stables; so, with no other *impedimenta* beyond the necessary ammunition, I shouldered my smooth-bore and dashed after the cry. No one, who has not followed a deep-mouthed pack of hounds in rocky and woodland glens, can form an adequate conception of the grand volume of music produced in such places by the united choir of echo and hounds; nor can I do better than describe it in the language of the million-minded Poet, who, in his "Midsummer Night's Dream," could not have painted the scene so faithfully, if he had not himself heard the "sweet thunder" of Sir Thomas Lucy's or some other Warwickshire Squire's hounds :

> "Never did I hear
> Such gallant chiding ; for besides the groves,
> The skies, the fountains, every region near,
> Seemed all one mutual cry. I never heard
> So musical a discord, such sweet thunder."

Ten couple of these huge rough hounds, in the full enjoyment of a fresh drag, on which every hound threw his tongue freely, might well be a sound to gladden a hunter's heart ; but, so filled was the valley with the reiterations of a thousand echoes, that it was impossible to make out in what direction the hounds were pointing ; and had it not been for the worn, wet paths, impressed by the footmarks of the eager pack, which I traversed with rapid strides, I should have missed seeing the grandest passage in the day's sport, namely, the rousing of the boar in that pile of rocks. Verily, he was a monster, but active as a mountain cat, in spite of his ungainly shape and huge size. When first found, he was lying in the open, under cover of an impending ledge, mantled with ivy and stunted oak ; but the ground being exposed, and at some distance above the grand clitter, he rapidly descended the broken ground, bounding like a chamois from the head of one boulder to another, clearing chasms in his stride, and at length disappearing in a subterranean passage beneath the rocky mass. Several shots had been fired by the peasants ; but whether or not he had been wounded at all was a matter of much doubt among those who had reserved their fire.

The fate of the hounds became now a matter of the most intense interest to all. The whole pack had been uncoupled, and were hard and close upon his quarters as the brute took refuge in the superincumbent mass. In one instant every hound was lost to sight ; and then commenced an uproar and a wailing such as torture only could upraise—the shriek of hounds in their agony! Kergoorlas had not yet arrived; but St. Prix, standing on the top of a boulder and listening to the murder, seemed for a moment petrified with horror. Descending at a bound, however, from this pedestal, he and a dozen peasants after him at once rushed forwards, and clambering as they best could over the huge fragments of granite that barred their course, they soon gained the spot under which the fray was surging with a terrible din.

"He'll murder every hound of them," shouted St. Prix, seizing his horn and blowing it like a madman; but this taking no effect upon the combatants, he quickly laid it down, and springing to the base of the rocks, on the very brink of the river, he drew his *couteau*, and was about to crawl, for he could not walk erect, into the hollow chasm where the fight was going on. Keryfan seized him by the arm, however, and with the timely aid of three or four peasants dragged him forcibly back. "Stay, M. de St. Prix," said one of them, "enter not there, or you'll rush to certain death. Let us light a fire behind the boar; and that, my word for it, will unearth him at once."

To this proposition he reluctantly gave way; and, in a few minutes a pile of heather, fern, leaves, and dead wood were dropped through a cranny exactly over the spot known to be the far end of the cavern, and probably exactly upon the boar. Then a whole box of lucifer matches was cast in a state of ignition right into the heather, and in a few seconds a dense volume of smoke, followed by a roaring flame, shot upwards. Instantly the rattling of pebbles and a strange rumbling commotion was heard below; and, almost before a peasant could snatch up his gun, the huge, swarthy beast burst out, and, dashing into the bed of the torrent, swam straight for the opposite shore. Before he landed, however, the messengers of death were hard upon him. Pierced by several shots at the same moment, he rolled a lifeless carcase on the river's edge. His lower tusks were seven inches in length, and he was said to weigh nearly 4 cwt. A grander brute neither Kergoolas nor St. Prix had ever seen ; and, as may be supposed, the homage they received from the peasantry was only such as the ancients were wont to pay to demigods who had rid them of some terrible enemy.

CHAPTER XI.

ERE a single horn had proclaimed the "*mort*," and while yet the monster boar was lying with his head and feet on the gravelly bank, and his hind legs still quivering in the stream, St. Prix on hands and knees was crawling into the cave—the first, as he always was, to give aid to the suffering hounds. Fourteen couple only had crossed the river; while three shivering, limping hounds, out of the remaining four couple, were standing on the water's edge, as if utterly unable to stem the torrent in their maimed and helpless condition. Five hounds were therefore wanting to complete the number of the hunting pack.

An interval of more than ten minutes had elapsed, during which time many a peasant volunteered to enter the cave, exhibiting intense anxiety for the fate of the hounds; when St. Prix again appeared on the surface, dragging after him a hound by the hind legs, literally disembowelled and dead. The four others, he said, had been so cruelly mauled that, not being known by the hounds, he dared not handle one of them. M. de Kergoorlas's chief piqueur, the very man who had been nearly roasted with his hounds in the shed at Gourin, then stood forward, and, divesting himself of his goat-skin jacket, entered the gloomy aperture. One, two, three, four were at length brought out singly and tenderly by the patient piqueur; and a more piteous scene was never witnessed.

"How was it possible for them to escape," said St. Prix, energetically, "when eighteen couple were crowded together in that narrow cavern, cheek by jowl with that terrible tusker? It is a mystery to me that so few have been killed!"

"Too many, too many!" said Kergoorlas, with a groan; "but who could foresee that the brute would run to ground, and there butcher my hounds in this fashion?"

Two out of the four died almost immediately after their wounds were washed; another having several of his ribs protruding through the skin, and his stomach rent, was destroyed on the spot; while the fourth, sorely maimed, was carried to a distant cottage on a goat-skin jacket, which, with a peasant at each corner, served the purpose of a most convenient ambulance. An old army surgeon was fortunately present, and spared no pains, with brandy, bandages and needle, to alleviate the misery of the other wounded hounds.

For a short time only, however, did this episode cast a gloom on the general field; most of whom cared little about the hounds, but were deeply interested in the destruction of the swine that had ravaged their crops, and terrified the women and children throughout the district. The hounds, as yet, had scarcely done an hour's work; and fourteen couple, a larger pack than St. Prix ever used for boar, were available and fresh for further operations. About a league from the ground where the carnage described took place, up stream and in some thick scrub hanging under the mountain-brow, several full-grown boar had been harboured by the piqueurs; and, as that part of the forest had been quite undisturbed, the hounds were trotted thither without much delay.

The evil of working too large a pack for boar could not have been more severely exemplified than in the recent massacre, although the circumstances, to be sure, were somewhat exceptional; the cavern proving a fatal trap in which the mischief was aggravated by numbers; and the animal hunted being a "*soli-*

taire," one of the fiercest and most powerful of wild beasts. So, when M. de Kergoorlas, with his love for a full choir of music, cast off again his whole pack, he might fairly calculate on neither running a pig to ground, nor finding another "*solitaire*" for that or many a day to come. But this consideration did not prevent St. Prix from impressing upon him the doctrine of which he was himself so practical an observer : " Better slip three or four couple at a time, Kergoorlas," I heard the Louvetier remark ; " and then throw in your relays—when the first have well settled on the game you mean to hunt."

But no ; the master of his hounds would be master still ; fourteen couple were cheered to the drag, and in less than half-an-hour three pigs were viewed in the distance, pointing downhill, and galloping in frantic fright for the river below. Being in single file, and following a leader, the hounds did not divide ; and as the pigs plunged across the rapid stream, in helter-skelter hurry, even Kergoorlas's love of sylvan music must have been more than gratified by the wild harmony awakened in the glen. Nor was it all mere towling, for four or five couple of hounds were dashing

"Abreast, like horses of the sun,"

into the gurgling waters, before the last pig could shake his bristly hide on the opposite bank. Crack, crack, went a smooth-bore within a few yards of the rock on which I stood ; and I saw that Keryfan, taking a snap shot at the hindmost pig, had rolled him headlong into the scrub. Instantly, however, he rose again, and hobbling back into the stream on three legs, he stood there at bay up to his belly in water, confronting the whole pack. "Now then for more mischief," I said to myself ; and scarcely had the thought crossed my mind than the boar charged, and I saw one hound at once float down the stream as helpless as a lumber-log—again, quick as lightning came the thought that, unless instant aid were given, the best hounds would be murdered or maimed wholesale in no time. Keryfan, too, saw the danger; and descending the steep ravine with the impetus of a kangaroo, reached the water's edge in time to stop another charge. His *balle-mariée* then, at the distance of only ten yards, put an end to the fight, passing through both shoulders of the beast, and rolling him dead into the hounds' jaws.

At that very moment St. Prix was on the spot, his *couteau* bared, and he in the very act of springing into the thick of the fray; he paused, however, on the brink of the stream, as the report of the smooth-bore rung on his ear; and it might have been fancy, but I could not help thinking a shade of disappointment passed over the fine fellow's face, as the adventurous work of closing with the boar and delivering the hounds from their instant danger was suddenly snatched from his hand. If it were so, the cloud vanished without breaking; and he turned round to thank Keryfan heartily for the ready help he had given the hounds. The pig was a tusker, and pronounced to be three or four years old: his lower tushes, calculating that portion of them imbedded in the jaw, were about six inches long, not much curved, but sharp and pointed as a barking knife; a pair of terrible weapons in a close fight. The peasants point out the stumps of oak trees on which they whet their tushes by way of keeping their armour in order; and as many of the trees near the water's edge were scored and seamed deeply all round their boles, they afforded pretty good proof that the boar of Kœnig were not only a numerous, but a very warlike race.

Louis Trefarreg, St. Prix's first piqueur, was so thoroughly versed in all the habits and slot-signs of the beasts he hunted, that he could approximately tell the size and age of a wolf or boar, not only from their track-marks in the ground, but he could gauge the height of the latter by the altitude at which he had scored the trees in whetting his tusks; every inch in the length of the boar's legs enabling him to strike higher or lower according to their length.

When the bristles from the last pig killed were extracted from his neck (a process immediately undertaken by some Cordonnier peasant, if he is not interfered with), the difference in size and strength between them and the bristles of the "*solitaire*," was quite remarkable; the latter being more like wire-rods than the growth of a pig's back; long, strong, and stiff as an awl—the very requirement adapted for the cobbler's use. No wonder then that these connoisseurs pounced with such avidity on so tempting a prize; nor that their discomfiture was expressed in bitter terms, when Louis Trefarreg prevented them, as he sometimes did, from indulging in this spoil. A fight, St. Prix told me, had more than once occurred between the piqueur and the spoiler over a dead boar; but that, in every instance, Louis had proved himself the better man. On the present occasion our pastime was undisturbed by the semblance of a broil; on the contrary, while the "*mort*" was being sounded, and the usual obsequies duly enacted over the fallen prey, every bristle was extracted from its neck; and, in the absence of the gendarmes, not one of whom intruded on the scene, all went smoothly and merrily as a marriage bell.

It has been already remarked that our Gallic neighbours, previous to the business of entering on the *chasse*, are the most deliberative of human beings; and now, even with the game afoot and before them, much useful time was wasted in deciding how the pursuit of the two other pigs should be continued; one party deeming it best to clap on the hounds at once from the river, and to stick to the line of scent; the other preferring to lift the pack and throw them into a thick scrub-cover, about a league off, into which it was pretty certain the pigs had gone. St. Prix and his piqueur stoutly advocated the latter plan, explaining how it would rest the hounds and tell against the game; but "music won the cause," Kergoorlas deciding that, if the hounds were lifted so far, they should lose so much sweet hunting, and probably not hit upon the line again.

"It appears to me," he said pointedly to St. **Prix**, "that the month you spent with Mr. Brockman's hounds in East Kent has warped without improving **your** former good judgment on Brittany hunting. **You** could not have gone, so Keryfan says, to a better school for **a** lesson in fox-hunting; but a fox and a boar **are** two different animals."

"So they are, Kergoorlas; but why you should prefer trailing with a cold scent over a long league of rough country, when you could clap your hounds quietly and quickly on the very back of the boar in half the distance, **beats my** comprehension."

The remonstrance was in vain; and in a few minutes the hounds, cheered **to the scent,** were picking it along merrily, but certainly not with **that** crash of music which was the delight of Kergoorlas's heart. Gradually, however, it improved; and in **half-an-hour, as the hounds** entered the scrub-cover, **the** "field" being a mile behind, and scattered in every direction, **a** roar **of thunder burst on our** ears, and told of hot work in the cover above. .Then came the blast of many horns, announcing "the boar afoot" with a **din** that, like Virgil's Fame, seemed to gather strength as **it** went rolling **along the** valleys below; **until**

"Tot linguæ, totidem ora sonant, tot subrigit aures."

The peasants, rejoicing in the well-known signal, hastily planted themselves, in small groups of twos or threes, at various **points by** which the chase was likely to pass. Some occupied **the summit of** a granite boulder far above the reach of the tusky foe; while others, preferring the ambush afforded by the trunk **of a tree,** took equal care to **post** themselves under an impending bough, into which, in case of attack, they could instantly spring **out of** harm's way. Keryfan, who was standing near me, listening attentively to the cry as the hounds' mouths were turned towards us, now suddenly started, and, turning to to me, he said, confidently, "The hounds have changed; hark! that's St. Prix's horn sounding 'Le Loup, vrai caffard:' he must have viewed a wolf, in spite of the signal given, 'Le Sanglier,' by the other horns."

He had scarcely spoken when, crossing an open space below us, a gaunt, grey old wolf went lopping along over some stony ground, his both ears pricked well forward, as if he expected foes in front as well as behind, and his stealthy gait betokening intense fear; he of course saw us, but as there were several peasants posted on the opposite side of the glen, he held on straight down the valley, pointing for the great cover below. Our both barrels were raised simultaneously; but before a trigger was touched, either by Keryfan or myself, we saw him stagger forward, and then instantly heard the reports of at least three guns fired at him by peasants lying in ambush within fifty yards of the spot.

"Bravo!" shouted Keryfan; "they've stopped the riot, at all events; he must be hard hit; a body-shot or a leg broken for certain: let's after him."

The hounds were now not a hundred yards from the wolf, rattling on like a storm of hail in his rear; and it occurred to both of us, if we could but catch another view of the wounded brute and give him his *coup-de-grâce* quickly, we should probably save the leading hounds from a terrible and disastrous encounter. So rushing at once forward, Keryfan diverging towards the river and I still holding to the upper ground, we both managed to view him again as he limped heavily towards the stream and was about to cross it for the opposite shore. This, however, it was not fated he should do: for Keryfan and myself, firing four barrels into him, killed him almost instantaneously. The pack then rushed in, and every hound seizing his mouthful of hide, a fiercer worry was never witnessed. But they did not "tear him and eat him," after the manner of English foxhounds running into their game: they did not even break a particle of his skin, and scarcely disfigured the thick, close jacket in which his carcase was encased: yet, for at least half-an-hour, every tooth in their heads and every muscle in their bodies was concentrated on the wolf's body, biting, shaking, and dragging it furiously.

This had been an old Tartar and the scourge of the neighbourhood for years: his four front teeth, above and below, were worn down to the gums; and his once formidable "holders," broken and blunted by age and use, had been reduced to mere stumps. He had frequently been found by St. Prix's hounds; but invariably, on breaking away, had stuck to an interminable line of covers fringing the Black Mountains; and reaching the forest of Dualt, had either thrown them off by a change with another wolf or run them into dark night. His head was more than grey, it was almost white; and doubtless, had his legs been as lissom as on former occasions, he would not now have turned short and run into the very jaws of death. The exultation of the peasants over this, their old enemy, was expressed in the strongest terms; and, if St. Prix had been capable of jealousy, it might easily have been aroused by the laudation which, on every side, he heard bestowed on Kergoorlas's hounds: for to them alone was attributed the fate that had at length overtaken this ancient and shifty robber.

In reality the hounds had been guilty of a great fault, and no man knew it better than St. Prix; they had changed, while in full chase, from one scent to another; and, in the deep forests of Brittany, where so many kinds of game abound, the disposition to change is looked upon as a serious blot in the character of their hounds, and the habit simply as the reckless riot of an untrained pack. So, when the Breton peasants were lauding the hounds, Kergoorlas was busy in apologizing for their misdeed:

"I know," he said, "the wolf must have jumped up in view before them, and so lifted their noses from the old scent. I had hoped the frequent infusion of the grey-griffon blood—and that, too, of your kennel, St. Prix—had cured that love of change so inherent in the smooth Vendean hounds."

"A mere accident," responded the Louvetier, "to which the best bred and best trained hounds in the world would always be liable: a view is a fatal temptation at all times."

Kergoorlas was very proud of his hounds, and for many years had devoted the closest attention to the improvement of their blood as well as to their discipline in the field: and, although St. Prix's observation was perfectly true, it scarcely sufficed to allay the vexation he so keenly felt, owing to this flagrant riot having been witnessed by all.

"Would I could pitch on the ringleaders," he said, angrily, "I'd make an example of them they would not readily forget."

"Well," said St. Prix, always the hounds' friend, "it is rather late now, after the worry, to chastise them for a fault, thereby condoned. Punishment, to be effectual, should instantly follow the riot, *flagrante delicto*, or the hound will suffer without knowing why or wherefore."

"By the death of this wolf, M. de Kergoorlas, you have done a rare good service," interposed M. Richard, the mayor of the commune; "and I propose, with the sanction of M. de St. Prix, to hand over the Government bounty to your piqueurs. We have yet other days for hunting the boar; and I trust you will be able to give a satisfactory account of them ere the week ends."

"With all my heart," responded St. Prix, gladly helping to turn the conversation into another channel, and hoping to soften the irritation M. de Kergoorlas too evidently felt. "They have done their work admirably; and, so far from begrudging the tribute to their fellow-piqueurs, my men will only be too happy if it is given as M. Richard proposes."

It had always been M. de St. Prix's custom to divide the Government award—thirty or fifty francs, according to the sex of the wolf slain—among his piqueurs; just as in former days, in this country, when a fox was killed, cap-money was levied from the "field" and usually handed over to the huntsman, in token of the sport and success achieved by the pack under his management; so that to "give Joe his half-crown" was looked upon as a happy privilege by those who were fortunate enough to live with the chase and to see it crowned with a kill. Therefore M. Richard, being well aware of St. Prix's practice, and deeming that they, whose hounds had done the work on the present occasion, were best entitled to the reward, proposed its distribution accordingly; and before M. de Kergoorlas could say aye or nay in the matter he handed over thirty francs to the chief piqueur, the very man who had been singed, while drunk and incapable, on the previous night.

The selection on the part of the mayor was not a happy one; and for this and other reasons Kergoorlas appeared anything but gratified by the transaction; however, he so far mastered his feelings as to thank that official with the utmost courtesy, and at the same time, drawing a handful of five-franc pieces from his pocket, he beckoned to Louis Trefarreg, and at once made ample amends for the loss of the largesse which he and his followers were entitled to expect for a wolf slain by hounds in the Louvetier's country.

But the Breton noblesse are a proud and fiery race: and St. Prix winced ominously at the unexpected and large compensation made to his men, in lieu of the paltry sum paid by the mayor to Kergoorlas's piqueurs; and Keryfan subsequently told me that, if such a liberty had been taken by any one less friendly than

Kergoorlas was with St. Prix, the latter would have chucked the money at the other's head. Then the inevitable result would have been a sword duel—not usually a fatal affair, but always a bloody one. But a *Deus ex machinâ* appeared and averted the danger at once: a peasant messenger, in wild haste, rushed up to announce that a single hound had been all along in chase of the two hunted pigs, and had driven them to bay in a pool of the river, about half a league from the spot on which we then stood.

In an instant all personal aggravations were cast to the winds; Kergóorlas deliberately unwound his horn and commenced playing "La sortie de l'eau" with a fervour that, if he had been nearer to his game, would have been certainly more suitable; while, the peasants, impatient of delay, dashed off to the scene of action with an impetus that knew no control. Nor did the hounds, which stood round their master, lifting their heads on high and solemnly joining in the wild melody, move a yard from the spot before he had finished that formal announcement on his horn. The peasants seemed to be well aware they had no need of their services, and that the one hound, having brought the pigs to bay in water, was amply sufficient to keep them there, until they could come to his aid; so, without hesitation, away they all scurried, leaving the hounds and their master to their present enjoyment.

I felt for the moment somewhat embarrassed, longing to scurry away too and see the finale to this unusual day's sport; but, observing the studious composure of Keryfan and the fiery St. Prix, neither of whom stirred a step while Kergoorlas and his choir were executing this piece of music, I became aware, if I did so, that I should be guilty of a breach of etiquette which would degrade me at once in the estimation of these high-class Breton chasseurs; so I submitted to my fate and waited a long three minutes for the conclusion of this strange ceremony. The horn being re-slung into its usual place, we then followed the peasants.

Before, however, we could overtake them, the reports of several guns, rapidly succeeding each other, fell on our ears; and by the time we reached the pool, where the hound had brought them to bay, two fine boar were lying stretched out, side by side, on the river-bank, still quivering in the throes of death. The hound that had stuck so gallantly to his game was called Troubadour, and a grander specimen of the veritable griffon no man could wish to see; he was rufous-grey in colour, had a long, sensible face, with a high crown to his head, deep chest, good feet, long powerful thighs, and legs without lumber; above all, he carried a bold stern well-arched over his back, and feathered deeply to its very tip. I can see the brave beast before my mind's eye at this very moment: two long gashes furrowing his ribs and streaming with blood, but apparently skin-deep only, as he seemed to pay little or no attention to these ugly-looking wounds.

"Oh," I said to myself as I marvelled at his real hound-like beauty, "would that I had powers of persuasion strong enough to induce some master of hounds in England to break through that fashionable routine of breeding, which is fast destroying the character and scenting qualities of foxhounds, such as they were in the days of the sixth Duke of Beaufort; when his long-headed and long-feathered badger-pies hunted like weasles, or drove their fox, like a flash of fire, over the cold fallows of the Gloucestershire wolds! The blood of Troubadour, judiciously infused, I venture to believe, is all that is wanted to bring back the modern foxhound to that grand type of former days."

Captain Anstruther Thomson's recent testimony on the value of Welsh hound-blood, is worthy of the utmost attention on this point.

CHAPTER XII.

It has already been mentioned in a former chapter how difficult it is, in the deep and rocky forests of Lower Brittany, to check riot and to keep hounds steady and together on the game which it is the object of the day's *chasse* to pursue. Hence the necessity of the piqueur and lime-hound in the first place, and of the relay system afterwards; by which, the right game being harboured and roused, the oldest and staunchest hounds are laid on; then, as the chase waxes hotter and hotter, the less steady are thrown in; then the rest of the pack, in batches, according to their degree of steadiness and love of the game pursued; and thus the chance of change is greatly diminished, even in a pack of hounds accustomed to run every beast of the forest from a roe-deer to a wild boar; and that, too, in the trackless depths of a Brittany cover.

The use of the lime or lyme-hound can be traced to a classic age; and several authors of antiquity, both Greek and Latin, have recorded his characteristics so minutely, that his identity, in point of use, with the Breton *limier* of the present day, is beyond all doubt. The *lymer*, so called from the *lyam* or leash in which he was led, was, from the nature of his employment, necessarily mute; and, as muteness in a well-bred hound is rarely met with, this indispensable pioneer was always a hybrid—the result of a cross between a hound and a mastiff, or pointer; the puppies favouring the hound being rarely kept for the purpose. Thus, this "canis ductor" is defined by Skinner as "Canis vilior ex cane sagace venatico cum Molosso copulato prognatus:" by which the mastiff blood is shown to be the cross adopted; but, if I mistake not, in Brittany the preference is usually given to a Spanish pointer for that purpose; that race being less addicted to throwing their tongue than even the mastiff or Molossian breed.

That the practice of commencing the chase by means of lymers, or, as Seneca calls them, the "canes tacitæ," should still prevail in Brittany and other parts of France, after the lapse of so many centuries (for the use of these tufters can be traced back to a boar-hunt in Mount Parnassus, as described by Homer in the 19th Book of the Odyssey) would indeed be extraordinary if, in a country abounding with a vast variety of wild game and endless forests, the same tactics in sylvan war were not as necessary in the present day as they were three thousand years ago.

In England, with a single exception, the services of the lymer have long ceased to be required; the cultivation going on, and so many of our wild beasts disappearing before it, the system has gradually dropped into disuse. The Devon and Somerset stag-hounds, however, still have their "tufters" and their "harbourers," both of which perform duties similar in many respects to those of the *Limiers* and *Piqueurs* of former days, and to those in France at the present time. But that pack, under the able management of Mr. Fenwick Bissett, is the only one now left in Great Britain that hunts the wild red deer in his native haunts. Long may it continue to flourish and represent the far nobler fashion of our forefathers in their pursuit of this grand beast than that so widely practised in the present day; long may those deep covers of Exmoor, erstwhile the hiding-place of the Doons and the red deer, continue to produce their warrantable stags; and long may the fastnesses ring with the chirrup of his hounds and the merry blast of Bissett's horn.

On our return from Kœnig that evening an agreeable surprise awaited M. de St. Prix, and, indeed, several of the Breton chasseurs, including myself, then gathered at Gourin : an Englishman, called Shafto, had arrived at the Cheval Blanc, after an absence of some months passed in Norway, whither he had gone for the purpose of salmon-fishing during the preceding summer. I had often heard of this gentleman during my stay in Brittany, but hitherto had not been lucky enough to meet him, much to my regret ; as, almost invariably, on being introduced to a strange chasseur, the first question he asked me was, if I knew my compatriot, Mr. Shafto ? And the look of surprise and disappointment expressed, on hearing I had not that honour, made me quite feel I was arguing myself unknown, and that the sooner I made his acquaintance the stronger would be my credentials in that country.

Well, here he was at last ; and a heartier demonstration of welcome and kindly feeling than that shown him, from the host of the Cheval Blanc to M. de St. Prix, was never yet witnessed. They actually hugged him ; and would, I think, have saluted his cheek, but for his natural repugnance to that kind of salutation. They would, however, have found that a difficult matter, as his face was as hairy as that of a Carlisle otterhound, and looked as if it had never been visited by the edge of a razor.

When St. Prix had formally introduced me to him, he said pleasantly, " Very glad to meet a fellow-countryman in such good company ; but how on earth did you find your way here ? I have lived twenty years in the country, and never met an Englishman before at Gourin."

I explained that my object in visiting the country was to get some good wolf-hunting, *more antiquo;* and that my friend

K

the Baron de Keryfan, having introduced me to M. de St. Prix, the Louvetier had kindly invited me to join his party on the present occasion.

"The man and place of all others for the sport," he observed; "but, happily,

'Non cuivis homini contingit adire Corinthum ;'

and this little town, the centre of the best wolf and boar-hunting, and, I may add, cock-shooting, in all Brittany, is, and I hope will long continue to be, a *terra incognita* to tourists in general, and gunners in particular. These latter, especially from the Channel Islands, have so overrun the covers and country bordering on the sea-coast, that henceforth it is proposed a *permis-de-chasse* should be granted to no foreigner who has not resided at least six months in the country. It is no mere figure of speech to say that these men have sent cart-loads of game to the Paris and English markets from this country; and hence the need of a more stringent law for the protection of the game, and the native chasseur."

The very fact that I was a friend of Keryfan's, and in St. Prix's company, was a sufficient guarantee to him that my sole object was wild sport; and feeling this, he not only did all in his power to promote that object, but bid me frequently to his "Hermitage," and showed me the most cordial hospitality during my two seasons' residence in Brittany. Of Shafto and that Hermitage I could fill a volume. However, I will only give a brief description of each for the present. The dwelling, so called, consisted simply of four square ground-floor rooms, such as might be constructed from a parish pin-fold, if roofed over and divided into compartments. It stood in the centre of a large yard, surrounded by a high, strong, stone wall, the entrance to to which was by a *porte-cochère*, massive as the gates of a Norman castle. Situated in a wild, solitary ravine of the Black Mountains, and surrounded on one side by deep woodlands, and on the other by long ridges of granite rocks, the building had originally been intended as a place of refuge for cattle during the heavy snow-storms of winter; when the wolves pack, and are driven by hunger to attack, even by daylight, the horses and dogs of peasants at their very doors.

Alexander Selkirk's abode could scarcely have surpassed this spot in desolation and solitude; but, while his company consisted of a cat, dog, goats, and a talking parrot, varied by the occasional visit of a tribe of savages, bent on a cannibal pic-nic—who, by the way, left him a valuable legacy, and did him far more service than harm in the long run—Shafto's court-yard was furnished around with pipe-casks from Bordeaux, every one of which had brought its quantum of good wine to the Hermitage, but was now converted into a comfortable dog-kennel. Setters, Sussex spaniels, and wire-haired Brittany wolf-hounds, numbering altogether about fifteen couple, had their separate lodgments in these *barriques*, and formed a useful and appropriate garrison for that tenement. The wolves, however, in the winter season, notwithstanding this fomidable force within, were continually reconnoiting the premises; and of all serenades ever listened to, the most dismal is theirs, wailing their hunger in the dead of night. The cat-tribe are said to make night more hideous by their cries. They, we know, are mere love-squabbles, and our ears, if doomed to city life, soon become familiar with, if not reconciled to, the nuisance; but there is something so mournful, so expressive of distress, so appalling in the howl of a wolf under your window, when all else is silent around, that he who has once heard it will never forget it while life lasts. The first time St. Prix slept at the Hermitage, at least half a dozen wolves howled in concert around its walls the live-long night. Some fresh meat for the hounds had been hung in the shambles hard by, and with this attraction for their noses their dismal serenade was unceasing, till, like Richard, he must have said :

> "Methought a legion of foul fiends
> Environ'd me, and howled in mine ears
> Such hideous cries, that with the very noise
> I trembling wak'd——."

Saving Shafto himself, and the sturdy Breton peasant, Owen Mawr—whose domicile was the stable-loft, and who, with his wife, fulfilled in a wonderful way the various offices of cook, groom, piqueur, and general purveyor—no other human being lived at, or within a league of the Hermitage. However, Shafto had sundry advantages over the hero of Defoe's story, in his four-roomed house; two spare beds were always ready for visitors during the hunting season; and these were kept tolerably well aired by kindred spirits, who, having once lodged there, were as regular in their visits as woodcock in their migration ever afterwards. When Frederick the Great furnished Voltaire's apartment for him at Sans Souci, he humorously decorated the walls with pictorial epigrams on the character and habits of that philosopher; and among others, the figure of a stork represented the regularity of his visits to that favoured spot. But here, at the Hermitage, the sole garniture of the panelled walls consisted of roe-deer and stags' antlers; on the tines of which were suspended whips, hunting-horns, spurs, rods, and fishing gear; while the floors were covered with skins of the wolf and the fox; trophies of the chase serving the purpose of a carpet, but more durable and far softer to the tread than the finest Axminster ever manufactured. Then each bed had its otter-skin coverlet, beneath which it was a luxury to lie on a cold winter's night; it was so warm, so soft, and withal light as an eider-down quilt; the French artists far surpassing ours in their treatment of fur-skins. The grisly hide of the boar was also turned to profitable account, and supplied a capital door-mat to each apartment.

Shafto's sire was yet alive, a large landed-proprietor in the north of England; but, having a numerous family by a second wife, he had given a willing consent to the self-imposed exile of his son and heir; with whom, owing to his devotion to the chase, and refusal to adopt a learned profession, he had held little or no intercourse for years, beyond paying him his regular allowance in quarterly instalments. When this was exceeded—a by no means uncommon event—and a request made for a "farther advance," the vials of the old man's wrath, charged with the bitterest invective, were poured unsparingly on the son's head. An old college friend once told me that his father had denounced him as a prodigal anticipating his inheritance, and "eating up the calf while yet in the cow's belly." To which the son, not without some reason, thus replied: "Father, I am the oldest heir-apparent in Great Britain; and you would have me wait till I've no teeth left either for cow or calf."

Shafto had naturally given the paternal roof a wide berth; and for twenty long years, the best years of his life, had adopted the Hermitage as his home, and the forests of Lower Brittany as his chief hunting-ground. From his open-handed liberality, giving his game wherever he killed it, keeping his wine-tap always going, and his tobacco-pouch well stored and ready for every peasant's pipe, he was literally adored by that class; and thereby enabled to save many and many a wolf's litter from the inevitable fate of being knocked on the head, instead of getting the chance given them of showing sport on a future occasion. Consequently, among the Breton noblesse, not only on this ground was he popular, but because he was, as they call him, "Un chasseur de première qualité," good company, and a thorough gentleman.

Having introduced my compatriot and his belongings thus briefly to the reader, let us hark back to the party who were receiving him with so cordial a welcome at the Cheval Blanc.

"We've expected you daily for the last week," said St. Prix

still grasping Shafto's hand; "and to-day you ought to have been with us, as we have not only killed the great boar of Laz, but the old wolf that led you so many dances from Scaer to Dualt, and kept your hounds without their blood for so many days."

"Bravo! that is a great triumph; but Keryfan tells me you were obliged to borrow a Vendean pack to achieve it."

"Quite true," shouted Kergoorlas: "though, to speak fairly, the old brute had not a tooth left, and might have been galloped to death by a donkey. However, his skin goes to the Hermitage; for all agree he was an old friend of yours, Shafto; and that you have a prescriptive right to that memento."

"I should have liked to be in at his death, I must confess," said Shafto, turning to me, and parrying the taunt pleasantly levelled at his hounds; "but I could not control the winds and the sea. Good sport though I have seen with my old friend Reginald James in the Norway waters, I would not again undergo the misery of that voyage from Christiansand to Bordeaux for the freehold of Torjedahl. Fancy, one-and-twenty days in a Norwegian timber-brig, with nothing but a 'hurricane house' abaft the mainmast to live in, for captain, crew, and passengers; no 'tween decks, all occupied by timber; and the wind blowing as if all the bags of Æolus had been ripped at once. The ship scudding wildly, with two men at the helm, under close-reefed topsails and reefed foresail! It's a lesson, believe me, I shall never forget. The only moment of merriment I enjoyed throughout the voyage was to hear a Devonshire man declare solemnly it was 'They qua'ter-noxes a-blow'ng,' although it was a good month after the usual period of the equinoctial gales."

That night was one of wassail at the Cheval Blanc; and the ceremony of drinking healths and toasts and singing Breton songs, suggested by the return of Shafto and the unusual success of the day, was prolonged to an hour better suited to the habits of confirmed Bacchanals than those of a party met for the enjoyment of wild sport. Hunting and head-aches don't go well together; and he who would really enjoy the former must forego the indulgence of "cakes and ale" for the time; must imitate, by his moderation and early habits, the example of that "Prime Minister" of the North, the Rev. John Russell, who though

> "So prone to the chase that he followed each scent,
> From the stag in the forest to bubble-a-vent,"

Yet the poet adds—
> "Not a lover of wine,
> He was sure to be fast on his pillow at nine;"*

and, like the student who would attain his object, he must be careful to keep body and mind in healthy condition; to abstain from all that tends to enervate either; or the goal will not be gained. It is impossible to carouse and at the same time enjoy the charms of the chase; nor ever in classic legend do we find Bacchus and Diana associated together.

Notwithstanding St. Prix's hounds were appointed to meet some four leagues off at eight in the morning, the wassail was still going on merrily long after midnight. Prominent among the nightingales, too, was the chairman, the Louvetier himself. The popular peasant song of the country he sang with great effect; it was called "Ann hini goz," and declared the passion of a young man for an old woman for the sake of her wealth; the refrain, in which every Breton joined heartily, creating roars of merriment. The chairman's power appeared to be imperative; and, on whomsoever he called for a song, that person was bound to sing. Shafto and myself responded to the request as well as we could; he, by singing, "'Twas on a dark day in December;" and I, the "Kilruddery Fox-chase." But when Kergoorlas was appealed to, he proved a recusant; and no solicitation could induce him to change his mind: he was willing to make a speech, though; and this commutation being accepted by the chairman, he commented

* That poet was his friend, Mr. George Templer, of Stover.

in the most humorous style on the Breton song "**Ann** hini goz;" and ended by especially recommending its **burden** to St. Prix, who was **then** a bachelor.

Apropos to this musical supper-party, still the **fashion in** Lower Brittany, **and formerly** one of the most popular of **institutions at** Oxford, **not** long since a lady, an octogenarian, made **her appearance at** Torquay; and, meeting a mutual friend, she **expressed a wish to have** an interview with Henry, Bishop of Exeter, the late Prelate—whose claim by the way, to the title of "*Fidei Defensor*" **was a** strong and a real one compared with that of his Royal namesake—"For," said the lady, "**I** should like **to** ask his lordship a question, while he yet lives; **and** he is the only man **now** living who **can give** an answer to **it**. I want to know **whether, on** the occasion of **a** supper-party at **Magdalen** College, Oxford, he did or did not say, **what he is reputed to** have said, to **my old friend Dymoke,** father **to the late** king's champion." It appears that they **and a lot of** jovial Demies had met together in the common room; and under the influence of a mighty **bowl of "** Bishop," **it was agreed that every** man present should either sing a song, tell **a** story, or drink a pint of salt and water. The lot fell on Dymoke to begin; but he sang so execrably ill, that **every** one present **was relieved** when the song came to an end. Next, it devolved on Henry Phillpotts to fulfil his part, or suffer the penalty. "I cannot sing," said he, "and I should be very loth to drink a pint of salt and water; but if I must *tell a story*, I should like to hear Dymoke sing that song again."

The lady and **the** prelate met soon afterwards, and the **question** being put, his lordship at once owned to the impeachment, **and greatly** delighted the lady by naming the very song Dymoke had so maltreated.

The **clock at the Cheval** Blanc struck three, A.M., as the last of the revellers **quitted** the *salle-a-manger* for their short night's **rest; and the consequent** knocking, kicking, and shouting that ensued at the doors of the various tenements to which they sought admission, must have disturbed every soul in Gourin. On retiring to my own apartment my misery may be better imagined than described when I discovered that my bed was already occupied by a chasseur, fast asleep, and breathing loudly and heavily under the influence of the wassail, of which he had been one of the chief promoters. He proved to be a M. de ——, a large landed-proprietor from the neighbourhood of St. Brieuc; a duellist, too, of no favourable reputation throughout Brittany. The very first day he joined our party Keryfan called my special attention to him, and said, " Whatever you do, don't quarrel with that man : he is as much given to duels as the editor of a Paris brochure."

I had taken him twice or three times by the shoulders and endeavoured to rouse him by a lusty shout, close to his ear; when, the light falling on his face, I discovered who the intruder was; and at the same moment, as Keryfan's warning flashed across my mind, I said to myself almost audibly, "Well! now I am in for a row; but it can't be helped; he has no business here, and out he shall come, *coûte qui coûte.*'" I was in the act of taking him by the ancles, for the purpose of ejectment, when, hearing Keryfan's light step on the staircase, I paused an instant, thinking he would readily lend me a hand, and that two of us could manage the matter better than one. But, he knew the man too well for that; he knew that bloodshed would be the inevitable result; and although he was bold enough to take a lion by the beard, if necessary, yet he was sensible enough to hate a brawl and to advise caution when danger was nigh.

"Don't touch the man," he said, emphatically; "he is evidently fast asleep and very drunk; why not drag the mattress from under him, and with a blanket around you take your rest on the floor; you would be just as comfortable as on a wooden bedstead."

So I followed this timely **advice**; and putting **on a** warm pair of slippers, and rolling myself in a blanket, the mosquito-net being superadded, I slept soundly and sweetly for four hours, when **the blast of Shafto's** horn, ringing out "**Le** point du **Jour**," told **the "coming of the morn**," and roused me from **further** slumber. **Let me add,** the occupier of my bedstead, instead **of** provoking **me to a deadly** encounter, made an ample apology **for** the wrong he had **done** me; and many a day afterwards he and I hunted **together on the best of terms.**

CHAPTER XIII.

THE meet on the present occasion was nominally at Pencoet, a desolate farm-house situated on a spur of the Montagnes Noires, in the direction of Châteaulin, but really was intended for the long chain of covers lying on the south-western side of that hilly region, which has been appropriately called the " Backbone of Brittany." These covers, consisting chiefly of oak, hazel, chestnut, and black pine trees, occupy for many leagues the hollow valleys of that district : and the nearest of them being at least a league beyond the farm-house, the hunting ground was not reached by the hounds till long after the appointed hour ; while the " field," after the orgies of the previous night, were yet more unpunctual.

Shafto alone had left Gourin at break of day; it having been arranged between him and St. Prix that he should bring six couple of his hounds to join the Louvetier's pack, the latter consisting also of a like number : but it was past ten o'clock ere the allied forces met at Gwernez, the precipitous cover they were appointed to attack first. The din of war had so disturbed the wild tenants of Laz and Kœnig, during the past two days, that it was confidently expected many of the survivors, especially the oldest and the craftiest, would cross the mountain range during the night and seek the quiet and secluded haunts of this cover ; and the report of the piqueurs fully confirmed this expectation. The heavy showers of the last few days had so moistened the surface of the rugged waste lying between the southern and northern slopes of the mountain range that, covered as it was with stones and stunted heather, the occasional track of a boar's heel, and the long, pointed, claw-scratches of a travelling wolf, were ever and anon revealed to the eye as we trotted along to the cover-side. The hounds, too, as they crossed the frequent line, could with difficulty be restrained from breaking away and carrying the drag over the barren ridge ; so that it was evident no time would be wasted in throwing off, either by drawing unprofitable ground or getting upon game not intended for the day's *chasse*.

The peasantry at the meet numbered in all not more than twenty men ; but every one carried his long fowling-piece openly and boldly on his shoulder, as if qualified by law to use it, and dreading neither man nor beast with that weapon in his hands. Their costume, too, was far more picturesque than that of the Gourin or Carhaix peasants, who, as a rule, wear tight sackcloth breeches, buttoning at the ankles, and a goat-skin jacket above ; whereas many of these sported the spacious trunk-hose, as worn by us in the sixteenth century, with claret-coloured cloth leggings and jackets of the same hue and texture ; while their waists were girthed up with broad leathern belts and mighty buckles. Two only were mounted on rough Brittany ponies, carrying saddles very similar in shape to the pack-saddle used by our millers : neither side of the saddle had stirrup-irons, but a single strap, running fore and aft on the near side from the pommel to the cantle, served the purpose efficiently, as the rider only required support on one side, and rode just as a lady would in this country. It is a strange contrariety, but, nevertheless, it is a fact that, in the interior of Finisterre and Morbihan, the women ride astride, while the men balance themselves on the saddle and carry both legs on the same side. During the two seasons I was in this part of Brittany I never saw more than one side-saddle ; nor, in the region I chiefly frequented, do I ever remember seeing more than one Breton woman ride after the feminine fashion in other countries.

The isolation of the land, and the slow growth of civilization among the people, who have no more affinity in race or habits with their Gallic neighbours than the Celts of Galway have with the Anglo-Saxons, will account, perhaps, for the non-introduction of the side-saddle into the primitive and poverty-stricken district of Cournouaille. Yet, when it is remembered that this convenient article of horse-furniture, which Johnson badly defines as "a woman's seat on horseback," was introduced into England by Anne of Luxembourg, the wife of our Richard the Second, and thus, as Stowe in his "Commentaries" tells us, superseded the use of "whirlicotes, except at coronations and such like spectacles," it is a marvel the side-saddle should still be unknown even in that land. Catharine de Medici, too, if not the originator of the side-saddle, is said to have greatly improved its form, and, from her devotion to hunting and rare seat on horseback, it must have been brought into general use throughout France even in those days. Still it appears not yet to have penetrated the neighbouring region of Cournouaille, or surely the habit of riding astride would not still be the common practice of the women in that country; and surely, here or there, the wife of some well-to-do peasant would have adopted its use for comfort's sake, if not as a "seat" more in accordance with the fashion of modern civilisation.

On the very edge of the great cover of Gwernez the two lots of hounds, belonging to M. de St. Prix and Shafto, were now assembled, awaiting impatiently in their couples the consultation held by those gentlemen and their friends, the result of which was to determine the operations of the day. Suddenly, but not unexpectedly, the trusty piqueur, **Louis** Trefarreg, emerged from the forest, and with his favourite Lymer, a big-headed half-bred hound, attached by a leash to his wrist, was advancing towards his master, when Shafto, anticipating his report, shouted out, " Bravo, Louis ; always the first to bring good news : you've tracked them home, I see, by your face. How many are they, and on which side of the valley ? "

" Pe'var moc'h vras, ha daou vihan" (four big pigs and two small ones) said the piqueur, in his own vernacular language ; for, although he understood the import of the questions put to him in French, he never trusted himself to speak a word in that tongue : and at the same time pointing with his club-stick, which, like the Bretons of that district, he perversely carried knob downwards, he indicated the rocky hollow in which he had harboured the game. " A couple of hounds," he continued, " will be ample for rousing them ; and when they divide we can clap on more."

" Quite enough at first," said St. Prix ; " or, with six pigs afoot at the same time, we should soon be in trouble. Uncouple Vetéran and Harmonie, give them the wind, and, when you hear my horn, let go three couple more."

" Mine, or your own ? " inquired Shafto, deferring with scrupulous etiquette to the Louvetier's word of command ; but, in truth, a little eager to see his own lot uncoupled and busy at work.

" Yours, by all means," responded St. Prix, divining his friend's ardour, and willing to indulge it ; " but let them be your steadiest hounds, Shafto, or, by St. Hubert, you'll never see some of them again."

While this conversation was going on, Louis Trefarreg had uncoupled the tufters, and trotting them rapidly across the moorland waste, lying to leeward of the gorge into which he had tracked the boar, the two hounds gave quick notice of hitting upon the drag, and with sonorous tongue carried it merrily forward into the very heart of the cover. Exactly in front of us, on the opposite side of the glen, lay the rocky recess, directly for which the hounds were now pointing; and, as it appeared like a vast amphitheatre, having its area encompassed with granite boulders, piled one above another, we were able to command, as spectators, every yard of the ground from our present position; so while Shafto, St. Prix, Kergoorlas, and others moved farther down the valley, taking the relays nearer to the scene of action, Keryfan and myself remained stationary on the moor, watching every stroke of the two hounds with a field-glass, and expecting every moment to see a grand find.

Hitherto the hounds had carried the drag together into the very centre of the semicircle; but suddenly they now divided, the tan-coloured bitch, Harmonie, holding one line straight up for the summit of the clitter, while the dark badger-pied Vétéran owned to another equally hot scent round the outside edge of the rocky ground. "The pigs have divided," whispered Keryfan, quietly; "the smaller ones not caring, probably, to occupy the same quarters with the larger pigs; or, it may be, the shorter legs of the former were unable to surmount the massive boulders, and they've entered the clitter from the upper side."

This was undoubtedly the case; for we could plainly see Harmonie, though throwing her tongue vigorously, was making but slow progress in her upward course; again and again, in clambering the face of a boulder, over which the pigs had evidently passed, the brave hound missed her hold and came toppling backwards to the ground—still, she never flagged a moment; still pointing upwards, scrambling, climbing, and springing over perpendicular rocks and chasms that would have made an Alpine guide shudder in his shoes. Her perseverance was marvellous; but, withal, in ten minutes she had scarcely advanced twenty yards, and the main stronghold of the clitter was yet a good hundred yards above her. In the meantime Vétéran was lashing his stern and making his tambourine tongue ring through the gorge; and now gaining the head of the clitter, he turned short into it, and swinging straight downwards—a far easier course than that of the brave Harmonie—he suddenly doubled his tongue, and with a thundering note proclaimed the presence of the pigs. The roar seemed to say, "Here you are, you villains; turn out, and trust to your legs." In an instant out bundled a brace of half-grown hog from a dense holly-bush, and springing, like goats, from rock to rock, made the best of their way towards the lower ground; and fiercely, in pursuit, dashed the gallant hound, "swearing hard words" close at their heels.

A clump of stunted pine for one moment hid them from view: but, as they emerged from this, out scampered also four huge grunters, apparently in as wild a fright as their smaller fellows, and rushing helter-skelter over the boulders straight into the face of Harmonie. My heart stopped beating as the collision, which was inevitable, took place between the foremost pigs and the brave hound; and I fancied, even at the distance at which I stood, that I could hear a simultaneous grunt from the herd, as they swept her headlong from a boulder into a chasm below. The pigs passed on, Vétéran thundering after and driving them like chaff before the wind: but for some seconds nothing of Harmonie could be seen, and Keryfan, who had been standing close to me, watching the scene with intense interest, turned and said, "Frank: that hound's back is broken; or, my word for it, she would be now in front, for a gamer animal never entered a cover."

Keryfan was wrong though; for the next instant she had clambered again to the head of the boulders, and, springing from one to the other, was following the leading hound with fiery zeal and uninjured vigour—"Bravo, Harmonie," fairly screeched out Keryfan: "the bitch is all right, I see; it would have broken St. Prix's heart to have lost that hound."

A deadly *cordon* of tirailleurs—the peasants to a man—had

now surrounded the lower portion of the rocky amphitheatre ; and every open spot, by which the pigs could possibly break, was guarded by two or three sharp-shooters, whose heavy slugs were not likely to allow a single pig to escape alive or unscathed into the cover below. The two smaller boar were toppled over before they were clear of the rocks ; and as the stronger beasts, close followed by the hounds, gained a patch of open ground and presented a fair broadside to the peasants guarding that pass, an involuntary shrug of the shoulders from Keryfan too plainly indicated his thoughts, and seemed to say, " All's up with that lot: we shall have to draw again, or get no hunting to-day."

But he was wrong again : two only of the bigger boar fell to the volley, the other two bounded away apparently unhit, and instantly were lost to sight in the dense and umbrageous cover into which they at once plunged. Vétéran and Harmonie, however, were after them, singing a lively duet and delighting Kergoorlas' ear with the sweet harmony. Then sounded the signal from St. Prix's horn ; and quick as lightning in uncoupling his relay, Shafto threw in the eager lot well to the head ; and if at that moment he could have borrowed Mercury's wings and witnessed the flinging, and twisting, and emulation of his hounds, his happiness would indeed have been complete : but, lacking these, he trudged manfully after them, and did all a mortal could do to see the sport and enjoy his life. A rare, enthusiastic, unflagging lover of hunting, was Shafto, as ever followed a hound : the habits of the game he pursued, and the power of instinct displayed by the hound, were his especial study ; and every hit made by the one or shifts practised by the other, in the longest day, seemed to be imprinted on his memory, like a picture on a plate of steel. Over a bottle of Bordeaux wine and among kindred spirits, years after some memorable run had taken place, how pleasant it was to hear him reproduce the scene, and record every incident of the chase as freshly and faithfully as if it had occurred but a week before! not a hound omitted, nor a friend forgotten throughout the story.

Again and again rang forth the signal to uncouple more hounds; till the Louvetier, determined to give the pigs a "burster," and, if possible, to run them fairly down, had summoned the twelve couple to his aid, and brought his whole force to bear on the flying game. His tactics, however, turned out to be somewhat premature; the two pigs had separated; and while the pack, hard at work with one, had at length brought it to bay under a rock impending over the river, the other was viewed leisurely trotting back to the high *genet* adjoining the moor where it had first entered the cover. Here, far away from the roar that accompanied its less fortunate mate, it was doubtless quietly resting, catching its wind and nursing its strength for further emergencies.

The notes of the Louvetier's horn now changed; and the welcome signal, "La sortie de l'eau" brought Keryfan and myself with rapid strides to the river's edge, where a grand picture of sylvan life was presented to our view. There, in the deep solitude of that mountain glen, on a bend of the stream, barred in its course by a rugged, perpendicular rock, thus forming a pond above and a cataract below, stood St. Prix up to his knees in water, his horn in one hand and his *couteau* in the other, not daring to advance into the gurgling eddies, and yet wild with excitement at the danger to which his hounds were exposed. And there, too, confronting him and the hounds, piqueurs and peasants, all of whom had understood the last signal of the horn, stood the grisly boar, up to his belly in soil, his eyes glaring with rage, his back arched, till every bristle stood erect on it like a porcupine's quill, and his stern bearing firmly against the rock, as if it was his last stay and refuge.

At sight of the brute in this position, to compare small things with great, I could not help thinking of James Fitzjames' gallant stand, when, beset by Roderick and his clansmen,

> "His back against a rock he bore,
> And firmly placed his foot before:
> 'Come one, come all! this rock shall fly
> From its firm base as soon as I——'"

The boar had chosen his ground with the utmost strategic skill: the instinct of a brute is ever sharpened by danger, and self-preservation suggests shifts that often baffle the ingenuity of the cleverest human reason. Look at the hare, for instance, retreating at break of day to her form! what jumps and gyrations does she practise to elude discovery; and, when sinking in the chase, how marvellous are her wiles and doubles, running the hot foil and squatting suddenly, so as often to puzzle the most observant huntsman and the keenest-nosed hounds? Or, look at the shifts of a deer in his last extremity: he takes soil, and carefully sinking his whole body, even to the tips of his brow-antlers, beneath the wave, his nostrils alone being exposed above the surface, he will remain immersed, like a crocodile, for a considerable time; nor will he allow a leaf or a twig to touch him, lest it should convey a taint to the air and reveal the secret of his whereabouts to the inquisitive foe. A fox, too, has been known to practise this very artifice, in addition to scores of others improvised in the moment of distress.

Surely this is a faculty very closely allied to reason! And who shall say where one begins and the other ends; or who shall divide them? That boar, finding his wind and strength failing him, must have reflected on his condition, and deduced from it the necessity of immediately choosing 'vantage ground on which to make his last stand, and await in the most favourable position the attack of his enemy. Is not this precisely what the ablest general would have done under like pressure? But the tactics of the one are attributed to reason; those of the other to mere brute instinct; though what the difference is my philosophy is unable to explain.

Mr. Trelawny has remarked more than once that to record efficiently the grandeur of the chase, its brilliant passages, and the wild, romantic scenery to which Diana often leads her votaries, every pack should have its artist—himself, too, a fellow-worshipper of the goddess—who, as an eye-witness, should illustrate the varying and glorious scenes of the hunting-field. Would that Horace Vernet or Landseer had been among us on this occasion! that boar and those hounds, that rock and river, St. Prix and his peasants, would have been, beyond all doubt, committed to canvas; there to delight the world's eye for ages to come.

The Louvetier would not allow a shot to be fired; indeed, so surrounded was the boar by hounds swimming, scrambling, and striking at him that, unless the marksman had been a Kentuckian, he could scarcely have hit the one without endangering the lives of the others. So the boar for some time had the best of the fight; the ledge of rock giving him firm standing-ground, and the depth of the pool compelling the hounds to swim to the attack, and the men to remain helpless lookers-on from the opposite bank. Ever and anon, as a gallant hound attempted to land and seize him in the flank, the boar, with a sudden swirl of the head, but without moving an inch from his rocky pedestal, struck the intruder a blow and a gash with his tusk that hurled him at once wounded and bleeding into the depths of the tide. Six or seven of the hounds were seriously injured in no time, and St. Prix became well-nigh frantic at the spectacle.

At length Shafto dashed into the river some twenty yards above the scene of the fray; and crossing it, waist-deep as it was, he quickly managed to mount the precipice from the rear, and, looking down on the boar, he dropped a huge pebble exactly on the brute's snout. Much to Shafto's surprise, the blow proved fatal; and down went the pig, like a cormorant, head-foremost into the flood, but never more to rise again alive to the surface, and down he was carried a lifeless mass over the cataract, the hounds, many of them, pouring after him, as if still in full chase; till it was a good hundred yards below ere he was fairly landed and the *mort* sounded over his carcase.

Shafto's *coup de main*, so adroitly directed, elicited, on behalf of the hounds, the warmest expressions of gratitude from St. Prix, who, unbuckling the belt that carried his *couteau-de-chasse*, a well-proved and priceless weapon, presented it to Shafto, telling him at the same time he was quite sure its brightness would never be tarnished in his hands. That *couteau*, at this moment, hangs in the old hall at —— Tower, and is not only valued for its history, but is the subject of many a stirring after-dinner story in that festive room.

It was past two o'clock ere the orgies enacted over this last boar were brought to an end; and, when the hounds were over-hauled and counted, it was found that eight couple only were sound and available for further work. However, this fact had little weight with the peasants, who, in addition to their genuine love of the sport, had yet a long score unpaid by the pigs for the damage done to their crops during the past autumn. So, one and all, knowing another pig to be within reach, and believing him to be harboured in the *genet*, declared for more war: and St. Prix, nothing loth, at once trotted off the hounds for that cover.

"A fresh hat in the ring" is always looked upon as a formidable matter by the already half-beaten wrestler; and though he be a champion, doughty as Cann or Polkinghorne of old, the inferior but fresh athlete will often prove an awkward customer; and the handicap is thus rendered tolerably fair for both parties. The boar, refreshed by two hours' rest, never waited a moment for the hounds to rouse him: but, as the music of their tongues rang on the stale line, he instantly broke cover for the open moor, and, before the pack were well on him, he was crossing the mountain ridge and going at a round gallop straight for Kœnig. Fortunately, our horses were at hand, held by Kergoorlas' drunken piqueur and Owen Mawr; but, though we managed to view him frequently, and the hounds carried a fine head over the heathery waste, "the fresh hat" proved too strong in the struggle, and reached the great covers of Kilvern ahead of us all. This was tantamount to a "fair backfall;" and as the shades of night were already taking possession of the woodland glens below, and the hounds were more than half beaten by their hard day's work, St. Prix blew his horn and stopped farther pursuit.

On our homeward route to Gourin the hound Vétéran frequently ranged alongside my horse, and, observing his high crown and long face, I remarked to Shafto that I had never seen a more sensible countenance than his in my life.

"Quite right!" he exclaimed; "that hound reminds me always of old Eldon; and, had our late archbishop ever heard him throw his tongue, he would infallibly have pronounced him to be a sound, dependable, orthodox hound. By-the-bye," continued he, "that Devonshire fellow-voyager of mine, on board the Norwegian timber-brig, gave me rather a novel definition of that word 'orthodox.' It appeared that a parish adjoining his own, in the north of Devon, had for some months lacked the services of a curate, although the rector,* an energetic parish priest, had spared no pains to obtain a right man. The rector was also the master of a rattling pack of hounds; and his churchwarden, Tozer, paying the market-town a visit about this time, was thus accosted by his grocer:

"'Well, Mr. Tozer, have ye got a coorate, yit, for Bridgwell?'

"'Not yit; they don't all suit master: but here's his advertisement, so I reckon he'll soon get one:

* The "Prime Minister" before alluded to.

"'Wanted, a curate for Bridgwell; must be a gentleman of moderate and orthodox views.'

"'Orthodox, Mr. Tozer. What doth he mean by orthodox?'

"'Well,' said the churchwarden, thoughtfully, and in deep perplexity, knowing the double nature of the curate's duties, secular as well as sacred, 'well, I can't exactly say; but I reckon 'tis a man as can *ride* pretty well.'"

CHAPTER XIV.

The last day at Gwernez had been a hard one for the hounds. So many had been wounded in the river, and so many lamed by want of condition, and by the sharp granite roads over which they had been compelled to travel in their long day's work, that it had been found necessary to leave two couple of Shafto's lot at a peasant's hut, some two leagues short of their kennel, which they reached in sad plight on the following day. The piqueurs, too, were many of them footsore; and the wonder was how they had endured the incessant toil and broken night rest to which they had been subjected for three successive days, shod as they were with iron-heeled huge sabots, weighing at least four pounds a pair, going incredible distances, and carousing the livelong night on their return to Gourin. Nothing but the inborn love of the chase, and that indomitable spirit, possessed by no nation stronger than by the Bretons, that carries men on till they drop rather than give in, could have sustained them under such circumstances.

Napoleon the First well knew the character of the Breton peasantry, and had too often tested their courage, hardihood, and physical endurance under the cruelest privation; hence the conscription, in his stormy day, fell with disproportionate weight on that primitive race, and more than decimated their land. Their power of bearing fatigue, however, he was wont to attribute as much to mechanical reasons, arising from their low stature, as to the brave spirit by which they were ever inspired; for the great General maintained that the heart, in impelling the blood to the extremities, would have so much less work to do in a small frame than a large one, in a short than a tall man; and therefore would become fatigued, and strike work in one more quickly than in the other: hence his preference for soldiers of low stature on long and arduous campaigns. What country could have met his requirements so fully in this respect as Lower Brittany, or where could he have found little men with bigger hearts than among this Celtic population?

The chasseurs, too, over and above their field-work, had kept the ball rolling with considerable vivacity during the past three nights at Gourin. So that when Kergoorlas proposed to give the piqueurs and hounds a day's rest on Thursday, and hunt at Kilvern on the following day, there was not found a dissentient voice among the party to object to the arrangement. As for St. Prix, he hailed it with delight, wolf-hunting being far more after his fancy, and also more in accordance with his duty, than the more dangerous sport of hunting the boar. Not that he cared for danger; but it was a real grief and vexation to him to see his hounds gashed and mutilated, as they so often were, by the tusks of that fierce animal.

"The peasants of the district have already expressed the utmost satisfaction and gratitude at the result of our *chasse*," said St. Prix; "and if we could not give them another day, not a man would grumble from Gourin to Concarneau."

"That's just as it should be," said Kergoorlas; but, at all events, they shall have the benefit of my hounds on Friday; and then, if our sport be as good as it has hitherto been, they will consider their wrongs amply redressed—at least, for the present year."

"Aye, but no longer," rejoined St. Prix; "for as sure as

autumn comes round with its crops of corn, potatoes, and chestnuts, so sure will the ravagers again appear, and heart-rending messages will reach us for further help, and——"

"More bacon," interposed Shafto; "and quite right, too, for, to my certain knowledge, not one man in ten of those Kilvern peasants gets a mouthful of butcher's meat, saving and excepting the produce of your *chasse*, from one year's end to another."

"And the produce of their own guns and gins," added M. de Kerjeguz, the chief cover-owner in the Kilvern country. "I had a fair stock of roe deer, as well as boar, in Laz and Kœnig a few years ago; but of late the supply from those covers has been barely sufficient for my own table. The scarcity is attributed to the wolves by the tenants of the adjacent farms; but my *garde-forêt* tells me the wolves that get the best share are habited in goat-skin attire. However, so long as the Louvetier can find a wolf and a boar, when he is good enough to bring his hounds and his friends into my covers, I care little what becomes of the roe, which, dress it as you will, is but sorry venison at last."

This imputation on the part of the *garde-forêt* was no doubt a just one. The peasants are free-traders in game, and look upon the *feræ naturæ* fed upon their farms, for which they pay a rent, as more their property than the landlord's; and, although checked by the necessity of paying for a *permis-de-chasse* if they openly carry a gun, their ingenuity in devising snares and gins of countless variety for entrapping game, is only equalled by their skill in setting them. Go where you will through the broomy land, if you are accompanied by dogs, you may consider yourself fortunate if, for any length of time, they escape the toils of the peasant poacher, either in the shape of a wire noose or a rusty spring-gun. This last, except it is intended for a wolf, is rarely a formidable engine; for, although I have had many a dog caught in one, the entrapment was never followed by worse results than a piteous cry and a broken skin.

On one occasion a wolf-gin was very nearly the cause of my getting into a serious scrape with the peasants of Trefranc. I was out woodcock shooting in that district; and, being in the act of jumping from the top of a high bank into a piece of sedgy ground, my trusty Breton servant, who had mounted the bank at the same moment, called my instant attention to a huge wolf-gin which was lying with open jaws very close to the spot on which I must have alighted, had I made my intended jump.

"That's a dangerous trap for man or dog," I said to Noel, with more irritation than gratitude at my narrow escape. "Pull it up, and cast it into yonder bog."

He immediately proceeded to obey orders; but, as there was some difficulty in extracting the iron pegs with which the gin was moored to the ground, I passed on with the spaniels, and was not aware that, instead of pitching it into the bog, he had consigned it to my *carnassiere*—a circumstance that afterwards saved him from serious discomfiture.

We had proceeded some half-a-league down the valley; he on one side, for the purpose of marking, and I on the other drawing a hanging cover, when an uproar in my rear apprised me that at least half-a-dozen peasants, armed with pitch-forks and clubs, were coming up in hot haste, and that I was the object of their pursuit. As they approached within twenty yards of me, I wheeled round and faced them—a movement that had the immediate effect of bringing the whole party to a halt; and before I could inquire what their business was, a simultaneous and angry shout informed me I had stolen their wolf-trap, and bid me restore it there and then. I pointed to Noel, and told them he knew more about the trap than I did, and would show them what he had done with it if they inquired of him.

This answer, and probably the half-cocked double gun I held in my right hand, turned their attention at once upon Noel, who, by-the-bye, had seen the whole affair, and even heard the conversation that had taken place between us. So when he saw the lot of angry peasants dashing down-hill directly for the meadow in which he stood, Noel's courage utterly failed him; and, dragging with all haste the wolf-trap from the depths of the *carnassière*, he cast it, in view of them, to the ground, and then, with a yell of terror, started off at top speed, and disappeared from the scene.

The abandonment of the spoil appeared to satisfy the peasants, as they instantly picked up the trap, turned on their heel, and quietly retraced their steps towards Trefranc. It was a case of *relictâ bene* on Noel's part, most clearly; for, had he been weighted with that incumbrance, he must inevitably have been overtaken, and would certainly have suffered rough treatment at his captors' hands.

After this adventure, which occurred soon after I first arrived at Carhaix, I made a memorandum never again to remove a peasant's trap. My dogs, of course, I liberated when caught; but I always allowed the engines to remain where I found them. While on the subject of poaching, let me record an ingenious and, to me, a novel mode of catching pheasants, which an old soldier —one who had done good service in India, but received no pension for it—practised some time since in a western county. Meeting him one day by the side of a river, with his creel tolerably well filled with trout, I found his conversation so full of wild-life anecdote that I gladly shared my sandwiches and sherry-flask with him, for the sake of his good company. As we wandered along, chatting, fishing, and sipping sherry, the old man's heart expanded, and, after deploring the want of a pension, to which he considered himself fairly entitled, he consoled himself by assuring me he knew a thing or two more than his neighbours, and that he could earn many a shilling while they were abed and asleep. "For," said he, taking me into full confidence, "so long as my Lady up to Grandton or Sir John up to Brigsham keep a swarm of pheasants, I shall never trouble the parish for a loaf of bread."

I felt somewhat surprised at this announcement, never before having met with an old soldier turned poacher; but, not to check the flow of his conversation, he being quite in the humour to decant his stock of knowledge to the dregs, I said, "So you get a head or two of them now and then, do you? How do you manage it? Are there no keepers?"

"Ay, a swarm of them, too; but they're a sleepy set, and so long as they don't hear a gun or find a wire they're easy enough, and don't take alarm."

"Then you match them with brimstone, or noose them with a pole and wire when at roost?"

The old soldier shook his head, and bid me guess again.

"Well, then, you take a game-cock with steel spurs on in a bag, and he pins them for you?"

"No, I don't: a cock would make too much noise to suit my book. I feed the ground with a handful or two of peas on the edge of a cover frequented by the pheasants, and I make half-a-dozen little holes, about the size of a coffee-cup, in the earth, dropping a couple of peas into each. When these have been picked up, I know they'll come again for more next day; so I twist up half-a-dozen little brown-paper bags, such as in shops they give you a pennyworth of comfits in, and, after smearing the inside of the bags with fresh bird-lime, I sink them in the holes, dropping lightly a pea or two into the bottom of each paper. Then, as the pheasants go picking along the line of peas (for they must be sown in line, not broadcast), they pop their bills into the bag, and suddenly find themselves hoodwinked by the paper adhering to their feathers. Then, being unable to see where to run or where to fly, they instantly squat like dead things. So that's my opportunity—I jumps out of the cover, catches them by the neck, and in they goes into my wallet, without a squeak of noise.

Why, 'twas but last Sunday morning," continued he, warming on the subject, "when other folks were to church, and the keepers abed—for that's *their* regular roosting time—that I got six fine fellows, a bird for each bag; and I wasn't above an hour or so about the whole business."

A few days after my interview with the old soldier, I met at a friend's house a general officer, named Taylor, a Waterloo hero, who for many years had commanded the 10th Hussars in India and elsewhere, and was himself a wood-craftsman of no ordinary ability. I described this *cornet-de-papier* dodge, and, to my surprise, he was already fully informed on the subject, having practised it extensively in India, but more especially in catching pigeons than birds of the game tribe; and we came to the conclusion that the old soldier had doubtless gained his experience in the same country.

It having been decided by the chasseurs, in conclave assembled, that there should be no hunting on the Thursday, a party was at once organised for paying a visit to the Marine Observatory, established at Concarneau by the Academy of Sciences. This institution—one of the first, if not *the* first of its kind in Europe, owes its origin and support to the liberality of the French Government; and under the able superintendence of M. Coste, backed by the Minister of Public Works, the habits and instinct of various sea-fish are here studied, and many secrets of the deep, hitherto unknown, are now daily being revealed to the inquiring eye. The attainment of a better knowledge of the science of Pisciculture is, of course, the ultimate object of this institution; but the business of actually breeding the fish is not practised here as at Arcachon and other localities better adapted for that purpose. It is strictly an observatory, not a water-farm, in which stock are bred and cultivated by artificial process; an aquarium, not a nursery intended for the development of ova and the care of young fish in the first stage of their existence.

M. de Kergoorlas having kindly volunteered the use of his

drag for the occasion, M. de St. Prix, Keryfan, Shafto, and myself determined to accompany him; while the rest of the party, consisting chiefly of the chasseurs from Upper Brittany, preferred a day at the woodcocks, large flights of which had been driven in to Conveau and the neighbouring covers by the recent storms. At daybreak on Thursday, accordingly, as heavy clouds from the north-west came scudding up over the little town of Gourin, scavenging the streets ever and anon with a fitful deluge, and saluting the window-panes with volleys of hail, hard and big as rifle-bullets, Kergoorlas's drag rattled over the stones, and came to a standstill at the door of the Cheval Blanc. The team, which matched neither in colour nor size, nevertheless had the appearance of a rough, useful lot, well suited to the country and work for which they were required; but one of the leaders, both being stallions, had a strong iron muzzle fitted over his nose, and seemed, from the caution shown in handling him, to be a downright vicious brute. Fight, and hold on like a bull-dog, he would, if man or horse provoked his wrath; and, although his groom professed to keep him on half-rations of hay and no corn, the spirit of this war-horse could not be subdued. He went by the significant name of "Vampire," having drawn blood so often, and would have been as fit a subject as "Cruiser" for Airey's taming power. Notwithstanding his hard treatment in the way of food, however, he was a rare beast in harness, and, according to Kergoorlas, could and did do the work of two ordinary horses, or long since he would have fed the hounds. A set of rope-traces did not add to the beauty of the team; but, if not

"Brilliant in Brummagem leather,"

a coil of additional rope tossed into the fore-boot insured a ready restoration to the gear, in case of disaster on the day's journey And constant need there appeared to be for this precaution, inasmuch as the off-side wheeler, now the coach was loaded, obstinately refused to start and go up to his collar; and every time the double-thong curled over his ribs the brute plunged frantically forward, and did more or less damage to the unfortunate harness.

However, rough and hilly as the road was over the Black Mountains, we reached Scaer soon after ten o'clock, without any serious mishap; and here, tarrying a while to bait our horses, and watch the usual process of frying omelets and broiling cutlets for our *déjeuner*, Shafto, Keryfan, and I strolled over the new bridge, to take a look at the stream that rushes, seething and gurgling, 'neath its pretty arches. To judge from its appearance, now somewhat turbid from the recent rain, a more favourable river for salmon and trout could not be seen between Dunkeld and Inverness. Immediately below Scaer bridge there is a beautiful run; and, if the reports of its well-stocked condition be true, an expert fisherman would be likely to fill his basket here without much trouble. The river is called the Elle, and falls into the sea at Quimperlé, a pretty little town, containing the grave of St. Gurlot, to which the Breton peasants resort for the cure of rheumatism, the arm being thrust into a hole perforated in the tombstone for that purpose.

The road, viâ Rosporden to Concarneau, presented no features of interest along its wild, sterile tract of moor and heathland, beyond occasional memorials of the terrible Chouan struggle which, indicated by wayside crosses, had been carried on so long and so savagely in this district. Within a short distance of this road was perpetrated that atrocious massacre of a party of bishops and priests who, by order of the Revolutionist Government, were proceeding to Brest, for the purpose of administering the rite of confirmation and consecrating a church in that town. They were dragged from their carriage with a cry resembling the whoop of an owl (this being the party signal of the Chouans, and hence their name), and cruelly butchered on the spot. A granite cross, rudely cut with the words "Siste Viator," arrests the wayfarer's attention, and is pointed out by a white-haired old mendicant, said to be the son of one of the actors in the above tragedy, as the very ground on which the murder was perpetrated. Not one word of pity or remorse, however, escapes the lips of this true Breton, who glories in the knowledge that the Chouans fought for a righteous cause—their legitimate Bourbon king—rather an old-fashioned virtue in the present day.

On descending the westward slope of this mountain-land a glorious view to the seaward meets the sight on every side. Below us, and at no great distance, the broken coast-line, indented with inlets, bays, and promontories, rugged and jagged by the ever-restless waves, might be seen as far as Pont Aven to the east; while, further away westward, Penmarch, Pont l'Abbé, and even the storm-beaten headland of Bec du Raz, forming one horn of the bay of Douarnenez, could be just descried by the naked eye. Then, further yet, and outward, rolled the great Atlantic, immeasurably spread beyond all.

"See you yonder little island off Quimper, on the Pont l'Abbé side of the bay?" said St. Prix, pointing to a spot of land looking not much bigger than a man-of-war moored out at sea.

"Quite distinctly," I replied. "I can even see the white foam of the waves as they break on its shore."

"Well, a strange adventure occurred during the last Anglo-Gallic war to the owner of that island, the Baron Daoulaz; and, as he told me the tale himself, you shall hear it as it came from his lips. The Baron, you must know, was a great farmer, and having cultivated a portion of this isolated land, was in the habit almost daily of rowing himself over, and paying a short visit of inspection to a plantation he had recently formed, accompanied by a black Newfoundland dog, his sole companion. It so happened at the same time that an English frigate stood off and on that coast for weeks together watching the French fleet, then lying securely in Brest Harbour, but preparing for sea under Admiral

Villeneuve, before the great battle of Trafalgar. The Baron's visits to the little island had not been unobserved from the frigate; indeed, they had already been made the subject of comment on the quarter-deck, and excited some curiosity.

"One day, however, the wind blowing gently off shore, and the sea being unusually quiescent, the signal-man again reported the boat afloat, a man and dog on board, and bound for the island. Instantly the order to 'man the galley' was given by the captain, and, by the time the Baron had landed, a crew of six men and a coxswain were pulling the ship's boat stealthily and speedily over the smooth water, and were soon in a position to intercept the Baron on his intended return to the mainland. Finding his retreat cut off, he very quietly resigned himself to his captors, by whom he and his dog and boat were forthwith conveyed to the frigate. But of what use were they, now they were captured, either to his ship or his country?—an incumbrance, if detained, and clearly of no profit to either, thought the captain to himself.

"'You say you are a farmer, Baron; and if so, you probably feed some fat stock. Now what have you in that hive?' said the Captain, interrogating him closely.

"'Sold all my bullocks at Brest last week to the Government navy purveyor, and I've nothing but a few fat pigs left.'

"Then did visions of pork cutlets, spare-ribs, and fresh sausages, incline the gallant officer's judgment to the side of mercy; for salt junk, and nothing but salt junk, had passed the enclosure of his jaws for many a long week, and his mouth fairly watered at the prospect of some fresh meat.

"'Send us,' said the Captain, a bright thought striking him, 'half-a-dozen of those pigs, the biggest and fattest you have, and I will at once give you your freedom, Baron.'

"'I can't send so many—my whole stock consists of four fat pigs only; but, if you will accept them as my ransom, they shall be sent without delay to your ship.'

"This offer was at once accepted; but a difficulty arose as to how the negotiation was to be completed, the danger of intercourse with the shore presenting a serious obstacle against the fulfilment of the bargain. However, the ready wit of the Breton nobleman, now sharpened by necessity, quickly suggested a safe expedient. 'Let the dog be my messenger,' said he. 'If you put him ashore at Penmarch Point, with a private letter of mine attached to his collar, he will speedily reach home, and the result, I feel certain, will be satisfactory.'

"Accordingly this was done. The dog and the letter were soon conveyed to the said point, when, screeched at by the bluejackets, he started homewards at full speed. Nor were they kept waiting long for the pigs: a couple of wild Breton peasants were seen from the ship pricking forward the four huge hogs slowly but steadily towards the shore. They were soon transported to the frigate; and, when he was restored to his boat, the Baron's feelings may be better imagined than described as he bid adieu to the captain and crew, with tears of joy and gratitude in his eyes. For years afterwards, whenever he met an Englishman, the Baron never failed to make a joke of this capture, and to boast of the value at which he had been estimated by a hungry British sailor— at four pigs only."

By the time St. Prix had finished his story Rosporden had been passed, and the team was trotting merrily over the stones into the little seaport of Concarneau, a town that once possessed fortified walls and a strong castle, built by Anne of Brittany, but is now famous only for its sardine fishery and marine observatory; but of this more anon in the next chapter.

CHAPTER XV.

No matter how wild and attractive the sport of wolf and boar-hunting may be, followed as it still is in Lower Brittany after the fashion of a bygone age, with hound and horn of ancient style, and customs of venery elsewhere unknown, nevertheless the bare subject, however seasoned with adventure, will at length pall on the sense, and become intolerable even to the strongest appetite. The course of nature itself is one of perpetual change and marvellous variety; and man, if he has one instinct beyond that which he exhibits in ten minutes after his birth, namely, searching for something to sustain life, certainly shows it in his crave for change. Harping on the same string, even though touched by the finger of a Paganini, pleases only as a passing charm; and he of the Sabine farm warns us that the feast too often repeated grows bitter* in the end.

Therefore on this ground a digression from the forest to the sea-shore—from the musical thunder of Kergoorlas' pack to the loud-sounding roar of the restless Atlantic—will not, probably, be unacceptable to the general reader. The little seaport of Concarneau, however, to which he is now introduced, possesses a Marine Observatory, in the waters of which a great variety of sea-fish not only seem "to live at home at ease," but to disport

* "Nempe inamarescunt epulæ sine fine petitæ."

themselves like creatures unconscious of captivity and in the enjoyment of perfect health. Whither, then, would he wish to turn from the rugged tracks of forest life, from the haunts of the wild boar and the wolf, if not to this attractive spot? Every hunter is, or ought to be, something of a naturalist; and here, at Concarneau, the faculty of his observation will be directed to a new study—to the nature and habits of animals, not such, perhaps, as he has so long loved to pursue, but to denizens of the deep, the finny tribe, vertebrate and non-vertebrate, whose ways have hitherto been inscrutable and beyond the power of man's ken.

Of late years science has been busy in revealing what the bowels of the earth contain: while its surface has been combed in all regions to supply the beasts of the field, fowls of the air, and creeping things of every kind for the use of our zoological institutions and the cultivation of natural history; but till recently, although man was given "dominion over the fish of the sea," as well as "over all the earth," by the great Creator of the Universe, the study of life in the waters has received little or no encouragement from the scientific of this or a former age, the shroud of the fathomless deep acting as a barrier to all investigation. Nevertheless, this neglect is somewhat remarkable, especially if the great value set upon fish in the luxurious days of old Rome be borne in mind, when seas were ransacked for the most delicate of their kind, and the poet could tell his friends what fish were best boiled and what roasted; that the *Peloris* of the Lucrine was a better fish than the *Murex* of Baiæ; and that

"Non omne mare est generosæ fertile testæ."

Again, one might have supposed that the interdiction of flesh-meat to the whole Roman Catholic world at certain seasons of the year, when a fish-diet, as tending to the mortification of the body, was universally allowed, would long since have stimulated inquiry and experiments as to the best mode of producing so useful a food in the greatest quantity. But no, it was reserved for men of the present day, such as, in our own country, Mr. Willughby, Colonel Montagu, Couch of Polperro, Pennant, Yarrell, Sir Humphrey Davy, Dr. Parnell, Sir Wm. Jardine, Dr. George Johnston of Berwick-on-Tweed, Mr. Donovan, Smith of Deanston, the sub-soiler and inventor of the artificial salmon-ladder, Dr. Knox, Mr. T. L. Parker, Sir Francis A. Mackenzie, Mr. John Shaw, R. Buist of Perth, Ffennell, Lee, Ford, Thomas Ashworth, the king of cultivators, as he was called in Galway, and last though not least, Mr. Frank Buckland, to originate the study of fish-life and fish-culture in river and sea; and doubtless great results have already been achieved by those pioneers and by the united interest of capital and science, now fairly awakened to this important point.

That it is an important point to the public, especially at the present period of high-priced provisions, may be gathered from the Report of the English Sea-Fishery Commissioners (1866), which informs us that "London alone consumes annually 80,000 tons of sea-fish, not estimating salmon, herrings, sprats, eels, crabs and lobsters, oysters, mussels, and shrimps; this in the aggregate greatly exceeds in weight the consumption of beef in London. The most frequented fishing-grounds are much more prolific of food than the same extent of the richest land. Once in the year, an acre of good land, carefully tilled, produces a ton of corn, or two or three hundred pounds' weight of meat or cheese; the same area at the bottom of the sea, on the best fishing-grounds, yields a greater weight of food to the persevering fisherman every week in the year.

"Five vessels, in a single night's fishing, brought in 17 tons of fish, an amount equal in weight to 50 cattle or 300 sheep. The ground which these vessels covered, during the night's fishing, could not have exceeded an area of 50 acres."

The late Mr. Thomas Ashworth, the most practical, persevering, and successful of pisciculturists, commenting on the above Report, says—" If we estimate the annual profit of 50 acres of the best land at £2 an acre, that is £100, and compare this with a single night's fishing of five vessels, producing 17 tons of fish, at £7 a ton, say £119, we may form some idea of the wonderful powers of production of a 'fish-farm' at the bottom of the sea, which, without any expensive tillage, produces more food *in one night* than a similar area of the best cultivated land *in an entire year!*"

That the Marine Observatory at Concarneau was established by the Academy of Sciences, not for breeding sea-fish artificially, but for the purpose of studying their habits, with a view to their better culture and propagation in a state of nature, has been explained in a previous chapter; and as the institution from its commencement has been entrusted to the management of M. Coste, a man eminently qualified for the post, great results have already been achieved, and greater may yet be anticipated.

On our arrival at the little seaport, the news rapidly spread from the hostelry to the gendarmerie, and thence, with official weight, to the ears of Mr. Coste, that a party of savants had arrived at Concarneau for the express purpose of visiting the Observatory and reporting thereon; so, while M. de St. Prix was engaged in writing a note to the Director, soliciting his permission to view the establishment, that energetic officer had anticipated the formality and reached the hotel: nor was the warmth and courtesy of his welcome at all chilled when he discovered—as he very quickly did—that we were only a party of wolf-hunters, eager to improve our acquaintance with the living wonders of the deep; mere amateurs in the science of natural history, and no savants at all.

"Come along, gentlemen," he said in the heartiest manner, proposing to lead the way directly towards the Institution; "and

I hope, after you have seen the few novelties we can show you, that you will give me the pleasure of your company at supper this evening at seven o'clock?"

"Thank you a thousand times," said M. de Kergoorlas. "But I fear we cannot accept your kind offer of hospitality, as my hounds are appointed to meet to-morrow morning at Kilvern, for a day's boar-hunting in that forest."

"Ah! you hunt the boar as well as the wolf? Well, that's a more profitable *chasse* than the other, for you destroy the destroyer, and eat him afterwards. But if you can defer your hunting to Saturday, and will do me the honour I ask, you would then have ample time to-morrow to see our Druidical monuments, of which there is a vast assemblage at Carnac and Plouharnel, in this neighbourhood; and they are acknowledged to be unequalled in Europe."

"That would be a great treat," responded Kergoorlas and myself at the same moment; Keryfan, too, chimed in, and hoped the change might be made in the hunting-day.

"With all my heart," said St. Prix, always ready to promote good-fellowship and the wishes of those around him; "so let us bow to the majority, Shafto, and accept M. Coste's hospitable offer and the treat in store for us to-morrow."

Now, so insatiable was Shafto's appetite for sport, that a day lost to hunting was almost equivalent to a day lost to his existence: and when thus appealed to by St. Prix, it required no little effort on his part to conceal his disappointment and assent to the proposal: but he did so manfully, nevertheless, although he would far rather have viewed the white tag of a living fox flashing across a path than have discovered the whitened bones of an arch-Druid at the base of a tottering cromlech.

"By all means, if you wish it, St. Prix. And"—he added, gracefully—"as we are so near, I think it is a duty we owe our forefathers to make a pilgrimage to their tombs."

"If tombs they be," said M. Coste; "but that at present is an unsolved problem."

Arrangements were then made for dispatching a mounted messenger to Gourin to proclaim aloud in its streets the postponement of the hunting-day; while Louis Trefarreg was charged, in a letter from the Louvetier, to inform the peasants of Kilvern on the same point: the fixture not having been advertised, this notice was deemed amply sufficient for the chasseurs and peasants of the surrounding district. Matters having been so far settled, we ordered beds at the Lion d'Or; and then, under the guidance of M. Coste, trotted off at once to the Observatory.

The site of this building is admirably adapted to its wants; inasmuch as, dependent on a constant supply of fresh sea-water for the sustenance and well-being of its occupants, it is founded on a rock literally overhanging the sea; the water of which, from the absence of a muddy tidal river and shore, is usually pellucid as the fountain of Blandusia: then, Concarneau being a fishing town and possessing a fleet of small craft numbering at least 400, engaged in the capture of sardines and all kinds of fish incidental to that coast, it offers peculiar advantages for the stocking of the establishment, both as to the variety of the captives and their quick conveyance from the wide sea to their narrow home. Nor are the fishermen uninstructed on this point: the moment an unusual prize is captured, the boat making the capture, if it possess not a suitable kettle, which some of them carry for the purpose, hastens back to port and deposits it with all care and expedition in the tanks of the Aquarium: a service which is liberally requited by M. Coste on behalf of the French Government.

The building itself is a long, rectangular, stone edifice—what the French call *une maison carrée*—bearing a terrace on its flat roof and a spacious reservoir, into which, being the topmost of a succession of reservoirs, the water is pumped directly and continuously from the sea. As the reservoirs are formed like a flight of steps, one below the other, a stream flows steadily through them, and thus, by its motion, the air of the water is constantly renewed—a process rendered necessary by the respiration of the fish, which would soon exhaust the fresh air of a still tank and die from the want of it.

An ingenious over-shot wheel had been designed for doing the laborious work of continuously pumping the water to the topmost reservoir; which water, on quitting the lowest reservoir, was to fall rapidly over a wooden shoot into the boxes of the wheel and thus give it the needful rotatory power. Allowing for waste and evaporation, it was expected this wheel would supply the reservoirs with sufficient water for nine days out of ten, but that on every tenth day it would be necessary to make up the deficiency by the usual manual labour. This contrivance, however, at the time of our visit, was in embryo; but I doubt not its proportions have been developed long since, and that it is now doing its giant work with the utmost effect.

A few words more on the construction of the reservoirs. These, forming a length altogether of about 80 metres, are divided into at least 100 cells by galvanised wire-net partitions, which, while they keep the different species of fish separate, permit a free passage to the running stream; so, in each compartment each kind gets the food peculiar to it, and seems to enjoy life as though unconscious of captivity. Nor, regulated by the outlet, can the usually pellucid water ever become too deep in the reservoirs; and thus the habits and instincts of the fish can at all times be watched by M. Coste and his observant staff—a point of considerable importance in the interest of ichthyological science.

So much for the building and its mechanical fittings; now for the live stock contained within its walls. On approaching the first reservoir, and before it was possible for the fish to see us,

M. Coste called our attention to the popular error with respect to the sense of hearing, denied, as so many think, to fish. "But," said he, "if they have no visible ears, the internal structure of the head exhibits in most species a thin, yielding cartilage, which serves the purpose of a tympanum ; and any vibration on the air affects that membrane sensibly at once." To illustrate this remark, he struck the edge of the tank sharply with his knuckles ; and instantly a rush was heard as of many fish bustling towards the spot. M. Coste then mounting a step higher and calling on us to do the same, we saw some fine grey mullet with their heads almost out of water, eagerly expecting the food which usually followed that summons. It reminded me of the "lake dinner-bell" at Charlottenburg, near Berlin ; the sound of which brings a shoal of carp and tench to it on the edge of the water, whenever the bell is rung. The Chinese call their fish together, at feeding time, with a sharp whistle.

So ravenous were the mullet, and so little timid, that, before M. Coste could convey to them the food prepared for their use, they were literally jostling each other and endeavouring to snatch it from his grasp, ere his hand touched the water : moreover, they permitted him to handle and stroke them, not only without resistance on their part, but apparently with a confidence that his attentions were kindly meant, and therefore most welcome. St. Anthony himself, the patron saint of fishes, could never have had a tamer flock than this small shoal of mullet : nor were they the only subjects exhibiting the results of kind treatment in this establishment. The sticklebacks, a naturally bold, pugnacious class, were equally civilised ; taking the food from his hand like a pack of pet spaniels ; a little eager and jealous of one another, perhaps, but still well-behaved on the whole, and betraying no fear whatever of the hand that fed them.

On one point only, however, they were not to be trifled with : each male fish selected a particular corner for his abiding place, and any invasion of this sanctum was instantly followed by a fierce encounter, which never ceased till the trespasser was ejected from the premises; tooth and spine were freely used on both sides, and the death of one, pierced by the spines, was the not unfrequent result of the battle.

It has been observed by M. Coste and other ichthyologists that the colour of the sticklebacks depends on the colour of the ground they occupy; for instance, one living in an earthenware jar in the far corner of the reservoir had assumed a dusky, brown hue; while on the opposite side, another, whose castle was a white tea-pot, was so light-coloured that, but for the pink colouring of his vicious little eye, he could scarcely be distinguished from the surrounding water. This assimilation in colour to that of their habitats is, however, not peculiar to this class, and is doubtless a provision of Nature to secure them and other species from the attacks of their enemies. The sticklebacks were great pets of M. Coste's, who told us, with much concern, that when he had trained them to quiet habits and even good-fellowship, they rarely lived longer than two years.

The next compartment to which M. Coste directed our attention was that enclosing the turbot—the most important, so far as the object of the institution is concerned, of all the fish contained in the Observatory. One hundred thousand turbot, more or less, are brought annually to the London market by Dutch fishermen of Scheveling alone, who are supposed to earn thereby some £80,000, a large sum which our own north-country fishermen might well envy, and a share of which the French are now making great efforts to obtain.

In captivity—as M. Coste demonstrated—the turbot will take food from the hand; and although he looks so unintelligent, he is not quite so great a fool as he looks. He knows, for instance, one hand from another; and the intrusion of a strange one, too near him, is instantly resented by an indignant attitude and unmistakable irritability, his fans expanding and the spots on his body changing from a light to a dark colour, as much as to say, "Keep your hand off my person, sir; that's a liberty I don't allow to a stranger." The rapidity with which he catches and devours a mullet of five or six ounces in weight is quite marvellous, considering his apparently unsuitable shape for rapid motion through the water, and the small mouth he possesses for taking a fish of that size. However, one, two, and three mullet, taken from a bait-tank, kept for the purpose, were quickly disposed of by a turbot not weighing eight pounds—his jaws expanding like those of a snake.

Other flat-fish there were in various compartments, such as skate, ray, brill, topknot, plaice, and sole; the first two, however, claiming more attention than the rest, probably because they were of larger size and not so well known by our party of landsmen as their smaller and more common congeners. Of the eleven species of true rays found in the adjoining seas, no less than five specimens, one consisting of the sting ray, had been captured for the institution. This fish is furnished with a serrated spine about four or five inches long, placed midway on the tail, and giving it the appearance of being double-tailed. With this weapon, when attacked, it has the power, by twisting about its long tail, of inflicting wounds that are rarely healed without much trouble, for, although it has been ascertained that the spine carries no poison, the laceration it effects is usually followed by severe inflammation. So the first thing a fisherman does on landing a sting ray is to chop off the dangerous tail.

Then came the tank appropriated to several species of the ugly and ever-hungry dog-fish, own kinsman to the shark, the "hyæna of ocean," and only less formidable because less powerful than that terrible fish. But of all the piscine tribe the most attractive and interesting to a naturalist were unquestionably the pipe-fish, a number of which, varying from eight to eighteen inches in length, moved in strange and graceful fashion, apparently hunting for water insects, invisible to the naked eye, in their narrow pellucid home. Sometimes they seemed to stand literally on their heads, the dorsal fin moving with singular rapidity; then, reversing that position, to balance themselves on their tails perpendicularly, with "heads up and sterns down," but, unlike the beauties described by my quotation, at such time the pace was nil, and, barring the dorsal fin, they were all but motionless.

But the most extraordinary feature distinguishing these *Syngnathi* consists in their being didelphyc or marsupial; the male fish being furnished with a false belly or elongated pouch between the stomach and the tail, into which the female casts her roe. In this receptacle the young are fecundated; and to it they retreat when threatened by danger, just as the young of the opossum and kangaroo do under like circumstances. There is a plate in the work of the old French naturalist Rondelet, entitled "*De Piscibus Marinis*," in which the young of the pipe-fish are represented as swimming in and out of the male parent's pouch (the female not being so provided), and playing around it, as a litter of puppies do around their dam.

The evolutions performed by these fish, on receiving their food, resembled those of a tumbler exhibiting some wondrous feat of gyration. They twisted round on their backs, and then through their curiously-formed syringe-like beak they sucked in the food—an evolution rendered necessary by the mouth being under the beak and perpendicular to its axis. M. Coste's interest in the peculiarities of these fish never seemed to grow weary. He had watched them, he told us, for hours together, and scarcely a day passed without his noticing some new trait in their habits worthy of record.

It would be far beyond the scope of this paper to relate a tithe of M. Coste's pleasant remarks on his finny flock; but I must not omit a few words on the crustaceous tribe, some of which, for various reasons, occupy an important office in this Marine Observatory. In the first place, the hermit crabs not only clear away the uneaten food of other fish, but, when death visits the tanks, the bodies of the defunct, no matter of what genus or size, are reduced in an incredibly short time to perfect skeletons : a nest of ants never did the polishing work more effectually. M. Coste, in pointing out this valuable service, by which all taint is removed from the water, brought to my recollection the quaint language of my old henchman and friend, Will Patey, who, whenever a hound proved utterly useless for work, invariably thus suggested his doom : " He must go a-crabbing, sir, he must ! " If sentence of death followed, in a tide or two the animal was reduced by a swarm of small crabs to so clean a skeleton that it might have been sent forthwith to the Hunterian Museum.

Between the common crab and the lobster M. Coste described a singular difference in the habits of the male fish ; the lobster is a grand Turk in his way ; roving, like a Lothario, from one attraction to another, and rebounding, tail forwards, five or six feet at a time, when meeting a rebuff from a coy mistress ; then gradually sidling up to her again with the hope of winning his fair prize. The crab, on the other hand, exhibits the virtue of conjugal fidelity to the highest degree, and is true as a dove to the single object of his affection ; clinging round her with all his arms, swimming about with her, and, if severed by force, seizing her again with the most devoted attachment ;—a pattern husband beyond all suspicion.

The metamorphosis, never dreamt of by Ovid, which these crustaceans undergo, have furnished most interesting matter for observation ; and beautiful indeed is the appearance of the lobster on first escaping from his crusty prison ; he is then dressed like a court beau, and seems quite conscious of the striking effect of his " purple and golden suit." The power of reproducing a limb in case of injury is common to all the tribe ; and as casualties, of course, are constantly occurring to them in their present narrow seas, the opportunity of observing the gradual but very slow growth of a new claw is but too frequently given to **M.** Coste and his watchful attendants.

The shades of night, now fast deepening over this interesting exhibition, soon brought our visit of inspection to a close, much to the regret of all; but, as **M.** de la Villemarqué, the eminent Celtic scholar and archæologist, was invited to meet us at dinner, his own château being at no great distance from Concarneau and very near Quimperlé, a great treat was yet in store for us from the company of two such men as **M.** Coste and that savant.

CHAPTER XVI.

A FEW minutes before the clock struck seven, M. de la Villemarqué, arriving from his chateau near Quimperlé, reached the private residence of M. Coste; and the party being augmented by the Colonel-Commandant of the district, we sat down, eight in number, to a bountiful and most appropriate supper. Never shall I forget the astonishment of Shafto at the variety of form and sauce in which so many different kinds of choice sea-fish were served; nor was the occasional groan that escaped from his brawny chest at the prospect of losing a day's hunting, "for the sake of those pagan monuments," any longer heard, so engrossed was he with the interesting conversation of M. de la Villemarqué and our host on the quality and utility of the various fish set before us.

To describe all the dishes would, as old Homer says, require a hundred tongues, and then the science of a Francatelli would be needed to enter analytically into the subject. I will, however, venture to touch upon two—the oyster soup and the bouillabaisse. This latter was pronounced by all a triumph of art; the fish, saffron, sweet red pepper, and other condiments being so insidiously *mêléed* together, that the most sensitive palate would have failed to distinguish a predominance over the rest in any one of its many ingredients. Greenwich s not more celebrated for its whitebait than Marseilles for its bouillabaisse, at the hotels of which city it is, at all seasons, a popular dish. The fish chiefly preferred for it is the dab, but in Paris all kinds of pond-fish are pressed into the service; and so good was it held to be by Thackeray, who was in the habit of feasting on bouillabaisse at Terré's Tavern, Rue Neuve des Petits Champs, that his muse absolutely cantered into rhyme on the merits of "the rich and savoury stew," for which, he says,

> "A Cordelier or Benedictine
> Might gladly, sure, his lot embrace,
> Nor find a fast-day too afflicting,
> Which served him up a bouillabaisse."

"When Louis XIV. dined with his cousin the Prince de Condé at Chantilly," observed M. Villemarqué, "Vatel, the *chef-de-cuisine*, failing to obtain suitable fish for the banquet, in a fit of desperation fell, like Cato, on his own sword; but, surely, had the artist served up a dish of bouillabaisse, the fish for which might have been caught at any moment in the reservoir hard by, he might have acquired additional fame, instead of committing self-murder."

"True," replied M. Coste; "but, unfortunately, the dish is of modern invention, and was not known in the days of the Grand Monarque."

"Then a man of such genius as Vatel should have improvised it in the emergency," said Villemarqué, whose acquaintance with the history of French dishes was evidently not on a par with his knowledge of dry bones or a Celtic ballad, the data of which he could fix with rare accuracy.

When the present Lord Chief Justice of England was engaged as counsel on a great mining case in South Wales, in addressing the jury it devolved on him to comment on the evidence given by Dr. Buckland, the eminent geologist, and, if possible, to weaken it by ridicule. So, assuming an air of gravity and doubt in his countenance, he said: "You have heard, gentlemen, the evidence of the learned professor, who has told you far more about the bowels of the earth than he knows or cares about his own." This was quite enough for the Welsh jury, whose faith in Buckland was shaken from that moment, though subsequent events have proved his geological foresight was quite correct in this matter. The parallel between that fine old Oxford professor and M. de la Villemarqué struck me forcibly at this moment, both being devoted to science, but giving no thought to the body beyond its needful claim.

So much for the bouillabaisse; and now for a few words on the oyster-soup. Had Horace been present he would have made Catius describe its composition to the last pinch of salt required for its flavour; another Satire would have been the happy result, and we should have known the bay—aye, the very bed—that furnished the delicious bivalve. But, lacking his good company, the reader must e'en be satisfied with M. Coste's history of his oyster-soup, in answer, as it were, to the unqualified praise bestowed on it by all present.

"I never knew what *oyster*-soup was," said he, "till I tasted it in Jersey. My ichthyological duties led me, some time since, to visit that island, seeking information respecting a shell-fish called the ormer, said to be peculiar to those coasts. My quarters were at Jeune's Union Hotel, in the Place Royale, which, for comfort and good fare, justly bore at that time the highest character in the island. With a rare stock of old Burgundy in the cellar—so old that no hand but that of the experienced host could decant it without breaking the crust— and an accomplished artist in the kitchen, who understood English and French cookery equally well, no wonder M. Jeune's hotel was the most popular in Jersey. But the dish of all others, which attracted most attention, was the oyster-soup, the receipt for which was a dead secret, nor would money tempt the *chef* to reveal it. However, what the dollar could not do, the Burgundy did. Pierre loved a bottle of it as much as his master; and catching him one day in a fever heat, after a grand banquet served up for the baillie and judges of the Royal Court, I proposed treating him to a bottle of this choice wine. His delicate palate (it is not every cook that has a palate) watered at the prospect, and before he had finished three parts of the bottle his heart was fairly uncorked, and he would have decanted the innermost secrets of his soul had I cared to know them. 'Now, Pierre,' said I, 'what is it that makes your oyster-soup the delight of the epicure and the envy of all cooks?'

"'Nothing more nor less than conger-eel,' he replied, 'from which the stock is always made, and which gives it the rich, delicate flavour so highly esteemed by all good judges.'

"'Conger delicate!' I exclaimed, with amazement; 'why, we bait our crab-pots with that fish, and only cook it when we can get no other fish.'

"'That may be,' he replied. 'Nevertheless, the fine flavour of a Jersey conger, when used for stock in oyster-soup, is unquestionable, and I strongly commend it to your future notice.'

M. Coste having told us this secret, Keryfan remarked that, while on a visit to me in South Devon, he had often eaten excellent conger-cutlets, which the farmers on the wild coast of the Start Point and Prawle Head kept salted, in lieu of bacon, for winter food. "And, Frank," said he, "you will bear me witness that, after a hard day's shooting with our dear old friend, 'Dick Randall,' over that rugged land, a conger-cutlet, fried in fresh butter, was no mean dish after all."

With the nuts and dessert after supper, the song went merrily round, after the usual Breton fashion; but M. de la Villemarqué, the man of all others who was brimful of the old ballads of the country, could not be prevailed on to sing one of them. Either he had no voice, or he considered it undignified to sing the songs which he, with infinite pains, has collected together and published with so much success. However, his recitation of "Kan Maenwynn," a ballad of the sixth century, which he immediately translated into French, indulging freely in the liberties of the paraphrase, was a treat never to be forgotten.

The next morning, at break of day, M. de Kergoorlas's drag appeared at the appointed hour (seven o'clock) at the door of the Lion d'Or; and, although a groom with firm hand stood at the head of each horse, neither the Vampire in front, though still iron-muzzled, nor the off-side wheeler, hampered as he was with a double trace-rope, showed as yet any symptoms of the vice for which they had acquired so bad a character. After picking up M. de la Villemarqué and M. Coste at the residence of the latter, we trotted along at a brisk rate through Pontaven and Quimperló on to Henn-bont—that being the Celtic word for old bridge—the granite-laid roads throughout the distance being in tip-top order, and such as Macadam himself would have been delighted to see. Verily, the government roads throughout France, superintended by officers, curtly called, from their office, "ponts et chaussées," and attended to by a staff of cantonniers, each one of whom is responsible for the good condition of so many kilometres, are admirably managed even in the remotest departments of that country. At Henn-bont the team was taken out and stabled for the rest of the day; the return journey to Gourin, *viâ* Plouay and Le Faouet (the last word meaning, in the Celtic language, "the land of beeches"), being a long and heavy tug for the poor beasts, and against the collar nearly the whole way.

We had just settled into our *voitures* provided by the Hôtel du Commerce for the purpose of reaching Auray without loss of time, when M. de la Villemarqué, by whose side I sat, pointed to a creek at the mouth of the river Blavet. "There," said he, "landed that gallant knight, Sir Walter de Manny, in the reign of Edward III., when he relieved Jeanne, the heroic Countess de Montfort, shut up in Henn-bont by the armies of Philippe de Valois and Charles de Blois. The countess, who, in the form of a delicate woman, possessed the heart of a lion, had animated the garrison to resist to the last man, fighting herself hand to hand, and assailing the enemy in several desperate sallies, till at length, when eating her last loaf, and preparing for capitulation, the English fleet hove in sight; and Sir Walter de Manny, with a host of knights and archers, hastened to the rescue. Two or three fierce sorties, headed by the countess mounted on a war horse, compelled the besiegers to withdraw, when the English troops, bringing an ample stock of provisions with them from the ships, were received into the town with the utmost joy and gratitude. But you should read 'Froisart,'" added Villemarqué, " to enjoy the history of Henn-bont and the achievements of this noble dame, the wife of Jean de Montfort."

With many such tales as this, having reference to the surrounding locality, did our *savants* beguile the time between Henn-bont and Auray. At this latter place, a boat is waiting to convey us down the little estuary to Locmariaker; and, as the wind and tide favour us, we soon arrive at Hellu, a cairn of stones not far from that desolate village. The menhir and dolmen that now meet our eye on every side, some tolerably whole, but most lying in fragments around, the grim and silent witnesses of unknown rites and of a by-gone people, are of such a magnitude, that every one contemplating the scene must wonder that not a scrap of history remains to inform us who were the authors, what was the date, or what the object of such vast and remarkable constructions. But so it is; time has obliterated every trace of their origin; and, if they be graves of the dead, as many conjecture, not a single epitaph remains to tell who or what they were who lie buried here. What a moral on the perpetuity of man's monuments!

Some strange figures, it is true, may be seen on the under side of the vast slabs of the Dolmen, called dol-yr-Marchant; but they are not believed to be coeval with the construction of the dolmen; and, if they have a meaning, hitherto all experts have been puzzled to decipher it.

Time would not permit us to visit Gavr Innis, or Goat Island, a granite rock off Locmariaker, although M. Villemarqué's description of its tumulus and mighty cromlech—the latter having no less than ten cover-stones and fourteen upright props—made us loth to leave so interesting an object unvisited. The great cromlech at Duffryn, near Cardiff—the upper slab being a monolith, which the late Mr. Bruce Pryce was so delighted to show the many *savants* who came to see it—although the largest cromlech in Great Britain, is a child's table compared with this giant's work.

"Carnac is a good two leagues off," said M. Villemarqué; "and although our *voitures* meet us there, we shall have to walk briskly to that point, or night will be on us ere we reach Auray again."

So away we went, stepping along at four miles an hour, crossing the ferry of Kerysfeer, and then over the most desolate and rugged road it was ever man's lot to travel, till we at length sighted Carnac. And what a sight was it—that army, as it has been called, of petrified soldiers all once marshalled in regular array! Imagine twelve thousand blocks of granite, originally standing at equal distances from each other, averaging from five to ten feet high apiece, and planted upright in the soil over many a rood of land! But no description of pen or pencil can convey an adequate picture of the grim scene to the most imaginative reader's eye. He must see it himself to understand the place aright. It is greatly to be regretted that no measures have been taken either by the Government or owners of the soil to prevent the depredations committed on this mysterious assemblage of granite monuments by the peasantry of the district; for to houses, windmills, and walls in every direction have these stones been appropriated; and it is now no easy matter to distinguish the ten once regular avenues, with the crescent-shaped row at their head, owing to such spoliation. Verily, if time has wiped out the history of these monuments, man is guilty of a worse desecration by carting away the very monuments themselves.

In the act of closely inspecting a menhir on the outskirts of this ground, our ichthyological *savant*, M. Coste, very nearly met with an awkward accident. He had scrambled up to it, and was standing some three feet above the level ground on a point of the projecting rock, when a covey of red-legs sprung up close to him; and so startled was he by the sudden whirr that he lost his footing, and fell heavily down. But, fortunately, though much shaken, no bones were broken; and he continued his investigations apparently without further inconvenience. The appearance of the birds, however, seemed to act like magic on the drooping spirits of Shafto, who, having sacrificed a long day in making this pilgrimage to what he persisted in calling the burying-ground of his Celtic ancestors, was getting thoroughly tired with the monotony of the dreary scene; but so roused was he by the sight of the covey, and by marking them down in a piece of genêt hard by, that, if he could have procured a gun there and then, we should certainly have seen no more of him for the rest of the day. Indeed, without the interesting comments of M. de la Villemarqué, and the perpetual discussion carried on between him and M. Coste respecting the extent of area occupied by the Carnac monuments, and details connected therewith, the dismal spectacle was quite sufficient to damp the ardour of our Gourin party, to all of whom, as we quitted the ground, the sight of a couple of charettes waiting for us at the village hostelry brought unquestionable relief. The picture gallery was too sombre, too monotonous, and too long for any man who was neither a philosopher nor an enthusiast in such matters.

In concluding this subject, it may be as well to add that

between Carnac and Stonehenge no similarity exists in the general aspect of the two places. In the first place, the form of the stone assemblage at Stonehenge is circular, having a flat slab, called the altar stone, in the centre; whereas that of Carnac is a parallelogram formed by eleven ranks, and headed by a single row of rude, upright blocks in the shape of a crescent. These are all of rough granite obtained in the neighbourhood; whilst those of Stonehenge are a kind of hard sandstone brought, as demonstrated by Mr. **Tom Smith, on rollers** from the **Gray** Wethers, about **ten miles off; just as** the largest **pedestal** in the world—that which **carries** the equestrian statue of Peter the Great at St. Petersburg —a granite block, weighing 1,217 tons, **was brought** from a vast bog to that city. "Trunks of oak bound with iron, and pierced with holes for levers," furnished, as Mr. Smith suggests, the rollers on which the stones were conveyed to their destination. At Stonehenge far greater care appears to have been taken in the construction of its monuments than in those of Carnac, the latter being unhewn and single blocks only, whereas the horizontal slabs of the outer circle at Stonehenge are artistically *tied* by mortices **to the upright** props, each of which has two tenons that fit **into** the imposts. This is supposed to have been used as a Druidical temple or Pantheon; the **other at Carnac** as a burying-ground **alone.** Both, however, being "**anterior to all written evidence,**" and therefore **without** history, nothing **certain is** known about **either, except,** indeed, that they must be considered as among the **most** ancient monuments of man's labour.

We did not reach Henn-bont that evening before seven o'clock, the last hour from Auray being passed in a Stygian darkness, illumined only by two wretched dip-candles, borne in a couple of horn lanterns on either side of the *voiturier*. Without some such contrivance the man would have been liable to a fine by the authorities; **but** the light, if intended for our safety, could only have contributed to it by preventing other *voitures* from running into us, for it gave no sign whatever of the approximate fences on either side of the road. Luckily, the horses knew it, and so we arrived at Henn-bont without accident.

Here, after some hasty refreshment, we bid adieu to our kind and agreeable companions, M. Coste and M. de la Villemarqué; and the road being a broad and a good one between this and Gourin, *viâ* Plouay and Le Faouet, we travelled over it at a merry pace with our light load and spanking team, and arrived at the Cheval Blanc soon after midnight.

"Hollo!" cried Shafto, as we entered the *place* of the old town (his mercury had been rising rapidly after quitting Carnac with the prospect of grand sport at Kilvern on the following day); "hollo! what on earth mean all these gendarmes in the street, and so many houses alight at this hour, St. Prix?"

"There has been a row, doubtless, of some sort," responded the latter; "but I devoutly hope none of our men are implicated in it."

"So do I," said Kergoorlas; "though that drunken piqueur of mine is always getting into scrapes; and it will be a marvel if he has managed, during my absence, to keep clear of one for two days."

This was precisely the case, as Kergoorlas soon discovered on alighting from the drag, three or four gendarmes and a crowd of peasants, the latter all more or less in a state of intoxication, having surrounded it the moment it came to a standstill.

"Your piqueur, Bertrand Gastel," said the chief officer, "has, we fear, murdered a man, the braconnier Pierre Cantref. He lies insensible at the Gendarmerie, and Gastel is shut up in the prison ward at the same place. He is still very drunk, and more like a raving bull than a human being."

"Then I hope you'll keep him there till he recovers his reason," said Kergoorlas, with great excitement.

"That you may be sure we shall do," replied the gendarme;

"and probably the law may require his detention for a yet longer period."

A murmur of applause burst from the crowd on hearing these words.

"Pleasant prospect for the hunting to-morrow," groaned out Shafto aloud.

"Ah, Monsieur," said the gendarme, "if you depend on M. Kergoorlas's hounds for your sport, I fear me you'll be greatly disappointed."

Then came out the whole history of the affair from beginning to end. It appeared that no sooner had Kergoorlas and St. Prix departed on the excursion to Concarneau than Gastel and two or three other piqueurs, birds of a feather, had assembled together in a small auberge on the outskirts of the town; and then, not satisfied with the day's debauch, had prolonged it through the night, finally falling asleep in the chimney-corner of this miserable den. The next day (Friday) had originally been the one fixed for the hunting at Kilvern; but, in consequence of the visit to Carnac, it was postponed to the following day, and due notice thereof proclaimed aloud in the streets of Gourin.

However, some half-a-dozen sabottiers, who had not heard of the change, calling early in the morning at the auberge, and finding the piqueurs fast asleep, and, at the same time, being informed by the aubergiste that the hunting at Kilvern had been deferred to the next day, exhibited the utmost vexation; and vowed they would have their day's sport in the neighbouring covers, come what would of it. But, although bearing a musket or two, not a dog of any kind had accompanied them; and, while perplexed on this point, the braconnier Cantref, at whose cottage the piqueur Gastel and several couple of hounds were billeted, entered the auberge, seeking that individual.

"The very man to your hand," suggested the aubergiste, in a subdued tone, lest he should disturb the sleeping piqueurs; "the hounds would follow him to the chase, and there is a herd of fine, fat chevreuil now lying in the forest of Conveau. Why not up and at them?"

The suggestion was a tempting one; and, followed as it was by a *goutte* or two of brandy, timely administered to the braconnier, he expressed himself quite ready to join the sabottiers in this daring adventure. In two minutes from that time the whole party, leaving the piqueurs still snoring on the ground like a lot of swine, were off to Conveau with no less than eight couple of Kergoorlas's hounds; and, as that cover lies within a league of Gourin, they were soon in hot pursuit of the chevreuil roused in its mazes.

Louis Trefarreg, however, St. Prix's ever-steady and experienced piqueur, was speedily informed of the circumstance; and, rushing to the auberge, managed to stir Gastel to his legs, and to make him understand the magnitude of the mischief occasioned by his absence and inebriety. "Death and hell follow the villain," said the still half-drunken piqueur. "If I can only overtake him, he'll never steal hound of mine more. So saying, he and the rest of the piqueurs staggered off in pursuit. The hounds' tongues and a few random shots soon brought the two parties together; and before the braconnier could defend himself, Gastel, with his iron-shod hunting-pole, felled him senseless to the ground. Then were the gendarmes summoned; and all on whom they could lay hands, save Louis Trefarreg, were at once secured, and brought to the gendarmerie.

The assault had occurred some sixteen hours before our arrival at Gourin, but the poor braconnier was still insensible; and the hounds, which Louis Trefarreg had in vain attempted to call off, were supposed to be still running in the forest of Conveau.

CHAPTER XVII.

The murderous assault committed on the poor braconnier, Cantref, so well known for many a league round Gourin, created intense excitement among the peasantry, who, notwithstanding the protection of the gendarmes and police, could with difficulty be restrained from seizing Gastel and wreaking instant vengeance on him for the foul deed. In the very nick of time, therefore, did the drag containing Kergoorlas and St. Prix—the latter respected and beloved beyond any man in Brittany—rattle over the rude stoneway of the town up to the doors of the Cheval Blanc. A plot, the object of which was to force the gendarmerie during the darkness of night, was gaining strength in all quarters; and, but for the timely arrival of the Louvetier, another hour would probably have matured it, and seen a desperate affray, if not murder, in the streets of Gourin. The Breton peasantry are a good-natured but fiery race; and their ire, once aroused, is not easily appeased. This, too, was an act of such savage violence perpetrated on a neighbour by the piqueur Gastel, whom they all regarded as a foreigner, being a Vendean, and no Breton at all; that nothing less than the influence of St. Prix, and a promise on his part that Gastel should be brought to justice before the authorities at Lorient, could pacify the excited crowd. M. de Kergoorlas, too, who was painfully shocked by the occurrence, not only expressed the deepest sympathy for the braconnier, but declared in the strongest terms that, if he died from the injury, he hoped the law would send the drunken ruffian to the galleys for life.

When the excitement had somewhat subsided in front of the Cheval Blanc, and our little party had gathered round a blazing wood fire in the *salle-à-manger*, the fate of the missing hounds became the subject of earnest conversation, ere the programme was settled for the next day's hunting at Kilvern.

"Out of the eight couple," said St. Prix, "taken to the forest, two hounds only have been recovered by Louis Trefarreg. The rest, he thinks, had found an old wolf, and gone away for Locrist or Dualt. He followed them through Conveau, so far as the Botderû Monument, and then they broke away over the mountain waste, and he heard no more of them."

"Small chance have I, then, of ever seeing a hound of them again," said Kergoorlas, in a tone of sheer despair.

"Never fear," cried Shafto. "Most of them, I'll undertake to say, will be secured by the peasants, and brought either to St. Prix's or my kennels; and probably some may find their way home to your own kennels on the Loire."

"I wish I could think so," said the disconsolate owner, determined not to be comforted; "but fifty leagues of country, bristling with furze, broom, and forest, are not likely to be traversed by hounds already wearied by a hard day's work. Besides, if the pack breaks up, and they straggle singly over the wilderness, the wolves will eat every hound of them, to a certainty."

Shafto was on the point of relating a story about a pack of hounds which their owner, wishing to be rid of them, had taken into a far country, found a fox, and then left them running, a legacy to the land, when St. Prix, remarking the lateness of the hour, entreated the attention of the chasseurs to the necessity of at once settling the plan with respect to Kilvern, the meet at which place was fixed for eight o'clock that morning. "We have only four hours for rest," said he, energetically; "and as it is quite clear Kergoorlas will be unable to keep the appointment with the remnant of his pack, you and I, Shafto, must put our shoulders to the wheel, and help him out of this difficulty. But the piqueurs wait for orders, and we must decide at once how it shall be done."

"You are welcome to every hound of mine," responded Shafto, heartily; "but I doubt if more than six couple will be found available, after that last day at Gwernez."

"Quite enough, with six couple of mine," said St. Prix, always an advocate for a short pack, when boar and not wolf was the game to be pursued. Louis Trefarreg was then summoned, and the trusty piqueur received the fullest instructions with respect to the rendezvous and the hounds to be first uncoupled on the drag, the party of chasseurs broke up, and, with the exception of one, retired every man forthwith to his chamber.

That one was M. de Kergoorlas, who, in the complication of trouble that now beset him—the poor braconnier lying insensible from the murderous attack of his own piqueur, and seven couple of his noble hounds gone nobody knew whither, and gone perhaps for ever—was little disposed to seek the rest which, young, elastic, and robust as he was, even his frame required. Lingering a few minutes near the embers of the wood fire, still glowing with heat, till the last of the party had fairly quitted the *salle-à-manger*, he then hastily donned his hunting-cap, and, going forth into the dark street, directed his steps straight for the gendarmerie and the little hospital extemporised for the braconnier's use.

Without entering into all the details of the wretched scene he witnessed in this latter place, suffice it to say that all a man could do he did, by sympathy and substantial aid, to soften the grief of the poor stricken Breton woman who, by the side of the braconnier's bed, was bathing his temples with cold lotions, and tenderly adjusting his pillow to the varying motions of his injured head. Nor was his kindly visit wholly unattended by consolation, inasmuch as he was assured by the medical officer that—the braconnier's habits with respect to drink having always been most temperate—he yet entertained, notwithstanding the severity of the concussion, a confident hope in his ultimate recovery. This opinion produced unspeakable relief to Kergoorlas's mind; for if fatal results were to follow the blow inflicted by his own servant, the public would not fail to regard him as the indirect cause of the murder, and the stain, however unmerited, would probably cling to his name for life.

Far different was the spectacle in the prison-ward of the gendarmerie. There, close pinioned, and utterly powerless for the commission of any violent act, lay Gastel, the piqueur, his eyes glaring like those of a wild beast, fierce but without expression, and his whole visage distorted by *delirium tremens*. A more painful sight, Kergoorlas declared, it was never his lot to witness. The man was not then drunk; but, his brain on fire and his reason gone, except in form, he was far more like a wolf of the forest than a human being.

"*Absinthe* has done it all," said the doctor gravely. "He has been an inveterate dram-drinker for a long period, I understand; and if so, this attack will go hard with him."

"Quite true," replied Kergoorlas; "for although I have rarely seen him in a state of helpless intoxication, from morning to night he gave his stomach no rest. He began the day with *absinthe*; then it was for ever a *goutte* of this or a *goutte* of that, whenever chance threw liquor in his way; and so Nature has sent in her account at last."

"And a heavy one, too, it is. However," added the doctor, cheerfully, "we'll do our best to help him to meet it, bad as the schedule looks on the debtor's side."

"Aye, I know you will," responded Kergoorlas, earnestly.

A glimmer of light now crossing the poor wretch's brain, and the familiar sound of his master's voice falling simultaneously on his ear, he instantly recognised it, and, looking up with a piteous expression, begged to know where he was—why he was pinioned —and wherefore detained in that place?—and "Oh!" he groaned out, "such a horrid dream have I had!—hunted down by a pack of wolves, that have been crunching and gnawing at my skull, and lapping up the very dregs of my brain! Oh! such torture!" He then burst into a flood of tears, which, it was hoped, would have brought him some relief; but in another instant his reason again forsook him, and he shrieked wildly, "They're coming again, I tell you—they're on me!—on me! Fire, fire!"

Kergoorlas's nerves, though not easily touched, trembled like reeds in a running river at this awful sight; and, as he afterwards confessed, if he had not beaten a hasty retreat, the cold chill that seized him must have paralysed the action of his heart, and brought him senseless to the floor—so he rushed from the cell. He had intended, after visiting the gendarmerie, to look up the several quarters at which his hounds were billeted, as he was anxious to ascertain what hounds they were that were now missing—whether the puppies had gone or the chiefs of the chase, or in what proportion both had been abducted; but he was too much affected by the appalling vision he had just witnessed to think of anything besides. Bidding the officials a hasty adieu, he returned directly to the hotel, and casting himself at full length on his narrow pallet, he was speedily enjoying, by the suspension of his mental and bodily powers, the blissful rest that sleep alone can give.

There is a mode of taxing dogs in France by which, if lost, their recovery is greatly facilitated by the aid of the government. When the tax is paid for a dog, every mark, like the "signes particuliers" in a passport, by which the animal can be identified, is duly registered; and, thus instructed, the police, the gendarmes, and the gardes-champêtres, in "correspondance" with every station from one end of the country to the other, are able to trace and recover a dog, whether stolen or strayed, on almost every occurrence of such a misadventure. Of course early notice must be given of the loss, or a thief in possession of a valuable animal may take ship, or cross the frontier, and then there is an end of the "correspondance."

In Lower Brittany, however, a single dog on stray has little or no chance of escaping the wolves in the winter season; for, as already stated, throughout the ancient region of Cornouaille, comprising a large portion of Morbihan and Finisterre—a region of broom, heather, and forest—the inhabitants of the small towns are compelled to keep fires burning during a heavy fall of snow, to save their dogs at night from the prowling wolves. And not only by night do they commit these raids, but, when pinched by hunger, they venture on them even by day. During my stay at Carhaix an instance of it occurred at Quimper, and created no little sensation among the quiet, picturesque inhabitants of that old-fashioned town. An English lady, long resident in that vicinity, was walking on the high road in the suburbs of the town in company with a favourite spaniel, when a wolf, dashing out of a neighbouring thicket, seized poor Fido across the back, and, notwithstanding the lady's energetic screams, carried him, crunched in his jaws, to the adjoining forest. This, however, must have been a bold brigand, a kind of Dick Turpin among the wolves; for certain it is, that such a highway robbery by daylight rarely occurs even in the severest weather.

The Bretons of that country, a people of serious demeanour and primitive habits, retire early to bed as a general rule; but, as on the present occasion, if anything is going on in the way of hunting, especially that most popular sport the chase of the wild boar, no matter at what hour they seek their couches, they are sure to be up and stirring on the wished-for morrow long before daybreak. At six o'clock, then, not only was the Cheval Blanc wide awake, but the whole town of Gourin was ringing with a confused din of men's voices, the clatter of sabots, curs barking, hounds baying, and the notes of many brazen horns, creating a combined discord, worthy of the Eumenides.

At my bedside, before I was half awake, and before I could exactly comprehend what the row was, Keryfan stood erect in full hunting costume, and, with his voluminous horn in hand, was preparing to salute me with his favourite air, "La sortie du Chenil." "A cold pig," had there been water enough, would have been far less trying to my nerves at that moment; so, to avert the infliction, I screeched out, at the top of my voice, "Hold hard, Keryfan, for mercy's sake, hold hard! You've broken my rest, and you'll break the drum of my ear if you blow that horn now."

"Well, then, turn out, Frank," said he, provokingly. "Louis Trefarreg and Shafto have gone on with the hounds; and St. Prix means to be punctual at the meet, having made up his mind to return to Carhaix this evening."

"I'll do anything," I replied, "if you'll only keep that horn quiet; give me twenty minutes, and I shall be ready—not for a start exactly, but for that cup of coffee you know so well how to brew."

"You shall have it, Frank; but despatch, mind, despatch! that's the word; for St. Prix will not wait one minute after seven o'clock."

Hitherto our Gourin meeting, barring a few trifling discomforts, had been one of unmixed pleasure and success; and, as Shafto was very anxious to draw some large covers, lying westward of Kilvern, and to entertain our party at the "Hermitage" (though how he proposed compressing us into four rooms was never explained), the meeting would probably have been prolonged over another week, and Shafto's hospitality, only bounded by walls, tested to its utmost limits—*Janua patet; cor magis*, might fairly be applied to such a man. But, cheerful as this prospect was, we were constrained to abandon it, owing to the untoward events that had occurred during our absence at Concarneau and Carnac; events that could not but cast a gloom on every member of the hunting party.

To add to our regret, just as we were about to start, Kergoorlas had sent a message from his bed-room to St. Prix, begging the latter to pardon him for not coming to the front at Kilvern that day; as, he declared, it would be quite impossible for him to enjoy any sport, while his thoughts were so occupied by the scene of misery he had so recently witnessed; and that he deemed it his duty to remain at Gourin, while the two poor fellows at the gendarmerie were lying in such imminent danger. We were none of us surprised at this determination, though very loth to lose his good company; especially as we were not likely to see anything more of him during the present season.

It was a fine breezy morning, the wind blowing steadily from the west and directly in our teeth, as we trotted along over that dreary, serrated ridge, so well named the "backbone of Brittany," a region of stunted heather and granite rocks, arid, barren, and desolate, and at length, reaching the head of a deep ravine, the woodlands of which appeared to be interminable, we crossed a small brook and soon sighted the outskirts of Kilvern. The scenery of this country is certainly not so grand as that of our own Highlands; but the wildest glen of the Trosachs is no wilder than this vast gorge, rugged and seamed as it is, far as the eye can see, with rock and chasm, forest, and fierce torrents—a rare homestead in all weather for the wolf and the boar; which, so long as Nature holds her own, will always find shelter and security in the recesses of this rude domain.

The site of the rendezvous, as the meet is termed, was a clitter of rocks overhanging and frowning upon the dark cover below;

and in the wide world, it would be difficult to find a more appropriate spot for such a gathering, the savage grandeur of the scene being in perfect keeping with the throng of picturesque, half-civilized Bretons, who, all clad in jackets of the roughest goat-skin, stood clustering around the huge, fierce-looking, wire-haired wolf-hounds, gazing with admiration now on this hound and now on that, as the well-known leaders of many a bygone chase. But their caresses, when offered, seemed anything but welcome to some of the chiefs, especially to old Cæsar, whose surly growl, stiff stern, and independent attitude, looked very much as if he was inclined to say, "Keep your hands to yourself; I'm a rough customer, and resent liberties."

The report of the piqueurs was most favourable; a couple of full-sized boar had been tracked into a patch of scrub-cover close below us; while, farther down in the valley, several pigs had crossed and recrossed the main stream, and were supposed to be lying somewhere among the boulders that, in vast fragments, were piled one on the other against the opposite hill. A stronghold was this, overgrown with ivy and clematis, and looked exactly like the ruins of some ancient castle, the towers of which had been overthrown and disjected by a mighty earthquake. The consultation between St. Prix and his "field" was shorter than usual; it being at once determined to uncouple Harmonie and Vétéran, and clap them on the drag of the two boars. These two hounds had been originally entered on boar, and had never been allowed to join the pack on wolf-hunting days; consequently, they were not only staunch to the scent of the former, but had shown a marked distaste for that of the latter; so, where there was a chance of change from one game to the other, as would be the case in these deep covers abounding with wolves and riot of various description, two such dependable leaders were invaluable to the master, when, as on the present occasion, boar was the object of the day's chase.

The quiet way in which hounds are thrown into cover in Lower Brittany, at the onset, contrasts remarkably with the uproar of tongue and horn that instantly follows the rousing of the game and many subsequent features of the chase. Scarcely now did a single cheer escape St. Prix's lips, as Harmonie and Vétéran, released from their couples, swung over the tainted line, and with lashing sterns and doubled tongue, at once disappeared into the depths of the cover; nor, for a few minutes, was there a word spoken by that large and wild-looking group of chasseurs that stood in listening attitude, noting every variation in the hounds' tongues, and ready to slip any number of couples at the first signal given by St. Prix's horn. The example of the Louvetier was probably the cause of this steadiness on the part of the peasants; and, indeed, so long as they were under his eye, the control he exercised over his rude followers appeared to be absolute; but the first blast of that horn, announcing the game a-foot, acted like a galvanic battery on their nerves, and seemed to kindle their savage hunting nature at once into a wild flame.

In the mountains of Wales, not many years ago, the fashion in fox-hunting, so far as noise, outcry, and hubbub were deemed necessary to cheer the hounds and scare the prey, was very similar to that followed in Brittany at the present day. His Breton brother, however, at the commencement of the chase, is far quieter and less riotous than the old Cambrian hunter, whose halloos and cheers to individual favourite hounds never cease from the moment they are thrown into cover, hit upon a drag, or maintain the chase, till they kill their fox, or, failing that, till the stars appear in the sky.

The practice of hallooing hounds, now all but discarded in the modern chase of the fox, is made the subject of more than one of Beckford's admirable letters. He tells us that "such halloos as serve to keep the hounds together, and to get on the tail-hounds, are always of use; it is the halloos of encouragement to the leading hounds, when injudiciously given, that spoil your sport: they are pleasing to sportsmen, but prejudicial to hounds." And again—"If hounds are often used to a halloo, they will expect it, and may trust, perhaps, to their ears and eyes more than to their noses."

Exactly so; the power of that one sense given to the nose is weakened at once, if another sense, that of seeing or listening, is called into action at the same time. Therefore halloos, when hounds are running, must generally be a mischievous accompaniment to the chase, and do far more harm than good in the long run. That word halloo, by-the-bye, has, as I believe, a French origin, and is derived, not as the lexicographers say, from the word "haler," but from the practice of shouting "Au loop—au loop," which, phonetically written, would be precisely halloo—the very word used to encourage hounds to pursue their game at the present day both in France and England. Shakspeare, speaking of a hound's note, says,

"A cry more tunable
Was never halloo'd to, nor cheered with horn."

But hark! it is a lucky thing Harmonie and Vétéran have been clinging to the line closer than my pen. Hark! the two good hounds have unharboured a brace of boar, and St. Prix's horn is ringing out merrily, "Les animaux en compagnie;" while Shafto and a group of peasants, stationed a far way down the ravine and ahead of the cry, are uncoupling for their lives, and throwing in more hounds to back up the chase. Then the thunder of war bursts out in earnest; and horns and hounds, halloos and echoes, shake the old forest to its uttermost bounds; and if that tornado in their rear do not strike the flying boar with terror, they must have stout hearts indeed! Be that as it may, down the valley pours the chase like a cataract; and contrary to Louis Trefarreg's expectation, not often wrong in his tactics, the boar do not attempt to cross the stream and seek the shelter of the rocks on the opposite heights, but, holding on still to the same sideland, neither sinking nor breasting the hill, they trust to their legs and endeavour to shake off by wild flight the pursuit of the foe. So those peasant sharpshooters, posted by Louis on certain points of the stream, usually crossed by the pigs, never fire a shot; and a rattling good run is the fortunate result. For two hours or more the roar of war never flags for a moment; and although twelve couple of hounds are close on their haunches, the pigs are still making strong running in front of the fray.

"Oh that Kergoorlas were here!" shouts Keryfan to me, "just to hear that grand peal ringing through the vale; it would drive him half wild with delight."

The wish had scarcely been uttered, when we heard a clatter in our rear; and looking round, to our intense amazement, we beheld Kergoorlas coming up at a hand-gallop, his horse flecked with foam, and four couple of great, grim, wire-haired hounds following on close to his heels. The wild huntsman of the Black Forest could scarcely have startled us more than Kergoorlas's company at such a moment; and before we could inquire by what lucky spell he had been able to join us, he roared out, "I heard them a league off, and thought I should never catch you! But what a scent; and what music!"

Not another word did he fling to us, as he dashed past on Grenadier, eager to throw his fresh lot in at the head to increase the volume of music he so dearly loved to hear; and it was at least three hours afterwards ere we learned the cause of his welcome but most unexpected reappearance among us. It turned out that, immediately on our departure for Kilvern, he had gone to the hospital, and hearing a favourable report of both patients—the braconnier having recovered consciousness, and the piqueur's delirium indicating an abatement satisfactory to the medical officer—he ordered Grenadier to be saddled, and gathering together four couple of hounds—all that were effective of his late noble pack—he had followed us to the field. The parley at the cover-side had been unusually brief, and the find more than usually quick, or his stern chase would not have been so long.

After he had passed Keryfan and myself at that terrific pace, fully accounting for the foam with which his gallant steed was bespattered, we never glimpsed him again till we found him standing astride over a fine bristly boar, sounding the "mort" with all the breath left in his body, and six couple of hounds baying round the dead game in a fervent strain of joy and exultation. He was all alone; the hounds had divided; and these having brought their pig to bay, he had followed up, and, arriving just in time, had been lucky enough to administer the *coup-de-grâce* ere a single hound had been injured.

St. Prix's doings with the rest of the pack must be reserved for another chapter.

CHAPTER XVIII.

Notes ever welcome to the Breton's ear are those proclaiming the "mort" over the captured game; and when that game happens to be the wolf or the tusky boar, his pæans of exultation burst out into the wildest strains of gratitude and joy. The "who-whoop" of our countrymen, vigorous even as that of Osbaldeston when "it might have been heard at Cottesmore," is a mild finale compared with the demonstration enacted in a Brittany forest, when the sylvan war is brought to a close by a successful and decisive victory. Nor is the flourish of horns, commingled with the din of hounds and men, without its serviceable use, a mere *vox et præterea nihil*—an ebullition of joy, and nothing more, in that forest-land—but, on the contrary, by conveying the news of victory far and wide, the scattered forces of the field, thrown out by the ever-recurring vicissitudes of the chase, are gathered together from all quarters to share and enjoy the triumph over the fallen foe.

So when Keryfan and I came up to him, although Kergoorlas was then alone, standing over the boar in an attitude that, but for its animation, might have been taken for an antique statue, and blowing his voluminous horn till his cheeks were well-nigh cracked, in less than ten minutes a score of peasants had assembled at the spot, all uniting to swell the hubbub, and looking forward to a division of the spoil with eager eyes. However nothing surprised me more, considering the damage they had sustained by the pigs, and the real treat fresh meat must have been to them, than the orderly and modest conduct of the peasants on every occasion when the boar was cut up and divided amongst them. This business was always managed under the direction of the Louvetier, M. de St. Prix, who, as before stated, exercised a paramount influence over the peasantry throughout the district of Cornouaille. His word was their law; and if at the right time a blow had been struck in favour of the Legitimate claim to the throne of France, I verily believe he could have brought every man of that country to the field, one and all at his back, in support of his own views and the old Bourbon blood. But St. Prix loved hunting better than politics, and far preferred the sound of his own sylvan horn to the fiercer clang of the martial trumpet; though, if his king had called on him, he would have gone to the front like a man, and then other and abler pens would probably have recorded his glory in fields more sanguinary but less joyous than those of a Brittany forest. Mine be the simpler task of telling how gallant his bearing, and how skilful his tactics ever were in all matters pertaining to the manly chase.

The great size of the boar, seeing he was not a *solitaire*, appeared to astonish the peasants not a little, for it is a most unusual event to find an old male tusker, of a certain weight and age, in company with another pig. But St. Prix's success, as we afterwards found, revealed the secret. That other pig, his companion, was a young sow, full-grown, but lean and long-legged as a greyhound, and fit to go for her life. The old gentleman had evidently stuck to his mate so long as his wind would permit him; but that failing him, he turned short, and so let in a few of the tail-hounds and Kergoorlas's lot, which, throwing fresh strength into the struggle, soon brought him to bay and then to bite the dust, under the *couteau* that struck him to the heart.

One blow sufficed, and so rapidly was it given that not a hound was scratched in the affair.

Hog-hunting, as practised in India, is doubtless a most exciting and manly sport, requiring not only good nerve in the rider, but thorough skill in the management of his horse and spear, good hands, and a quick eye—these are indispensable gifts; and the honour of winning "first spear" and the tusks, no matter how swift the steed may be, will only accidentally fall to the lot of him who lacks such needful qualifications. But the danger of pursuing the boar in this fashion is not to be compared with the risk a man runs when he closes, *chasse-couteau* in hand, with the brute at bay. His charge then, if his wind has not been completely pumped out of him, is certain to do serious mischief; and woe be to the hunter who is a laggard in striking the blow rapidly and expertly so soon as the hounds have done their work—brought him fairly to bay. Kergoorlas would not have missed that feat for a dukedom.

But let us now follow St. Prix, who, when the big boar turned short, and the tail-hounds turned with him, kept his ear on the leading hounds, and sticking to them, found to his joy that, though the hounds had divided, the body of the pack was still with him, and the pig going straight for the river in the hollow vale below. There, he well knew, the beast would make a stand; and, as the stream was a broad and rocky one, his anxiety for the hounds' safety impelled him forward at a terrific pace. If Barbe-bleu, on which he was fortunately mounted, had possessed the legs of a mountain-cat, he needed them all in descending that steep ravine, obstructed as he was at every stride by the tangled brake and rugged ground over which he was compelled to travel so rapidly. But the gallant steed carried him, like a dragon on wings, through and over every impediment; though, as Shafto, who had vainly attempted to keep pace with him, afterwards told us, it was nothing short of a miracle how both man and horse escaped utter annihilation. However, by the time we reached him, at least an hour after Kergoorlas and the peasants had slung up the slain boar by the heels for future dissection, he was sounding "La sortie de l'eau" complacently on the river bank, and without a symptom of his usual lively excitement. The hounds, too, were sitting on their haunches, regarding with intent look the boar, as she stood mid-waist in the water, her back arched like a bow, her jaws smeared with froth, and her hind-quarters planted firmly against the roots of a gnarled oak-tree.

Shafto and half a score peasants were there, restraining the hounds with rate and lash, until the stragglers, especially Keryfan and myself, could be brought up by the well-known signal to see the finish. St. Prix had ascertained the sex of the pig; and, although the crunch of a sow's jaws is no joke, it is not to be compared to the rip of a tusker, who, if he gets a fair cut at limb or body, leaves a life, if not a death mark, on the unlucky victim. So St. Prix's complacency was at once accounted for; he had enjoyed, too, a fine run, and was now patiently awaiting the arrival of his "field," and resting his hounds, ere he 'loo'd them on to their last attack.

Men are all selfish animals; and even among those devoted to hunting, of all sports the most social, few there be who will not confess to a certain amount of satisfaction in being able, either by their own judgment or their steed's merits, or even by sheer luck, to see "a good thing" across country, and to find themselves living with hounds "alone in their glory," while the rest of the "field" are "positively nowhere." The tendency to self-glorification is, doubtless, at the root of this inward chuckle; though, in ten minutes after the ardour of the chase has evaporated, every good fellow will hate himself for allowing his heart to entertain so selfish a feeling. St. Prix, as he urged the gallant Barbe-bleu down that rugged hill-side, and felt as if he was carried by

"A creature winged, I swear,"

home to the stern of his hounds, might well be pardoned if a tinge of pride mantled to his brow at that moment; but the colouring, if it came, was as transient as the shade of a summer cloud, for no man on earth could be less selfish, either in the chase or at home, than St. Prix; no one could love to share pleasure with another better than he did.

"Bravo, Kergoorlas!" he exclaimed with delight, as, to his great surprise, he saw that chasseur in our company. "Bravo! you and your hounds are just in time to do us good service with yonder pig. I have been running her hard for three hours; but she has fresh caught her wind now, and will hold us a good tug yet."

The moment he had driven her to soil St. Prix had given an order that no gun should be used, and that he meant to kill the game beast by fair hunting alone; and now, with the reinforcement brought up by Kergoorlas, he expected to accomplish that object without much difficulty.

One cheer and a blast on his horn sent every hound plunging into the stream; but as it was some twenty yards across, and the pig's standpoint was under cover of the opposite bank, before a hound could reach her she dashed down the stream swiftly as a red deer, swimming the pools, and making the water fly from her heels as she scampered over the shallow bed. Never was heard a finer crack of music than opened in her rear; and so determinedly did the beast cleave to the river, in which she had already found such good shelter, that, press her as they would, the hounds fairly failed to make her land and seek for refuge elsewhere. So for more than half-an-hour the chase became literally more like an otter than a boar-hunt. Twice, when brought temporarily to bay, did St. Prix bound into the stream, thinking to bury his *couteau* behind her shoulder-blade, and twice did the wary beast elude the blow, flying down stream like a water-ouzel, and plunging in and out of pools, as if water were her native element.

"Now this is what I call sport," said Keryfan to me, just as the hounds had again brought the pig to bay. "It reminds me, Frank, of that day when you and I joined Mr. Trelawny's pack on the Plym river, and had the good fortune to see them kill a fine dog-otter under Cann Quarries. Such a dashing, crashing, amphibious lot as they were I shall never forget."

"True enough. That was the day when a hound called Wanderer made so many fine hits, and at last marked the otter in a holt that proved to be a wasp's nest—when, as they sallied forth to revenge the intrusion, old Limpetty, the huntsman, blew his horn like a madman, bolted off, and rode his horse Jack Sheppard head-foremost into a deep pool. But luckily the otter, as you remember, Keryfan, bolted too, or, backed as he was by such protection, we could never have touched him again."

By crossing a narrow strip of open ground, guided by the peasants, we now managed to cut off a long bend of the river just in time to head the chase, as the pig, with her mouth wide open, and reduced to a trot, came struggling through the flood right up to us. The hounds were close on her; but as there was no friendly rock, nor even the roots of a tree, against which she could bring her back to bear and face the foe, she still struggled on towards the precipitous bank on which we all stood to witness the scene. She was too beaten, however, to gain even that point; for, in attempting to cross a run of shallow water, a couple of the leading hounds, old Cæsar being one of them, seized her by the hams, and in another instant, as all three rolled over together, at least five couple more had fixed their fangs in her fore and aft, holding fast on, and tugging at her as if her hide must be torn in one minute into "a hundred tatters of brown." But not a bit of it—not an inch of her hide was broken; and it is impossible to say how long the desperate fight might have lasted, if St. Prix, observing one hound badly crunched, had not sprung in amongst them, and with a quick blow brought the struggle to an end. Cæsar had more scars on his face, some of them of very recent date, than his imperial namesake, a warrior all his life, could boast of on his whole body; but I was delighted to find the brave old hound had not added another notch to the ugly score on the present occasion.

"Two good boars slain in fair fight, and not a shot fired!" exclaimed Kergoorlas, in a transport of delight. "Rare work for one day, it must be owned."

"But the day is not over yet," said Shafto, whose appetite for hunting was positively insatiable; "at least half-a-dozen pigs have been harboured in the Castle rocks, on the Kilvern side; and, as it is but little after mid-day, we surely can't quit the cover without giving them a brush."

The peasants, especially those who had formed the deputation to Carhaix, with one voice entreated St. Prix to continue the *chasse*, denouncing the Kilvern pigs as destructive brigands, and asserting the impossibility of checking their ravages without his help. One of the speakers, called Tredwyn—a remarkably handsome specimen of the farmer class—became quite eloquent on the subject, and asked, with no little excitement, if the Government desired to see the peasants of that district extinguished by famine; or if the Louvetier, as their neighbour and countryman, would not do his utmost to rid them of the pests that had destroyed their crops, and well-nigh ruined the land. "Without hounds," added he, "we can neither follow them in these vast woodlands, nor dislodge them from that inaccessible pile of rocks, the stronghold in which so many take refuge."

The appeal was irresistible; but St. Prix, in making the draft for storming those craggy heights, positively refused at first to allow any but his drag-hounds to encounter the danger; and alluded, in piteous terms, to the massacre inflicted on his pack by the big boar at Kœnig, on exactly similar rocky ground. However, as this was to be the last day given to boar-hunting on that side of the country, and consequently would be the last opportunity for compensating the peasants' losses by a liberal supply of bacon, fattened, as they justly averred, on their own corn and chestnuts, St. Prix gave way, and, in deference to the wish of all, proceeded with his whole force, sixteen couple strong, straight for the rocks. In winding their way, not without many rude obstructions, up the tangled and declivitous path pointed out by Tredwyn, whose farm lay contiguous to the upper side of Kilvern, the Louvetier took especial pains to instruct the peasants on an important point affecting the safety of the hounds. He warned them not to head the chase before the boar and hounds were fairly clear of that stronghold, and that they must give the game ample room to break ; or, if headed back, the fate of many a brave hound would inevitably be sealed. All this they promised to attend to ; but St. Prix, not satisfied with this precaution, and knowing how little a Breton in the heat of chase was to be depended on, ordered Louis Trefarreg to couple up several of his fiercest hounds—Cæsar and Paladin being especially named— and reserve them as a *relais* in case of need.

"You may think St. Prix a little too careful of his hounds in making these arrangements," said Keryfan, as he managed to ride alongside me, over a bit of level ground cleared by the charcoal-burners ; "but, if you knew, Frank, how many a good hound he has lost, and how often his pack has been crippled for the season by encounters with boar, in these very rocks, too, you would not wonder at the precaution he takes on such occasions."

"A good general is always chary of the lives of his men," I replied ; "and to judge from the carnage that occurred at Kœnig and Gwernez, the tactics of the Louvetier appear to indicate a man lacking neither humane feelings nor sound judgment."

"Quite true, Frank; it would be a cruel and short-sighted policy on his **part to** allow **his** hounds to be slashed and ripped to pieces, if by any means he has the power **to** save them, and show sport at the same time; and this last, **you** will allow, **he** never fails to **do**."

It was nearly two o'clock ere we fairly reached the outskirts of the Castle rocks, which, covering an **area** of **several** acres on the side of a precipitous hill, were approachable only in Indian file over the last half league of ground. Happily, the rugged granite slabs, although opposing our horses' progress with a slanting, and sometimes an almost perpendicular, frontage, afforded their feet a steady hold; and, after some experience, my cob managed to creep up and down over their rough surface, and follow Barbebleu as if he had been trained to the work all his life long. It is quite marvellous how readily a temperate, courageous horse will accommodate his action to the ground **over which** he is required to travel: **shortening or** lengthening his stride; **jumping, creep**ing, and **feeling his** way at every step; or **even slithering on his** haunches, **as** circumstances may need such a mode of descent. How this last feat can be performed may be seen to great advantage when a good jack-hare is found near Thunder-Barrow or Telscombe Tye, on the Sussex Downs, the steep and glassy slopes of which the horses descend at a terrific pace, almost on their very haunches; the force of gravitation, and not so much their hind legs, acting as the propelling power. On Dartmoor, too, a stranger would hold his breath if he once **saw Mr.** Trelawny sitting back in his saddle, and **coming** down the steepest hill-side like an avalanche into the vale below, the greatest danger being a tendency, on the horse's part, if the pilot be a wavering **one,** to deviate from the straight line, and turn right or left on his downward **course.**

The **wind** from the rocks, as we now suddenly rounded a point of the valley, blew directly towards us; and the eager look of the hounds, as, with heads erect, they sniffed "the tainted gale," gave unmistakable proof of the presence of game in our immediate vicinity. The piqueurs had reported that no less than five full-grown boar had crossed the stream in this direction; and although they had not been fairly harboured, owing to the stony character of the ground, Louis Trefarreg was ready to stake his reputation that at least five, if not a larger number, were laid up in this craggy retreat. Already had the peasants disappeared; and every point on the river and north sides of the rocks, at which it was possible for the pigs to break, was guarded by parties of sharpshooters, thirsting for their blood. Some of them, however, as it turned out afterwards, were posted directly in front of one of the chief runs used by the pigs, in utter forgetfulness of St. Prix's orders; and the consequence, although not fatal, as great luck would have it, to more than one hound, proved well-nigh so to Barbe-bleu, who, but for his rare activity and sense of danger, must inevitably have come to grief in the narrow path on which he stood.

The hounds dashed into the cover like a set of dragons, and, in less than two minutes, the roaring peal of their deep-mouthed tongues, the blast of horns, and the wild response of a thousand echoes, created so startling an uproar that every wild animal, from a marten-cat to the bristly boar, must have quaked for leagues away at the sound of that terrible din. Two lots of swine were on their legs in a twinkling—one consisting of four, and the other of three animals, all full-grown, and long and lanky as a set of greyhounds. The pricked ears, and the rapid helter-skelter fashion in which they bundled over the rocks, clearing wide chasms at a bound, and pitching from the head of giant boulders down on the slabs below, like chamois descending a mountain ridge, indicated a degree of terror they rarely show when so many pigs are found together. On such occasions the master boar, or the old sow, is usually the hindmost of the lot, either from being less active or with a view to covering the retreat of the flying herd; but the moment he is pressed by the pursuing hounds, he wheels round, and, backed up by the others, fiercely confronts the whole pack. Now, however, the assault on their stronghold had been so sudden, the cry of hounds, the blast of horns, and the echoes so bewildering, that leaders and all seemed equally panic-stricken, and only eager to make themselves scarce with all possible despatch.

Downwards and straight for the stream poured the seven pigs, as if kicked by so many demons; while ten couple of hounds, roaring in their rear, drove them in the wildest confusion on the very guns of the enemy. Instantly a terrible fire opened upon them, and two, falling mortally wounded on the edge of the clitter, were soon despatched by fresh hands joining in the fray; four ran the gauntlet, passing unscathed by a dozen peasants, and escaping at top speed into the woods below; while the seventh, apparently the biggest pig of the lot, and evidently a boar, not relishing the cannonade in front, turned short back in the very face of the hounds.

Keryfan and I were standing about ten yards below St. Prix; and hearing him mutter a deep imprecation on the peasants' heads, to whose over-eagerness this mischief was alone attributable, I looked up and saw his lips compressed, and every muscle of his face quivering with alarm. "That's exactly what I feared would happen," he exclaimed aloud; "and now there'll be wild work among the hounds before that boar attempts to break again."

When the boar faced about, he paused for a moment as if uncertain what course next to pursue—whether to stand at bay, and meet all comers on that rugged battle-ground, or charge at once through the pack, now rapidly advancing, and seek refuge in the forest by a lateral track, the only egress now available, the front being hemmed in by a swarm of foes. That moment of hesitation, however, proved well nigh his last; for, as he stood out prominently on the ridge of a vast boulder, his figure defined and his head somewhat elevated, as if scanning the number and strength of the enemy, or the weak point at which he might best make his charge, a peasant, unable to resist the chance, recklessly drew his trigger; and while one heavy slug passed through the boar's ear, causing it to lop at once over his right eye, but without doing further injury, another struck a noble hound, called Helicon, right in the shoulder, and killed him dead on the spot. Luckily Kergoorlas, the owner of the hound, was stationed on the opposite side of the cover, and was not aware till afterwards of the loss he had sustained; but, had he witnessed the act, it is more than probable, from his feudal spirit and fiery nature, that the peasant would have rued that shot to the last day of his life. As it was, he made himself scarce and quitted the forest, without daring to face either Kergoorlas or St. Prix, and so forfeited all claim to a share of the meat when cut up and apportioned at the end of the day.

The report of the peasant's gun, and the smart cuff in his ear quickly settled the boar's doubts. Away he rushed, twitching his head violently, into the very thick of the hounds, striking several fiercely, and hoisting one fairly into the air, but still forging a-head fast as his legs could carry him, and in one minute, what with sheer force, wondrous activity, and a thorough knowledge of the ground, he succeeded in clearing the whole pack, and made straight for the sideland path on which St. Prix stood. Now there was no room on that narrow path even for two horses abreast, nor, from its ledge-like form—there being a wall on one side and a precipice on the other—was it possible, without advancing some distance, for St. Prix to wheel his horse round and avoid the imminent collision. The advance, too, would have been impracticable, as the boar even now was breaking directly in the Louvetier's face.

I held my breath as I saw the danger to which he was exposed, with no power on my part or Keryfan's to lend him a scrap of aid. He and I had voted our guns a bore on this occasion, and had sent them with our baggage to Carhaix; but, as that huge fierce boar, with the hounds hard after him, his ear dropped, and his face painted with blood and foam, lowered his head and prepared to charge Barbe-bleu and his rider, I would have given all I possessed, or ever hoped to possess, for my old smooth-bore at that moment. But, *mirabile dictu*, it so happened that neither the horse nor man required such help; for, just as the boar dropped his nose, to give him greater power in the use of his tusks, and when within three feet of the horse's legs, Barbe-bleu made a sudden spring into the air, and, clearing the pig, alighted safely on the path beyond, without touching a bristle of the brute's back. Never could there have been a more timely jump, nor one displaying a clearer instinct of impending danger, and the need of instant action.

The boar passed on; while St. Prix, unslinging his horn, rung out "La Vue," as coolly and cheerily as if he had viewed a fox away, and thought nothing of the danger he had so narrowly escaped. But he talked of it afterwards; and, while he extolled the adroitness of Barbe-bleu, he never failed to characterise himself as a born idiot for getting into that narrow, cramped path, and exposing himself and horse to such a risk.

However, "all's well that ends well," especially if the result be a profitable experience. Not more than eight couple of hounds got away with the boar; but they were ample for the work, and in less than half-an-hour brought him to bay in the rocky river, not far from the spot where we had killed our second pig. He was dead beat; and a peasant, coming up before he had recovered his wind, and consequently before he could do much mischief, sent his *balle-mariée* right through his heart. He was a grand beast, with bristles enough, strong as wire, for all the *cordonniers* in Lower Brittany, and his weight could not have been much under 300lbs.

CHAPTER XIX.

THAT last was a grand day at Kilvern, and gave, both by the sport and its result, unqualified satisfaction to the peasants of the district; but it was a long and a heavy one, and we did not reach Carhaix before ten o'clock that night—a late hour, considering the work done by the hounds and the brief rest enjoyed by the chasseurs, by night and day, during the whole of the past week.

"I feel as if I could sleep for a fortnight," said Keryfan, rising from a table that, by its *débris* of bones and bottles, bore witness to a vast demolition of cutlets and La Rose claret; and, seizing his candle, he begged hard that the usual *le réveil* might not be sounded on the morrow morn, at least within the walls of the Hôtel d'Auvergne.

"What! own yourself beaten, Keryfan?" said Shafto, always ready and fresh either for sport or badinage. "Well, I little thought to have heard such a confession from a man whom I have hitherto regarded as the Paladin of Breton chasseurs."

"Can't help it," said Keryfan, yawning. "I've worked hard and fed well, and feel just now more like a python than a man, so must have my whack of sleep, and then to work again."

Hereupon interposed Marseillier, the ever-obliging host, who promised to do his best to keep the house quiet, but reminded Keryfan that, the following day being Sunday, all Carhaix would be astir, and that every man possessing a horn would not fail to summon his neighbour and every dog in the town to the chase, long before a streak of light appeared in the sky.

"And you mean to join them, of course?" said Keryfan, growing half savage at the prospect of not being allowed to indulge in a long spell of sleep after so much fatigue.

"Of course," rejoined Marseillier, with an air of unfeigned astonishment on his good-natured face that such a question could be asked him; "to be sure I do. Why, it's the only day out of the seven on which business will permit a poor bourgeois to enjoy his life and give rest to his brain."

The disregard of the sabbath as a day of rest being the popular and general practice of that country, Keryfan had no notion, on moral grounds, of interfering with his neighbours' amusements on that sacred day. Its desecration was too habitual among all classes of the community to arouse within him the faintest scruple of conscience on the subject, for he had never been taught in childhood what every village schoolboy learns, as his first lesson, in this more favoured land—those words of "Poor Richard," that

> "A Sunday well spent brings a week of content,
> And strength for the toils of the morrow;
> But a Sunday profaned, whate'er may be gained,
> Is the certain forerunner of sorrow."

That the cup of sorrow has been drained, over and over again, to its bitterest dregs, by that people who, of all others on earth, do most dishonour to the sabbath-day, cannot be denied; though whether it be or be not for this very sin that the nation has been so heavily visited by God's wrath, it is not for man to decide.

Marseillier's renewed assurance that neither *le point du jour* nor *le réveil* should be sounded on his premises if he could possibly prevent it (for he had a most voluminous and discordant horn of his own, and was very fond of blowing it whenever he joined the town-chasse) seemed to satisfy Keryfan, who was well aware of his host's weakness on this point; and, having so far gained his object, he withdrew for the night.

The gap in our little circle, occasioned by the absence of the Comte de Kergoorlas, was the subject of great disappointment to all; but, encompassed as he was with so many troubles at Gourin, the result of which might probably involve him in serious difficulty hereafter, he felt it was imperative on him, both as a matter of duty and self-interest, to repair thither without delay after the sport at Kilvern; and to this necessity we were compelled reluctantly to bow.

But now to return to the forest. The obsequies over that last boar were soon ended; nor was his carcase honoured with the fanfare of horns that usually proclaimed the final triumph over the bristly foe. No less than five boar, suspended by the heels in various forest trees, awaited dissection, ere St. Prix could venture to quit the ground and take his hounds home to their Carhaix kennel. The day was waning fast; and as this work was the especial duty of Louis Trefarreg and his piqueurs, under the direction of the Louvetier himself, it was done, as may be supposed, in a rough-and-ready fashion, and with a despatch rendered necessary by the gloom of night that even now darkened the glen. It was marvellous, however, considering the tools used —two or three *chasse-couteaux* and one small battle-axe, which Louis Trefarreg bore in his belt—how adroitly the head and quarters were severed, and the chines divided with a precision worthy of a Paris *charcutier*. The distribution of all this meat, roughly estimated at ten hundred-weight, was quickly effected, and, as heretofore, appeared to give the peasants unqualified satisfaction; but if the tales about their crops were true, that amount of compensation could scarcely have been considered an equivalent for the damage they had sustained by the plundering habits of so many pigs. The sport was doubtless the first object;

for, to judge by the wild delight evinced on every occasion by the drag, the chase, or the kill, it was impossible to resist the conclusion that, after all, the sport alone would have gone a long way in satisfying the wrongs endured by these manly fellows.

When Kergoorlas turned his back on this wild woodland scene, of all that noble pack, eighteen couple strong, that he had brought with him but a few days before from Upper Brittany, seven hounds only remained to follow him home from the field. The others, either rendered *hors-de-combat* by death or wounds, or straying, after that fatal day at Conveau, over the trackless wastes of the Black Mountains, made up a list of casualties long enough and vexatious enough to break the heart of a man less sanguine and elastic than that of Kergoorlas. He was not one, however, to yield complacently to adverse circumstances, and cry out for help from Jupiter before he had put his own shoulder to the wheel; but, on the contrary, the loss of his hounds, which he felt grievously, seemed to rouse his spirit and at once to add fresh fuel to his natural energy; and, as he turned in his saddle to survey the scanty lot that, in answer to their names, instantly separated from the pack, and, with sterns erect, gathered in closely to his horse's heels, his last words were, " Helicon, Mareschal, and Niobe are, I grieve to say, past recovery, and many of my leading hounds are badly wounded; but, for the rest, if uneaten by wolves, I'll draw every hamlet and forest in Lower Brittany till I find them; so we may meet again."

He then bid us adieu, and set his horse's head direct for Gourin. On arriving in that town, his first business was to repair to the hospital—on which, indeed, even in the fervour of the chase, his thoughts had been intent throughout the day; for, though the morning report was favourable, he was fully aware that the lives of both the men, the braconnier and piqueur, must still be in the utmost jeopardy. "The painful suspense I endured" (he wrote to St. Prix on the following day) "ere I reached the gendarmerie, can never be effaced from my memory. With hasty strides I approached the building, and the nearer I drew to it, the stronger grew my presentiment that evil tidings awaited me within its walls. My nerves are not easily disturbed, as you well know; but you might have knocked me down with a marabout feather, when, in crossing the threshold, the medical officer blurted out, 'It's all over. In five minutes after you left, your piqueur Gastel had a fit, from which he never rallied; and he died at noon.'"

"And the braconnier?" I inquired, gasping with expectation of hearing still worse news.

"'Is doing well,' he replied, with confidence, 'and with care and rest, will probably be none the worse for the concussion in a week or two.'"

"You can easily imagine," continued Kergoorlas in his letter, "what comfort this information brought me; for the complication would have been indeed a serious one for me had the braconnier died from a blow inflicted by my servant, and, as the world would believe, on my account. Then there was the man's wife. It would have changed some of your scruples, St. Prix, had you witnessed, as I did, the unwearied, gentle tenderness and devotion with which she watched, and nursed, and soothed him in his agony. It was a picture I should like to paint—that homely but handsome peasant-girl—for she could scarcely have seen twenty summers—transformed by love into a ministering angel. Such a proof of what a woman can feel and do, as a help-meet, for the man she loves, would compel you, as it did me, to think better of the sex for the rest of your life."

The remainder of the letter described, in glad terms, the unexpected return of six couple of the lost hounds, which, to the great surprise of all, found their way back to their recent quarters at Gourin; and this, too, as was supposed, of their own accord. But it turned out afterwards that, luckily, a half-bred hound belonging to the braconnier had followed his master and the sabottiers to the forest of Conveau, and, having joined the pack when the wolf was roused, had held on with the chase; and this hound, well acquainted with the country, had doubtless acted as pioneer, and brought the rest back to his own home.

Not only hounds, but horses, buffalo, deer, and, in fact, all gregarious animals, when beset by danger or difficulties, are wont, as a rule, to adopt a leader and to trust implicitly to him for safety and deliverance. And it is no less marvellous than true that, in the selection of that leader, unerring instinct prompts them to distinguish the right animal for the right place, and to choose the one of all others the most capable and best qualified, either by courage, strength, local knowledge, or superior sagacity, to bring them in safety out of their trouble. Who that has read the passage can forget Lord Byron's description of the "trampling troop" of wild horses, and their mighty leader, in that story of Mazeppa? While the steed, to which he was so fast bound, fell at length, and, with glazing eyes and reeking limbs, lay immovable—

> "A thousand horse, the wild, the free,
> Like waves that follow o'er the sea,
> Came thickly thundering on.
>   *   *   *   *
> On came the troop—they saw him stoop,
> They saw me strangely bound along
> His back with many a bloody thong:
> They stop—they start—they snuff the air,
> Gallop a moment here and there,
> Approach, retire, wheel round and round,
> Then plunging back with sudden bound,
> Headed by one black mighty steed,
> Who seemed the patriarch of his breed,
> Without a single speck or hair
> Of white upon his shaggy hide;
> They snort—they foam—neigh—swerve aside,
> And backward to the forest fly,
> By instinct, from a human eye."

The remaining couple of hounds, still missing, were not heard of until ten days afterwards, when St. Prix received information from the gendarmes at Guingamp that a party of chasseurs, woodcock-shooting in the vale of the Frieux, in a forest formerly belonging to the Ducs de Penthièvre, had met with an old dog-wolf, so beaten and distressed by long travel that, with a charge or two of small shot, they toppled him over and brought his course to an end without any difficulty. This had scarcely been accomplished, when the tongue of hounds was heard at no great distance; and as the cry approached nearer and nearer, the chasseurs perceived a couple only of strange hounds, toil-stricken and leg-weary, but still struggling on and clinging to the line of scent, as if determined at all cost to gain their blood. On coming up to their prey, now powerless and gasping for life, they could do little more than fall upon the carcase and there lie, apparently well satisfied with the result, but utterly unable from exhaustion to worry the dying brute or throw out a single note in token of victory. The chasseurs found no difficulty in securing the hounds, which, after discovering from the Louvetier to whom they belonged, were forwarded to M. Kergoorlas's kennels on the Loire, none the worse for their long and adventurous chase.

It may here be remarked that the practice of rounding the ears and branding the sides of hounds is, so far as I know, never followed in Lower Brittany; but although it would be a great pity to mutilate the long, silky, pendulous ear of the native hound, and damage the appearance of his grand head, it must be owned he would find great advantage from the process in the unceasing cover-work to which he is subjected. As to the use of the side-brand, in no country would the plan be more useful, for an old dog-wolf, as just recorded, will often break country and go straight away to a far distant forest, making light of twelve and even fifteen leagues with the view of shaking off his pursuers—

a strategic manœuvre in which he is too often successful—on such occasions, from the frequency of deep valleys, roadless forests, and impracticable fences, which are like Devonshire banks, but far bigger; the most determined horseman soon finds himself nowhere, the piqueurs are left miles behind, and the hounds eventually throw up in a strange country without the power, if they have the instinct, to return to their own kennel. If, therefore, the plan of branding hounds with the initial letter of the owner's surname be found so useful in England, *à fortiori* would it be so in Lower Brittany.

Some five-and-twenty years ago I was riding to cover in company with Mr. J. Russell and sixteen couple of the N.D.H., when looking over a young hound, recently sent to him from a distant kennel, he discovered him to be unbranded. "This won't do," said he; "we hunt to-day in a wild, woodland country, and if we lose that hound, we shall never see him again." Then instantly dismounting and handing his horse's rein to me, he drew a small scissors from his pocket-book, took the hound between his knees, and in a twinkling cut out a great R in the hair on the animal's ribs. "There, Frank, no matter where he turns up now; he'll be sent back to my kennel for fifty miles round." So spake Russell, of all living houndsmen certainly one of the most experienced and most practical.

During our absence at Gourin, an Englishman had arrived at Carhaix and taken up his quarters at an old-fashioned house, exactly opposite the Hotel La Tour d'Auvergne; and, as our garrulous and good-natured host, Marseillier, made a point of ferreting out the business of every stranger who sojourned for a night or two at his own or a neighbour's house, he was not long in informing us that the gentleman was called "Johnson," that his object was the chasse, and that, with M. de St. Prix's permission, he hoped to be allowed to join the wolf-hounds while they hunted in that part of the country. Now, ubiquitous as Englishmen are said to be, they but rarely find their way to the uncommercial and remote little **town of Carhaix**; and when they do, the hotel, **with** its ready restaurant and appliances, is usually preferred to the pennyworth-of-pepper style of housekeeping entailed **by** private lodgings. The intention of making Carhaix his residence for a lengthened period was at once supposed by Marseillier to **be the ground for** Mr. Johnson's exceptional choice; and as, in that case, in **all** probability he would still become a daily *demi-pensionnaire* at the hotel, and 'a *compagnon de chasse* for himself, **the** wily host **lost** no time in persuading St. Prix to send him **a** polite invitation to join the wolf-hunt fixed for Locrist on the following Tuesday.

Some hours elapsed ere an answer was returned by Johnson, **but at** length it came, written **fluently in** Jersey-French, and **expressing his** gratitude in terms so extra-deferential, that St. Prix could not forbear shrugging his shoulders **as he read it**; as **if there was** something **beyond his comprehension, something very unlike the independent manner of** an English gentleman in the whole style of **the note.** A suspicion, like an electric spark, then flashed across the Louvetier's mind that it was not all above-board with this new comer, and that he himself had acted somewhat incautiously **in** adopting the course recommended by Marseillier. However, the thing was done; and if the stranger, thus invited, had proved to be a convict escaped from the galleys, St. Prix would not have revoked his invitation for that **day's** hunt.

"Whoever **he** may be," **said** Keryfan, perusing the note with the shrewdness of **an expert,** "**if** there is anything wrong about **the** man, he is already half-trapped **by entering** that house. Masson, the proprietor, is well known to be **a** Government spy; and, **depend** upon it, from mere habit, every movement of his guest, nay, **every** letter he **writes or** receives, will be subjected to the **closest surveillance."**

"Then I think," said St. Prix, "if he is in such good hands, we need not trouble ourselves with what, after all, may be nothing more than a groundless suspicion."

The subject then dropped, nor was anything seen of the mysterious stranger until the Tuesday morning; when, just as we were finishing an early breakfast, the hounds having gone on to Locrist an hour before, Marseillier rushed into our *salle-a-manger*, and, with an ill-suppressed grin on his countenance, announced M. Johnson as being in attendance at the hotel door, *vêtu à la cavalière*, and purposing to ride on with us to the cover-side. "But," said Marseiller, bursting into a fit of the wildest merriment, "he is mounted on butcher Kenwyn's 'Lunatique,' a horse that no man in Carhaix could ever sit beyond the first cross-road outside the town. See him in the butcher's *charrette*, and you'd consider him perfection; but he'll plunge and kick his hind shoes off rather than carry a saddle one kilometre."

"Then I fear," said Keryfan, "we shall not have the pleasure of his company as far as Locrist. But how on earth could Kenwyn venture to lend such a horse to a stranger?"

"For three francs he'd lend him his wife," replied the host. "Kenwyn is not particular when money stares him in the face; besides, he says that horse has shown him more sport by kicking off his riders than he ever saw at a *Jeux du Cirque*."

I did not half relish this last remark, and began to feel somewhat indignant at the prospect of seeing my compatriot thus turned into a laughing-stock, and probably maltreated, simply to satisfy the greed and humour of this Breton butcher; so I determined to rise at once from the table, and give Mr. Johnson a timely hint as to the vicious character of the horse he had hired for the day. But before I could effect my purpose the conversation continued; and Keryfan remarked that "it would be a sorry joke for the butcher if the rider's neck should be broken by his notoriously wicked horse."

"Not a bit of it," said Marseillier, evidently bent himself on seeing the fun. "Kenwyn has fully informed M. Johnson of the horse's tricks; and the only answer he made was, 'I should like to see him try them on with me, that's all.' So now, if his neck is broken, it will be clearly his business, not Kenwyn's."

At that instant St. Prix's drag rattled up to the doors of the hotel, and a general move taking place, we were quickly brought face to face with Mr. Johnson, who for the last five minutes had become the subject of some curiosity to all of us. There was the man, then, seated low in his saddle, apparently as unconcerned and as much at home as if he had been mounted on one of old Tilbury's park hacks, instead of a brute whose eye was as wicked as Waterton's cayman. His hunting attire, however, was simply awful: top-boots and yellowish cord breeches, a green coat with basket buttons, a red waistcoat and a bright blue bird's-eye throat-lash, with a black velvet cap above all, encased his body in a medley of colours, strangely inharmonious; nevertheless, with that love of parti-coloured paraphernalia which, in their hunting costume, is not unfrequently exhibited by our neighbours, his "get-up" appeared to attract unbounded admiration among the crowd of Bretons now gathering around him on every side.

"Where on earth does the fellow come from? and what can he be?" inquired Shafto, half indignant that so questionable a specimen of his countrymen should be described as an English gentleman. "He looks as if he had escaped from Portland or some other convict establishment."

The man's countenance, however, had more of the knave than the ruffian in it, with something about the glint of his eye, expressive at once of broad humour and intense cunning. I was so attracted at first by his extraordinary costume that for some moments I did not observe his face; but when at length I looked up and caught his eye, and then heard him address St. Prix in that broad *franc-patois* peculiar to Jersey, I immediately recognised the individual as a livery-stable keeper, with whom I had

had occasional dealings during my sojourn in that island. He, too, recognised me, and lost no time in making the fact known by asking how a bay horse had turned out that he had sold me the last time I had visited his stables. "I have come to this country," he said, "to attend some horse-fairs at Rostrenan, Chateaulin, and Morlaix; and, with a bit of luck, I hope to pick up a string of useful cobs that will sell well at Southampton; for, that's my market now, not St. Hellier's, where a lot of fellows have congregated who can't afford to pay for a pint of shrimps."

During this short conversation he was busily employed in rolling a huge horse-rug together and fastening it across the pommel of the saddle and in front of his knees, by way of a stay; the butcher standing at the horse's head, holding the bridle tightly with one hand and smoothing down his nose with the other, to keep the brute quiet, if possible, during the operation.

"Your friend seems to know what he's about," said Shafto. "That rug-roll, strapped in front, is the very dodge adopted in Australia, when a young 'bucker' is hampered and mounted for the first time; and I begin to think 'Lunatique' has found his master in that rider."

St. Prix's drag was now under weigh; and the clatter of hoofs and the crack of the whip seemed to electrify "Lunatique" in one instant. He reared twice on end, but Johnson dropped his bridle-hand, and, throwing his weight on the brute's neck, frustrated the back-fall that appeared to be imminent; he then made a succession of plunges, bucking on all fours into the air and coming down with his nose to the ground. But with all these frantic efforts, there sat the undisturbed Johnson, fast and firm, as if he had been glued to his saddle. A sharp, stinging cut with his heavy jockey-whip, then another and another over the off-flank, brought the brute at once into progressive action, and in five minutes afterwards he was cantering along, in the wake of our drag, as smoothly and submissively as a lady's pet palfrey.

This victory, so rapidly achieved and so decisive, brought Johnson into immediate favour with our Breton chasseurs, whose praise of him as a "bon cavalier" was unbounded. But the further adventures of this hero, as well as the sport at Locrist, must be told in the next chapter.

CHAPTER XX.

Notwithstanding the signal victory obtained by the Jersey horse-dealer over "Lunatique," the faith of his owner, butcher Kenwyn, in the inherent vice of the animal continued firm as ever; and under the conviction that another fight would ensue, and then probably with a different result, at the cross-roads near St. Katherine, he and many of the Carhaix people struggled after us for more than a league out of the town. The butcher, however, did not enjoy his expected grin, for up to that point, and beyond the bridge, Johnson and the "Lunatique" were still trotting after the drag, and seemed inclined to pursue the even tenor of their way amicably together for the rest of the day. They were then lost to sight by the butcher and his friends, who, on their return to Carhaix, expressed their chagrin in no measured terms at the facility with which the horse had been mastered and their sport marred, by the courage and skill of M. Johnson.

But there was another and a better reason for butcher Kenwyn's disappointment. Relying fully on the vicious habit of the horse, he had agreed to sell him for a lower sum than his intrinsic value, provided that on trial in the saddle the animal gave satisfaction; and that he was now likely to do so, being a rare stepper, and only five years old, made him all but crazy at the prospect of losing so serviceable a beast. However, the day was not yet over; and if, smarting keenly under a sense of the imprudent bargain to which he had committed himself, Kenwyn still cherished a hope that the horse-dealer would be brought home on a hurdle rather than on "Lunatique's" back, I do not describe, according to Marseillier, the injured pride and vexation of the man a whit too strongly.

Locrist, the fixture at which the hounds were appointed to meet, is, as I have before said, a small hamlet consisting of two cottages and an old water-mill, snugly situated in a valley which, from its beautiful trout-stream and dark hanging woods, is one of the wildest and most picturesque spots in Brittany. It is scarcely more than two leagues from Carhaix; and as the covers abound with woodcock, and the river in hard weather with teal and wild-duck, the visits of the town braconniers—men who get their livelihood solely by the *chasse*—were by no means unfrequently paid, as may be supposed, to that locality. On the present occasion it was quickly discovered by Louis Trefarreg that on the previous day a couple of braconniers had drawn every cover in the valley; and, as woodcock were then numerous, had kept up a continuous fusillade at that and other game from morning to night. Our old friend Kledan Kam, too, in spite of his recent wound, had sallied forth with his musket and profited largely by the toil of the men and their dogs on the opposite side of the valley; and although he with difficulty managed to hobble along on a stick, many a cock and a red-leg fell victims to this crafty dodge of the lame "Lion."

Now a fox, in a wild country, is a very wild animal, and speedily takes the hint to be off, if the seclusion in which he lives is intruded upon by an unwelcome visitor; but far more vigilant and suspicious of danger is the cowardly wolf, especially if by daylight the sound of man's voice and the report of fire-arms ring on his ears: wide is the berth he then gives to that hated locality, nor will he return for many a long day to it, even though it be his old haunt and the strongest cover in the neighbourhood. So when the trusty piqueur Trefarreg communicated the aforesaid information to St. Prix, that bright, hopeful look that usually illumined the Louvetier's countenance when about to draw a favourite cover, assumed a gloomy, portentous hue, and fell suddenly like the mercury in a barometer before a thunder-storm. Then the cloud burst. "It's no use whatever," he said angrily, "to waste our time in this valley; as well may we expect to find a wolf in Marseillier's cabbage-garden as in these disturbed covers. What with gunners and wolf-traps, my hounds shall never come near the place again."

It will be remembered that, on a former visit to Locrist, a favourite pointer of M. de Kergoorlas's had been caught in the jaws of a huge wolf-gin, and that it had been found necessary to destroy the animal on the spot—a catastrophe M. de St. Prix was not likely to forget for the remainder of his life. Holding the appointment of Louvetier—a post expressly designed for the destruction, not the preservation, of wolves—he yet held that to hunt the animal with hound and horn was the only legitimate mode of killing the brute; and he was just as tenacious of his official rights and interests as any M.F.H. in Great Britain could be. A steel-gin was his horror, not solely because he begrudged the summary destruction of a wolf, and the occasional curtailment of sport thereby, but because many a good hound of his had been entrapped in its fatal jaws.

Kledan Kam did well to keep out of the way on the present occasion; for, suspected as he had been in the matter of the gin, and having aided on the previous day in disturbing the whole valley of Locrist, although the intended meet of the wolf-hounds had been made known to him, he certainly would have found himself in the position of a lightning-conductor, on which the fulminations of the Louvetier would have descended with fearful force had he not thus adopted the discreet course of avoiding the shock.

To a remonstrance of Shafto's that, being on the spot, he might as well draw Locrist, as it lay directly in the line for Hengoet, the next great cover beyond this valley, St. Prix reluctantly gave way, remarking, with no little acerbity, that it would be too surely time and labour thrown away, and that the disappointment caused by a blank must rest on his shoulders. Then followed the usual animated palaver as to the best mode of drawing the line of covers, and the contingencies likely to result therefrom; so that, before Louis Trefarreg had received his final orders to uncouple the tufters, a good half-hour had been wasted in preliminary talk. This custom of our continental neighbours is, of all others, the most tiresome, for, no matter how urgent the need of despatch, nor how fierce and inclement the elements may be, the palaver must take place; and if, at such a time, a party of Indian chiefs (who, when assembled to discuss any important subject, are remarkable for their quiet bearing and dignified demeanour) could only witness the impulsive gesticulation and lively language of our civilised friends, they would conclude them to be little better than a set of lunatics. Wide as the gulf is between the noblesse and the peasantry of Lower Brittany, still the doctrine of equality and free speech is universally established even in this stronghold of the *ancien régime*, and peasants as well as peers will have their say at the cover-side. Consequently, although the object of the palaver is a reasonable one—it being intended to secure concerted action in the sylvan war—the Babel of talkers suggesting various plans, and each asserting his own plan to be the right one, renders it sometimes no easy task for the commanding officer to decide on the tactics he had best adopt.

Three couple of the staunchest wolf-tufters (and among them were some rare, deep-drawing hounds) were then uncoupled on each side of the valley, and every acre of gorse, broom, and woodland was steadily drawn, up to the table-land between it and Hengoet, but, as already anticipated, without any satisfactory result. Not a hound spoke, nor did there appear to be a whiff left of even a stale scent. More than one fox, however, was viewed, crossing the narrow green meadow from one side of the valley to the other, and inducing a wild shout of "Ah'r louarn! Ah'r louarn!" from some unruly peasants; but the hounds were steady, and held on heedless of riot.

During this long and very tedious process, St. Prix's patience, none of the most enduring, became fairly exhausted; and, denouncing the braconniers of Carhaix and Kledan Kam as the sole cause of the blank, he vowed it should be many a long day before he visited the valley of Locrist again with his hounds. "If they will mar our sport thus wilfully," he said, "let them take the consequences. The wolves shall teach them a lesson they will not soon forget."

We had now reached—hounds, horses, and men—a point of the table-land where the main road between Callac and Rostrenen intersects a narrow cross-country road leading direct to Carhaix. It is a wild, lonely district, bristling with granite rocks and endless broom, and is, by its sparse population, almost wholly uncultivated; so what the poverty-stricken peasants, who are born and bred in this desert, can find to live upon, is a problem I will not pretend to solve. There are trout, it is true, in the brooks, and a certain amount of game in the covers; but of this the wolf gets the lion's share, and the others are only to be caught in the summer season.

Up to this point Johnson and the "Lunatique" had been travelling together apparently in perfect accord one with the other; the former indulging in quaint and facetious reflections on the tailors of Carhaix and the butcher's ignorance of horseflesh, while he congratulated himself on the prospect of purchasing so valuable an animal on such easy terms. But he was whistling, as it soon proved, before he was clear of the wood: the Ides of

March were not yet over, and a desperate struggle awaited the horse-dealer in that narrow cross-road leading direct to Carhaix.

"Forward to Hengoet!" said St. Prix to his chief piqueur, in a curt and decisive tone. "It is now past mid-day, and we have two long leagues before us ere we reach the outskirts of that forest."

Louis Trefarreg's knowledge of the Louvetier's temper did not encourage him at that moment to suggest any difficulty—a practice to which, from his long experience with hounds, thorough knowledge of the country, and, above all, his acquaintance with the habits of the wild animals he hunted, he was somewhat too prone. He now, however, most prudently said nothing, but at once accepting the order, dashed off, hounds and all, towards Hengoet, taking the Rostrenen road in that direction. Close in his wake followed the field of chasseurs, peasants, piqueurs, and cavaliers—all save one, our facetious friend, the parti-coloured Johnson, whose horse, having no fancy for the Rostrenen route, and preferring much the one leading straight to his stable, had suddenly become a fixture. At first the dealer did what he could to coax the beast forward by gentle measures, stroking and patting his neck, and talking to him in the mildest of tones; but by such means he might as well have hoped to move an equestrian statue into action. Not a leg did he stir; but he cropped both ears close back viciously, while the white of his wicked eye indicated a temper ripe for a row.

Keryfan and myself dropped instantly back, hoping, by the example of our willing steeds, to induce the "Lunatique" to follow them towards Rostrenen. But not a bit of it; his head was turned towards Carhaix, and if not permitted to travel in that direction, not a yard would he go on the Rostrenen road. But the man on his back had a firm seat and a resolute will; and, finding gentle treatment of no avail, he brought down his heavy whip with a whack that sounded like a pistol-shot on the horse's back ribs. Then the fight began. Up went the beast on all-fours, bucking into the air as high as a five-barred gate several times in rapid succession; and ever, as he touched the earth, again plunging forward, as if impelled by a catapult. The man sat, like a Centaur, incorporate with his horse; and if his knees had been rivetted to the saddle, he could scarcely have gripped it with a firmer hold. Nor did his right hand cease its work for one moment; down came the stinging cuts on rib, flank, and thigh, half-a-dozen for every plunge, and leaving a weal big as a man's finger after every cut.

For ten long minutes did this fierce struggle last, when the horse, apparently exhausted by his frantic efforts to unseat the rider, reared straight on end, and, coming heavily backward, he fell prostrate, and there lay, not a kick left in him, beaten, dispirited, and groaning on the ground. With the agility of a mountebank had Johnson quitted his seat at the right moment, and, throwing himself off, had rolled through the wet, slushy soil, clear of all danger. He was on his legs, however, in another second, but not before he had been so plastered with mud that every article of his dress, lately so gay and varied in hue, was transformed, instanter, into one sombre colour—that of a mud-casing—from head to foot. Never was a metamorphosis more complete; never a proud horseman more rapidly converted into the form of a grimy brick-burner! Proteus himself might have envied the feat, but for the ugly fall. The consequence of this, however, was merely external, namely, the disfigurement of his person and the damage of his dress. Having long been accustomed to hunt with the Hambledon Hounds, and usually mounted on raw horses, Johnson was well versed in the art of falling, and knew well how and when to quit his seat when his horse was in a difficulty—a secret not sufficiently studied by men in general; hence his escape on the present occasion, with neither a broken limb nor even a bruised body.

My first impulse, I confess, was to burst out laughing at the strange aspect he had so suddenly assumed; but on second and better thoughts the inhumanity of doing so occurred to my mind, and I rushed up with the view of rendering him all the assistance his situation might require. Keryfan, too, did the same, with an unusually grave demeanour; but before we had fairly ranged alongside him, the horse-dealer had drawn a long clasp-knife out of his breeches-pocket, and was coolly proceeding to scrape the mud from his face and clothes, just as he would have applied an iron hoop to a horse's belly in his own stable-yard.

"Not hurt, I hope?" inquired Keryfan and myself simultaneously, as we reined up our horses close to where he stood.

"No damage done, gentlemen, except to my body-clothes. They were all new last week; and now Samuel Brothers, who supplied the rig, would not know a garment of them again, I'm blessed if they would."

"Oh, if that's all, they'll be all right again, and all the better, perhaps, for the seasoning," I replied, being somewhat surprised at finding the man took more thought of the adornment than the safety of his body.

"You think so, do you?" he answered curtly, now scraping away at his waistcoat, and bringing out its original scarlet hue, though in a sadly subdued form. "A spoke-brush and ten buckets of water wouldn't do it; at least, that's my opinion."

During this process and conversation the horse lay embedded in the mire, still as a log, and apparently utterly cowed by the rough treatment to which he had been subjected; nor, while he was busied in removing the soil from his person, did Johnson vouchsafe even a look at the animal that had brought him into so woful a plight. But that being accomplished, so far as his knife could do it, he lighted a cigar, and, taking the curb-rein in hand, he dealt the horse a tremendous kick in the ribs, shouting at him to "get up," and bringing the curb to bear sharply on his jaw at the same moment. The poor brute, however, never attempted to rise, but, in response to the blow, gave one or two audible sobs. The dejection, too, expressed by his eye seemed to say he would rather die on the spot than carry his hard taskmaster another yard. But the horse-dealer had handled in his time many such customers—"devils at first, and dunghills afterwards," as he described them; so, instead of manifesting any concern at the refusal of the horse to rise, he proceeded deliberately to gather large handfuls of dry grass and fern, which, placed under his tail, and set on fire, "would," he said, "bring him on his legs in a twinkling."

Both Keryfan and myself, however, at once interposed, and declared we would not stand by and see a dumb animal so cruelly treated, and that he must adopt some plan less torturing than that of fire to get the horse on his legs again. A gleam of fierce defiance instantly flashed from the horse-dealer's eyes, and, from the attitude he assumed, buttoning up his coat, squaring his elbows, and doubling his spare fist (for he still held his big iron-headed whip in the other hand), I fully expected he would attack us both, there and then, rather than be thwarted in the savage purpose on which he was bent. Notwithstanding this menace, however, Keryfan stepped forward, and with his heel stamped into the wet mire the heap of grass collected by the ruffian—an act that seemed to convince him at once that we, too, were disposed to be as resolute as he was—and perhaps the rapid calculation that two to one were awkward odds for that one to encounter had an electric effect in causing him to change his tactics, and, instead of a warlike attitude, to assume the air of a man whose right to do as he liked with his own had been grossly outraged. At all events, discretion stepped in opportunely, and instead of doing battle with his fists, he satisfied himself by doing it vigorously with his tongue.

"Who's going to pay for this horse, then?" he inquired

sarcastically. "Not I, let me tell you; not one sous. He's a dead horse, he is, if he lies there till he grows chilled and gets inflammation, that's certain. And you'll pay for him, of course, if you won't suffer me to save his life by getting him, as I best can, out of this mire."

The poor beast's nose was now resting on the edge of a rut, while his belly was deeply imbedded in the watery slush; so, as there was doubtless some truth in the horse-dealer's argument, I endeavoured to appease his wrath by a soft answer, telling him that, short of fire, we were quite ready to give him all the help in our power; and that, if he would make another effort, I would handle the bridle, while Keryfan or he cracked him up about the quarters with my hunting-thong.

To this he assented, but evidently against his inclination; and as he puffed away briskly at his cigar, he continued his evil vaticination—"He's a dead horse, I tell you, if he lies here much longer; and there's nothing will move him but fire; that I know."

I then took both reins over the animal's head, and, patting him gently on the neck, I fancied I could discern a slight improvement in the sad expression of his eye; and while Keryfan proceeded to touch him up with his thong, the horse-dealer gripped him by the root of the tail, and endeavoured to lift his quarters, or pretended to do so, clear of the mire. In an instant the beast sprung upon his legs, and before I could scramble out of his way, he almost jumped on top of me; he then set to kicking furiously, clipping his tail close between his legs, and looking like a horse driven mad by rage or pain.

We did not know it then, but shortly afterwards it oozed out that the burning end of his cigar—the actual cautery—had been insidiously applied to the tenderest part of the poor brute's quarters. Exquisite torture was, of course, inflicted thereby, and hence his frantic action the moment he was on his legs. This, however, when the pain had somewhat subsided, did not deter Johnson from again closing with his victim, and vaulting on his back, like a tiger springing on his prey. There was a ferocity now in his expression that I had not before observed, a vindictive, pitiless look, that seemed to say he'd cut him to ribbons if the beast again proved refractory.

Happily, however, we were spared a further exhibition of brutality. The animal, now fairly subdued, walked quietly away in the direction of Rostrenen; Johnson, too, soon regained his natural vivacity, indulging in stable slang, and boasting that he should be able to guide the "Lunatique" with a packthread for the rest of his life.

After this exciting episode on the highway, we did not overtake the hounds before they had reached Hengoet. St. Prix had already thrown his tufters into cover, and the occasional deep-sounding note of more than one pioneer gave token of a night-scent, not very fresh, but still improving, as the hounds advanced into the hollow glen.

"This is a travelling wolf," observed the Louvetier, "probably disturbed from Locrist; and if so, the drag, I fear, will be a long affair, and may lead us far beyond this cover ere we come up to the wanderer's lair."

I had just looked at my watch; and finding the time to be 2.55 P.M., and the glen below looking dark as the jaws of Erebus, I wondered how long and how far he would encourage his hounds to carry the drag, if they failed to rouse the wild beast in this grand forest, the distant boundary of which appeared to be at least a league away; so I ventured to inquire the name and distance of the next cover, if this should prove a blank.

"The stronghold of Dualt," said St. Prix, "lies about two leagues off; and this wolf being, as I suspect, an old skulker, it is more than probable he has passed on and sought the rocky fastnesses of that vast cover. In that case, the hounds will be encouraged to hold the line of drag to within a short distance of Dualt, then stopped, and taken to Callac for the night. At break of day we shall be at him again (for Callac is on the outskirts of the forest), and then, I trust, we shall get on better terms with this wary customer."

"A pleasant programme enough," I rejoined, "provided the necessary accommodation can be found for your hounds and horses in that primitive little town. Of course *you* will return to Carhaix for the night?"

"By no means," said the Louvetier. "M. Thomas's hotel has ample accommodation for all; and as it is so conveniently near the forest, it will save us ten leagues of road work if we rest there instead of returning to Carhaix."

"That is, doubtless, an important consideration," I replied; and not wishing to appear fastidious about my own personal comforts, when he and others were so ready to rough it for the sake of hunting, I expressed a cordial approval of the plan, though I confess sundry misgivings rose to my mind at the prospect of roosting for the night at a way-side tavern, without a rag of change, or even a tooth-brush to aid one's ablutions.

An occasional double note from the furthermost depths of Hengoet still reached our ears, proving the good hounds were clinging to the drag, though unable, except at intervals, to give hopeful tidings of the foe ahead. The Louvetier's expectations of a blank day were evidently about to be realised; and although such an event was fortunately one of rare occurrence in this country, it was not the less likely to chafe the temper of a man so sanguine and so fiery as he was. We were now threading our way, in Indian file, through a vast broom-field that skirted the cover for a league or more, when one of the piqueurs, advancing to meet us, informed St. Prix that he had tracked a couple of old wolves, apparently in company, to the far end of the valley; that the track-prints were clear of the cover, and, so far as he could judge, pointing directly for Dualt; moreover, that he was quite certain one of the wolves had but three legs, or at all events, carried one which apparently was of no use to it.

The Louvetier, on hearing this, at once sounded his horn, and, pricking forward briskly, clapped the whole body of his pack on the line indicated by the piqueur; but, well marked as the tracks were, it was only here and there that some fine-nosed hound, giving an extra lash with his stern, was able to throw his tongue on the all-but extinguished scent. The tufters, however, were not far astern, and, as soon as they came up, matters mended a little; but still the cry, as patiently and perseveringly those skilled pioneers picked up the scent, making a hit here and a hit there, over the wild, rocky waste between Hengoet and Dualt, would have given Kergoorlas the ear-ache, so cheerless was it up to the very edge of the latter forest. There, as the sun went down, the Louvetier stopped the pack, when all, with the exception of Johnson, turned their horses' heads direct for Callac, he and the "Lunatique," now apparently sobered and submissive, returning alone to Carhaix. Thus ended a blank day—the only one I was doomed to see in company with St. Prix's hounds.

CHAPTER XXI.

Having sojourned, as already stated, for two seasons in the least-frequented and remotest towns of Lower Brittany, mainly for the sake of the wild sport obtainable in that country, my acquaintance with the hotels, of which there is at least one more pretentious than the rest in every small town, became almost as extensive as that of any *Commis-voyageur*, hailing from Brest or some other neighbouring seaport. At M. Thomas' I had frequently halted for the night; and, well knowing the extent of his bed-room accommodation, it puzzled me not a little to imagine how he could possibly contrive to stow us all comfortably away, as St. Prix declared he was able to do, within the limits of his narrow domain. Besides our own party, consisting of Keryfan, Shafto, the Louvetier, and myself, four other gentlemen had joined us, not one of whom had the slightest intention of returning to his home till the hounds were taken back to their kennels near Morlaix. Three bed-apartments comprised the total amount of stowage-room available for night guests; and although a couple of small bedsteads, the furniture of which was clean and white as the driven snow, stood confronting one another in each chamber, two more were still wanting to supply the needful accommodation for all the party.

While this difficulty was under discussion, M. Thomas stepped forward and proposed a solution of it that, at all events, did him infinite credit as an obliging, if not a disinterested, host: he proposed that Madame Thomas and he should vacate their own apartment and occupy a room on the ground-floor. Now, on the Continent, especially among the French and Germans, the *rez-de-chaussée*, under the impression of its unhealthiness during the night-season, is usually occupied only by those whose circumstances compel them to sleep below stairs. This offer was at once accepted, though, in order to show his full appreciation of the sacrifice which the worthy couple were so ready to make, St. Prix made as many apologies to Madame Thomas for dispossessing her as if he were addressing the first duchess of the land. I discovered afterwards that the "room on the ground-floor" was no other than the kitchen, and their sleeping quarters a hole in the wall, some six feet above the floor of the apartment —a recess originally intended for the *batterie-de-cuisine*, but now converted into a dormitory, not unlike in the form of its excavation to one of those *loculi*, in which a couple of skeletons may be seen reposing side by side, sleeping the long sleep of death, in some Italian catacomb. But Thomas and his spouse were anything but skeletons; and how on earth the outside sleeping partner contrived to hold his or her own in such narrow quarters, without tumbling overboard, will remain a mystery to me to the end of the chapter.

This arrangement, however inconvenient to them, not only gave our party the needful accommodation, but also insured the early rising of the host and hostess—an important result, seeing that he performed the office of cook and she of waiting-maid to the establishment, and this, too, with an efficiency I have rarely seen equalled. Accordingly, before the peep of day, a substantial breakfast of mutton cutlets, omelets cooked to a second, and hot coffee smoked upon the board; and even Keryfan, who had been considerably disconcerted by the absence of his usual toilet accompaniments, was ready to endorse St. Prix's character of the hostelry, and declare that, modest as were its pretensions, he had met here with better fare and less discomfort than in many of the larger hotels in Brittany.

The hour of seven had just been announced by the old-fashioned clock in the *salle-à-manger*, and our meal so far dispatched that on every side pipes were being lighted and horns slung, in the immediate prospect of a start for Dualt, when Louis Trefarreg, entering the apartment, brought the startling intelligence that a carrion horse, killed for the hounds on the previous day, and lying within twenty yards of the kennel door, had been devoured by wolves in the night, and that nothing but the bones of the beast remained to tell the tale.

"I wondered," said the piqueur, "to hear the hounds baying so wildly in the dead of night, and more than once was tempted to rise and find out the cause of the disturbance. Had I done so, I might have saved the flesh and restored peace to the kennel."

"Aye, and the hounds would have been all the fresher for their day's work," said the Louvetier, greatly excited by these tidings.

"Quite true," answered the wily piqueur; "but still the wolves, having had time to gorge the whole of the carrion, will find themselves heavily weighted when the chase grows hot; and this advantage, methinks, will strike a telling balance in favour of the hounds."

"What's a half-starved Brittany pony among half-a-dozen hungry wolves?" responded the Louvetier; "for there must have been a pack of them, or they never would have ventured on so daring an act of aggression during the present open weather."

"There were only a couple; and what's more, I'll be sworn they were the same we hunted yesterday through Hengoet; at all events, the tracks were precisely similar: one was an old dog-wolf, and the other a bitch going on three legs."

"Then we must kill them both, Louis," said the Louvetier, "or that crippled wolf, unable as she now is to chase and catch her wild prey, will turn her attention to domestic stock, and, with the aid of her mate, will do more damage in a month than half-a-dozen other wolves in a whole year."

"That's quite certain," said Shafto; "just as a mangy old tiger betakes himself to villages and 'cantonments,' and becomes a man-eater, simply because from age and infirmity he is no longer a match for the stately sambar or the swift Indian antelope."

This information of the piqueur's rendered a change of tactics at once necessary; and instead of trotting them off to the forest of Dualt, three couple of the steadiest old hounds were laid directly on the hot drag within a hundred yards of the kennel door. Over the first fence they broke abreast, every hound throwing his tongue and dashing into the adjoining *genêt*, with bristles up and in full cry. "Let them all go," shouted Shafto. "With such a scent they're not likely to change; and the stronger the pack the better head will they carry between this and Dualt."

St. Prix either did not or would not hear him, for he instantly gave Louis Trefarreg orders to make the best of his way to that forest with the body of the pack, and to hold them in couples till the signal was given for slipping the first relay. This, as it soon appeared, was sound advice, as, while the drag-hounds were carrying the scent at a rattling pace through a thick gorsy cover, overhanging the brook on the south side of Callac, a fox and a brace of roe-deer broke away in the very face of the hounds, the scent of the latter being a temptation which none but the staunchest old tufters are ever able to resist. But, strangely enough, in addition to this chance of riot on view, the roe-deer took exactly the same line with the wolves, broke the fences exactly at the same spot, and finally entered Dualt within fifty yards of the granite clitter over which the wolves had passed in the gloom of that early morn.

Never could the sense of discrimination evinced by these hounds have been better tested, nor the steadiness with which they cleaved to the grosser game more admirably displayed. Not for one instant did they appear perplexed by the double scent, for whenever a divergence of the two lines occurred, the savage manner of the hounds and the angry tones in which they spoke, indicated, as truly as the piqueur's tracking eye, the line taken by the wolves. Then what a real hunting treat it was to see them, when at fault, casting themselves to recover the scent, with heads and bodies lowered to their work, how they twisted and turned like snakes over the ground; and then, the hound that caught it, how he dashed ahead! and what a struggle it created to catch him again! A neck-and-neck race between horses, be it on the Downs of Epsom or the Curragh of Kildare, gives, to my mind, but a faint and artificial picture of emulation, compared with the ardour of hounds struggling for a lead on a scent they love. With these, Nature is the jockey; but with the other, steel and whalebone are too often needed to bring their heads to the front of the fray.

Happily, it was most of it open moorland between Callac and the forest of Dualt, or, fairly mounted as we were, little should we have seen of many an interesting passage in that rapid drag. The pile of rocks was now gained, some of which, great granite slabs, stood on end, like giants on guard, barring access to the forest beyond; while the mass lay recumbent, forming natural cromlechs and dolmens of mighty size and grotesque shape. Over these the hounds clambered without difficulty, in full swing and melodious cry; but for the horses to follow them was now simply impracticable. A little *détour*, however, down-wind, in which Keryfan undertook the pilotage, soon brought us within ear-shot, though rarely within sight of the leaders of the chase—

for all was now dense forest for miles—and, except in small patches cleared by the charcoal-burners, or in the wider space occupied by clumps of beech-trees that crowned the heights and suffered no vegetation to flourish under their wide-spreading shade, we could only, ever and anon, catch a glimpse of the hounds forging ahead, but still on drag-scent.

At length the tone of the hounds changed, and a sharper, less prolonged note, quickly doubled, and more hurrisome, set my heart a-throbbing, like a sledge-hammer battering against my ribs. At the same moment St. Prix, leaning forward over his saddle, and with his ear turned in the direction of the hounds, had thrown Barbe-bleu back on his haunches. "By St. Hubert!" he exclaimed, "that's a find; and we need hold hard for a second to hear which way they turn."

The old horse, too, seemed to understand, as well as his master, the change in the hounds' tongue, for, like a war-horse when he hears the trumpet sounding the charge, his ears were pricked forward, his eyes dilated, and his very attitude appeared to say, "That's the signal for strife; and now the battle begins in earnest."

So it did; the game was roused, and coming directly, as the cry indicated, for the clump of beech-trees under which we then stood. St. Prix, on Barbe-bleu, holding his hand aloft to enjoin silence, was motionless as Marcus Aurelius in the piazza of the Capitol! He scarcely seemed to breathe! Nearer and nearer came the cry; and as every eye peered keenly into the various short vistas formed by the beech-trees, suddenly, and transient as an electric flash, a brace of wolves lopped across an open space, and instantly disappeared in the dense cover, to which they at once turned. The view was enough, however, to enable us all to distinguish that one was a cripple and the other a gaunt brute of unusual size. They, too, had seen us, for they separated at once, like two scoundrels at the sight of the police, the bigger villain quitting his partner at a tangent, and, in a few strides, leaving her in the lurch, as if "the devil take the hindmost" was the only thought uppermost in the brute's head.

"That's a lucky turn for us," said the Louvetier, trotting rapidly forward, and clapping the tufters, as they streamed in sight, close on the back of the crippled wolf. At the same time (for as yet not a hound of the relay had been uncoupled) he put his horn to his lips, and sounded a lively signal for the first batch; but before these had time to catch us, the tufters had driven the old harridan back to the rocks, and there brought her to bay under a granite ledge that protected her on every side, except in front, from the attack of her enemies.

Quick as thought St. Prix was out of his saddle, and Barbe bleu made fast by his chain-halter to a convenient tree; but, intent as he was on saving his hounds, and bounding, as he did, like an ibex, from rock to rock, over chasms, fissures, and such-like obstructions, he was unable to reach the ground in time to save old Cæsar from his usual fate. The brave old hound had gone in alone at the formidable foe (the passage to the holt being so narrow that it was impossible for more than one to enter at a time), and in the desperate fight that ensued he had come out savagely mangled about the head, which was literally a mass of blood. Notwithstanding this punishment, however, the very moment he caught sight of St. Prix springing to his aid, he dashed in again without a scruple of fear; then, locked together, jaw and jaw, the wolf and the hound renewed their terrible struggle at the mouth of that narrow den. Two bull-dogs never encountered each other with more fury; the courage of the hound, notwithstanding the immense superiority of the other in point of weight, muscular power, and length of teeth, giving the old hero a decided advantage over his cowardly foe.

At the risk of, at least, an odd rib or two in getting forward, Keryfan and I were soon standing at St. Prix's side, and able to lend him a hand as he dropped into the narrow arena occupied by the two combatants. The Louvetier's *couteau* never missed its mark; and with one stroke the gaunt wolf, though grip and grip with old Cæsar, fell dead at his feet. The fore-arm of the brute, on being measured just below the elbow, proved to be no less than ten inches in circumference, while the canine teeth, or holders, independent of that larger portion buried in the socket, were at least an inch and a half in length; so sharp and formidable were they, and so powerful were the jaws of the brute, that it was quite a marvel how the hound escaped with his life.

Then commenced the funeral obsequies of sounding the *mort* over the prostrate carcase, now raised to the surface and stretched out at full length on a table-rock hard by; and although the Louvetier knew perfectly well how important it was to get on with all despatch after the other wolf, he would as soon have omitted this ceremony as a Galway peasant would a "wake" over the body of some departed friend. But there was another business claiming the immediate attention of the Louvetier besides sounding the *mort;* that business was the extrication of old Cæsar, who lay bleeding and disabled in the fore-leg at the bottom of the fissure into which he had followed the retreating foe. This, however, was a far more difficult matter than might be imagined. The hound had a surly, savage nature of his own, and at the best of times would not suffer anyone to handle him save his master or Louis Trefarreg. The latter had not yet reached the death scene; and as the several blasts, sounded both by Keryfan and St. Prix, had failed to produce him, no other hand but that of the Louvetier could venture to tackle the old warrior in his present condition. So, as time was precious, St. Prix, running the thong of his whip through the keeper, and descending into the pit, adjusted the loop gently and carefully over the hound's head; then twisting the thong securely round the handle, which Keryfan and I grasped simultaneously from above, we landed the hero alongside his mortal foe amid a roar of growls that would have terrified a gladiator. The very moment he caught sight of the company he was in, forgetting his wounds, and by way of venting his ill-humour, he dashed at the wolf's throat, and never relaxed his hold till St. Prix, after wiping the blood from his face with a pocket-handkerchief, commenced pouring some brandy into the gashes with which his head was seamed. The torture inflicted by this treatment made him let go at once; and then came another roar, angry and fierce as that of Cerberus when Hercules rescued Alceste from Pluto's dread domain. But it was of short duration, that roar of agony: a few gentle words from the Louvetier seemed to satisfy the sagacious old hound that it was all done for his good; and, lifting his head, he licked his master's hand with a touching air of gratitude and affection.

While St. Prix still persevered in sounding the *mort*—for neither Louis Trefarreg, nor Shafto, nor the other chasseurs had as yet answered the signal, nor had a hound of the relay reached the rocks—it became evident that something must have occurred to take them in an opposite direction, and that, too, beyond the reach of the Louvetier's horn.

> "And still he blew a louder blast,
> And gave a lustier cheer;"

but echo alone answered the prolonged notes, and even they, growing fainter and fainter, soon ceased to disturb the silence of that lone forest for many a rood round.

"I see plainly what has happened," said St. Prix, boiling over with impatience, and weary of delay. "The hounds have crossed the line of the dog-wolf, and gone away with him nobody knows where."

"Except those lucky fellows, Louis and the rest of them, who are now enjoying their turn of luck, as we have had ours," said

Keryfan, affecting to hide the keen disappointment he felt at being shut out of a run that bid fair to be *the one* of the season.

"Killing a three-legged wolf may be of service to the community, Keryfan; but it has been sorry sport for ourselves, I confess," said the Louvetier. "Our friend Frank, too, knows so well what a flying fox is, that I should like him to see, ere he quits Brittany, what a flying wolf can do, when he sets his neck straight and goes for a cover in some far distant land."

"Let's be up and after them," I said in response. "Our horses are fresh, you know the country, and we may yet ' nick in ' for a fine run and a glorious finale."

In five minutes from that time we were up in our saddles again, St. Prix, on Barbe-bleu, leading us by short cuts and with rapid strides to the far end of the forest eastward. By this manœuvre leagues of cover had been avoided; and so lucky and judicious was the cast, that we had not reined up our horses for half-a-minute before we heard the hounds running hard and coming directly for us in full cry.

"We are over the scent, or we shall head him to a dead certainty," said the Louvetier, in an agony of despair. And scarcely were the words uttered when the hounds, flinging over the scent, came to a sudden check within a hundred yards of the spot on which we stood. True enough, we had headed the wolf back. The wily brute, hearing the clatter of our horses' hoofs, had turned short, and instead of breaking, as he meant to have done, sought again the darkest depths of that trackless forest. Not a word was spoken as the pack, bursting like a shell around us, felt eagerly for the scent, every hound doing his work as if the recovery of the line depended on him individually! Wider and wider they swept over the ground, busy as bees on every side, till a noble hound called Talleyrand, dropping his stern, threw his tongue like a clap of thunder. Then, what a scurry it was to catch him; and what a grand peal burst on the ear as the whole pack, getting together, rattled along with a roar of harmony that made the old forest rock to its very centre.

"That was a trying moment of suspense," observed the Louvetier, whose countenance had indicated intense anxiety during the check; "but I really think the untoward act of heading the wolf may yet turn to our advantage. Had he broken where he intended, his point would doubtless have been the rough covers of Bourbriac, some six leagues away; but now he may put his head for Hengoet, and give us a better chance."

So he did; and although some of the chasseurs, who carried their carabines and professed to know Dualt as intimately as their own pockets, rode hard for a shot at several points, the old villain never gave them a chance, but went, like an arrow, straight for the western side of the cover, and, breaking at the exact spot on which we had stopped the hounds on the previous night, he led us to Hengoet at a pace that would have blown a mountain fox. The jays screeched and the magpies chattered, migrating in dismay from their old secluded haunts, as the chase swept through Hengoet, pointing over the dreary waste direct *for* Locrist. The long-winded horns were now useless, indeed, an incumbrance to the chasseurs: the hounds, driving like fire over a prairie, needed not their aid, and the men had enough to do to manage their steeds and live with the cry.

"Go along, Frank!" said Keryfan, observing my cob still travelling as sweet as oil over the roughest ground; "go along! we've got a Tartar before us; and if they don't stop him in Locrist, he'll take us either to Trefranc or Conveau to a dead certainty."

"I only hope he may," said the Louvetier, as, clearing a bank higher than a parish pound, he landed in the road, where the fight took place between the butcher's horse and the Jersey dealer. At this point, however, the wolf turned, apparently mistrusting the safety of Locrist as much as the Louvetier; and leaving that valley to the right, he traversed the rough table-land, for many a mile overgrown with heather and stunted broom, direct for Trefranc. Thus far, but for the lanes and unfenced wastes, it would have been impossible to have lived with the pack. Six horsemen, however, thanks to St. Prix's pilotage, were not only well up, but were able, on descending the hill, to view the brute as he entered Trefranc not a hundred yards ahead of the hounds. Stout as he was, his heart must have quailed, as the Louvetier reined up his steed, irresistibly impelled to blow his horn and sound "*La Vue*" even in mid-chase. The three chasseurs, who carried their carabines, now separated, and galloping directly for the far side of the cover, hoped to intercept him if the wolf attempted to break away from this strong cover. For this fell purpose, happily, they were too late, though just in time to sound "*Le Débuché*," as the pack broke away, ten couple together, and every hound in his place, straight for Glomel, a cover of M. de Saisy's on a spur of the Black Mountains.

But he was doomed to fall ere he reached that sheltering retreat. A charcoal-burner, as the chase approached a small outlying coppice, snatched up his gun, and, firing at him in close quarters, shattered one of his hind legs, just above the hock; the hounds were on him in another minute, and after a terrible struggle, in which the peasant took an active part, the strong beast succumbed to numbers, and died fighting fiercely and mutely to the very last.

CHAPTER XXII.

Notwithstanding the unfeigned regret of the Louvetier that his hounds had not been permitted to pull down in fair chase this stout old wolf, I could not help remarking to Keryfan that the charcoal-burner's shot was a timely and fortunate stroke in favour of the hounds. They had run him incessantly, including drag and chase, from eight in the morning till three o'clock in the afternoon, and that, too, for a distance of ten leagues at least, over as rough a country as any in Lower Brittany. The wolf, however, during the latter part of the chase—that between Trefranc and Glomel—had been gradually increasing the space between him and them, and bid fair, judging by the beaten condition of the latter, to "knock them out of time," even if their courage and stamina had enabled them to maintain the chase for an hour longer, when night would have given him the victory.

It was fortunate, also, for the hounds that, by killing at Glomel, they were within such easy distance—only two leagues—from Carhaix; and certainly not less fortunate for our steeds and the running piqueurs, whose powers of endurance had been sorely tried by the straight-away tactics of this veteran wolf. Long and continuous, however, as the chase had been, the piqueurs, from their knowledge of the country and of the short cuts from one cover to another, managed to put in an appearance before St. Prix had sounded the *mort* for the last time at the death-scene. Nor was the change from Callac back to our old quarters an unwelcome prospect to any of us, great as had been the sacrifice and assiduous the attention of M. and Madame Thomas during our short sojourn at their hotel. Keryfan, indeed, indulged in the strongest expressions of thanksgiving on returning to Carhaix ; the separation from his dressing-case and clean linen having been the subject of sore misery to him even for one night.

Short, however, as the distance was between Glomel and Carhaix, the cross-country road over, or rather through, which we struggled proved by far the most wearisome work of the day, and did more injury to our horses than double the distance would have done on a better road. It was like travelling over Marsh Gibbon, or the Clayton Woods in Oxfordshire, after a wet November and a hard day with the Bicester Hounds—a heavy clay, that stuck like bird-lime to the horses' legs, and a slush, fetlock deep and more, so impeded their action that, had we not dismounted and driven them before us, Shafto's horse and mine would certainly never have reached Carhaix that night at all. The piqueurs and the hounds did better ; they travelled on the top of the hedge-banks, which, being broad and readily drained, afforded the driest footpath, or *troed-ffordd*, obtainable in those heavy lands.

By the time we entered the town of Carhaix it was dark night, and the glimmering old lanterns, slung on a single wire across the streets, and that, too, at long intervals one from the other, presented but a dismal light, and served rather to increase the gloom and render it only the more visible, as we groped our way through the narrow, silent avenue leading to the Hôtel la Tour d'Auvergne. Here and there, indeed, in a few of the best shop windows stood a wretched resin candle, imparting so faint a ray that, were it not for its locality, might well be mistaken for the glimmer of a glow-worm's tail : the object of the pale beacon being rather to show that customers would still be attended to than to exhibit the variety and quality of the goods within. Dismal as the aspect was, however, out of doors, right pleasant was it to see Marseillier's hearty and ever-cheerful countenance beaming with joy at our unexpected return, and bidding us welcome within his portals as if we had been old friends he had lost sight of for many a long day. Verily, his warm greeting acted like a cordial on our spirits as, wearied by the wet mud-work, and somewhat depressed by the surrounding gloom, we entered his comfortable hotel.

Then his tongue, which was as long as that of an ant-eater, rattled on like the clapper of a mill, the sole subject of its volubility being the rascality of Johnson, the Jersey horse-dealer.

"Butcher Kenwyn has had a narrow escape," said he; "and would probably have lost both his horse and his money if the police had not tracked this villain to his den in the very nick of time."

"What, our companion of yesterday?" inquired St. Prix, fairly taken by surprise at this startling intelligence.

"The same," answered Marseillier; "the man whom I introduced to your society as a gentleman, M. de St. Prix; for which act I owe you and your friends the most ample apology, as a greater rogue never assumed that honourable title."

"I did not at all like the looks of the man, I own," said St. Prix; "but inasmuch as he was a stranger, and apparently fond of hunting, I tried to overcome the prejudice one is too apt to feel, either for good or ill, at first sight, and so welcomed him to our hunt. But what has happened, Marseillier?"

The garrulous host then proceeded to relate the capture of the horse-dealer by a London detective, aided by a French commissary of police, and the circumstances, so far as he could learn them, that led to his apprehension.

"No sooner," said he, "had Johnson returned to Carhaix last

evening than he proceeded at once to Kenwyn's to claim the horse, 'Lunatique,' at the price agreed upon between them; and although the butcher was loth enough to part with so good a slave at so low a figure, his vice as a saddle-horse being heretofore deemed incurable, the threat of a *procès-verbal* so alarmed him that he reluctantly consented to accept Johnson's bill and give up the horse. But just as the latter was about to ride away in triumph, meaning to send off the horse next morning to Morlaix, for shipment to England, the officers pounced upon him, and, securing his wrists in steel manacles, carried him off to Port Rieux, thence to be conveyed to Jersey by the first vessel leaving the port for that island. The charge against him is that of arson, with intent to defraud an influential London fire-insurance society. It appears he had insured his premises and stock-in-trade for a large sum with that and other companies, and that, on three different occasions, fire had broken out most unaccountably in the lofts, consuming, as Johnson swore, a large quantity of hay and corn, for which he was twice paid in full by the insurance companies. Suspicion, however, fell upon him as the perpetrator; and his neighbours, after giving him the nickname of Guy Fawkes, did not scruple to warn the fire-office agents that foul play had been practised on them upon each occasion. So a vigilant eye was kept upon him on every side, even by his own stablemen; and when, for the third time, a fire was discovered in a loft, which no one but himself had entered for four-and-twenty-hours previously, a stringent inquiry was at once instituted by the chief insurance company; and, bit by bit, evidence was at length elicited which went to prove, beyond all reasonable doubt, that the premises had been fired by Johnson's own hand. In the meantime, while these preliminaries were being sifted, Johnson, not liking the turn affairs were taking, and probably cowed by his own conscience, quitted the island privately by night, taking passage in a fishing craft, which for a small sum landed him at Tréguier, on our own

s

coast. Secret as had been his flight, however, the non-return of the boat on the following day gave rise to inquiries, which soon brought the London detective on his track; and although no footprints remained to indicate his route o'er the pathless sea, the officer in pursuit, as if guided by instinct, drew the Brittany ports, one by one, from St. Malo westward, and at length hit off his man at the Tréguier Douanerie.

"From that point there was little further difficulty in the matter, for had the fugitive retired to the forest, and lived with the wolves, instead of coming here to hunt them and deal for horses, our police and gendarmes would have hunted him down, to a certainty, as weasels would hunt a rat in a bundle of faggots."

"Aye," said Shafto, "and would take care that he was sent to Cayenne afterwards, there to expiate his crime by expatriation and labour for the remainder of his life. In England convicts are kept at home, and fed on far better fare than falls to the lot of the honest, industrious labourer; and if they only happen to have plausible tongues, and a credulous chaplain, they are again let loose on the public to practise, as they too often do, with improved knowledge, their old craft of ruffianism and felony."

Apropos to ticket-of-leave men, a story is told of the late Lord Carlisle, who, when he was Viceroy of Ireland, undertook, from motives of philanthropy, to employ convicts thus liberated as domestic servants at Dublin Castle. Accordingly, one day after dinner, when two strapping ticket-of-leave men had been waiting at table, powdered and full-dressed as footmen in court livery, Lord Carlisle turned to an intimate friend, one of the wittiest and best known of diners-out in London, and asked him to give his opinion and tell him honestly what he thought of the plan.

"Well, my lord," said he, "I think if you persevere with it, you will soon be the only spoon left in this house."

This out-spoken opinion of course provoked a laugh, but did not prevent that kind, large-hearted man from going on with his scheme, and doing all in his power to find employment for the convict class released from prison on tickets-of-leave.

The next morning at breakfast, St. Prix, to our infinite regret, announced his intention of taking his hounds home to Morlaix so soon as they were able, after their recent hard work, to undergo the journey. "The duties of my office have now been fulfilled," said he, "in this district; and although I shall turn my back on you and it with much pain, the wolf," he added, dropping his voice to a whisper, "is a precious animal, and merits some consideration, at least on our parts, for the sport he shows in these wild forests. Besides, a blank day, such as we had at Locrist, I should be sorry to inflict on you ever again; and to guard against its recurrence for the future we must be careful not to diminish our present stock beyond a certain limit, or disappointment will be the sure result."

"No fear of that, I should hope," said I. "These forests of yours are so grand and continuous, and the population so sparse, that even if you had an Edgar ruling over you, the extermination of the wolf would be a thing impossible in such a country."

"True enough; it would take a long time and mighty efforts to exterminate the race; but still, as guns are now so commonly carried by all classes of the community, and every peasant, unless handsomely paid for it, murders a wolf as he would a viper, the stock might easily be so reduced as to render a find in these vast forests a matter of frequent uncertainty."

While this discussion was going on, the sound of a vehicle rattling over the stones, and brought to a standstill at the doors of the hotel, suddenly arrested the Louvetier's attention, who, springing from his seat, and announcing his belief that old Cæsar and the tufters had arrived from Callac, proceeded at once to inspect the condition of the gallant hound after the maltreatment he had met with on the previous day. A crowd of bystanders had already gathered round the *charette*, for, besides the maimed old warrior, whose head, fearfully swollen, was a mass of wounds, his gaunt enemy, the she-wolf, was lashed in a conspicuous position to the back part of the driver's seat, and looked even now

"Tremendous still in death."

The hound, of course, had his full share of admiration and pity from the sympathising townsfolk, who, however, saw enough of his crusty nature not to venture, beyond a few kind words, on caressing him in his present sore plight. But it was the wolf that excited the attention of the crowd to the highest degree. On it they never seemed to be tired of gazing; old people crawled out on crutches, and women lifted their infant children to take a view of the beast that all seemed to fear and hate equally. Nor was it strange that so destructive a brigand, living amongst them and yet doing his fell work so mysteriously that to catch him in the act is a matter of the rarest occurrence, should attract the curiosity of the suffering crowd, nor that, seeing him now powerless for further evil, the expression of joy and gratulation should be heard on every side. Accordingly, when the *charette* moved off towards the kennels (if the peasants' hovels appropriated to that purpose could be so called), the shout of exultation that followed it brought every soul, not already in the streets, to the open windows, and roused old Cæsar to such a degree that he roared like thunder in response. *Sejanus ducitur unco*, wrote the poet of a spectacle once exhibited in the streets of mighty Rome; and doubtless a similar shout might then have been heard to that which now followed the fallen wolf as, with a hook through its nose, its carcase was dragged triumphantly through the streets of old Carhaix. On examining the wolf subsequently, one of its hock-joints was found to be stiff, or anchylose, as the doctors would term it, from the bite of a steel gin, long since inflicted, and probably by that very gin consigned by St. Prix to the bottom of the Locrist river. From the pendant, long-drawn teats of the animal, it was inferred by Louis Trefarreg and other gnostics that she had produced at least four or five litters of cubs in her time, and had thus done good service to the lupine race, but incalculable damage to the community at large.

To have been quartered at Carhaix, even for one day, with nothing to do, would have been an infliction too terrible to bear ; and as the prospect of St. Prix's departure was imminent, Keryfan and I made up our minds to accept Shafto's kind invitation and pay him a visit at the Hermitage, where, he said, if the Louvetier thought wolves enough had been killed for the season, we might still find woodcock and wild-fowl to our hearts' content. However, as we still hoped to enjoy the good company of the Louvetier for a day or two longer, it was resolved, through Marseillier's influence, to request the *ouvriers* to gather together their trencher-pack, and give us a week-day hunt, instead of waiting for Sunday, the usual day devoted by them to that recreation.

A carpenter, who kept a couple of small, smart harriers, appeared to be the chief controller of this motley crew ; and he, on being promised a day's wages, readily consented to make every arrangement for showing us a grand *chasse* after the manner of the townsfolk, on the following day. I have already described the hubbub occasioned by the mustering of this party on a Sabbath morn ; but hitherto it had been quiet as a Quakers' meeting, compared with the discordant din that roused every soul in the town hours before daybreak on that especial occasion. So well had Marseillier managed the matter—he himself being a prominent member of the confederation—that every *ouvrier* who possessed a musket, or kept a cur, no matter how useless or how ignoble, made a point of joining the *chasse*, the object being not so much to enjoy the sport as to do honour to the Louvetier, who was looked upon as a public benefactor to Carhaix and the surrounding district.

Although the blasting of powder by those who were cleaning their guns, and the braying of horns, and the yelping of curs and the more distant thunder of St. Prix's hounds, began about five A.M., it was past seven before the whole body of the town chasseurs assembled in the *Place*, and thence, taking the Kergloff road, sallied forth to the chase of every beast and bird, from a linnet to a red-leg, or a squirrel to a roebuck, no game being too insignificant for their guns, nor too big for their capacious *carnassières*. But for a full description of the day's diversion the reader is referred to the next chapter.

CHAPTER XXIII.

CARHAIX is a very primitive town, and, so long as railways keep their distance, is likely to continue so for many a year to come. Beyond a couple of water-mills, to grind corn for the people, here are no other mills nor manufactories to induce commercial visits and increase the wealth of the place; nor, beyond the company of the Juge de Paix and the Doctor, both of whom had travelled beyond the precincts of their native department—the latter, indeed, even so far as Algeria—was there any society to which a stranger could fly for recreation when the business of the day was done, and night had drawn its dark curtain over the sombre town. There was one billiard-room in the place, it is true, but the seamed surface of its cloth indicated too plainly how many a game the moths had played on it, and scarcely would a schoolboy have been tempted to try his cue on such a table; and one café within a stone's-throw of the hotel; but, with the exception of an occasional *commis-voyageur*, and that, too, only after the breakfast meal, it was a rare occurrence indeed to see even the idlest lounger of the town cross its threshold.

So, a man sojourning at Carhaix, without resources of his own to fall back upon, either mental or muscular, literary or mechanical, sedentary or sylvan, would inevitably feel the worst horrors of isolation, and suffer the tortures of *ennui* to an unlimited extent; but to him who could be contented and happy with a moderate share of field and sylvan amusements, the forests of the immediate neighbourhood would afford a varied diurnal feast throughout the season: at least, this was the case at the period to which these papers refer. The *chasse* of the townsfolk, then, whatever that meant or might be supposed to include, was an outing we all accepted with pleasure, and, with the exception of St. Prix, we shouldered our guns and sallied forth, with the prospect at least of getting a good walk, if not of enjoying the day's sport. The only weapon carried by the Louvetier on the occasion was a club-stick, which, by the way, he handled in Breton fashion, grasping it by the small end, and making the knob do duty on the ground.

"No eye hath seen such scarecrows," exclaimed the immortal Jack Falstaff, when he flatly refused to march into Coventry before the ragged lot he was then leading; but Jack's experience would have been enlarged had he seen the strange medley of men and dogs that marched upon Kergloff that morn, for certainly in no quarter of the civilised globe could a wilder-looking set of bipeds be found than those of Cornouaille proceeding with their scratch-pack to the *chasse* in hunting costume. The latter, about twenty in number, with the exception of five harriers, were chiefly mongrels of the lowest type, from the form and features of which it would have puzzled the craftiest cynologist to discover to what class of dog they were most nearly allied, or what mongrel blood most predominated in their veins. In some, united under one skin, were the distinct characteristics of poodle, pointer, and butcher's dog, while others displayed a dash of hound's blood, grossly adulterated with that of the cur, the Italian greyhound, and the curly-coated poodle, the last of which appeared to be commingled with every description of dog that traversed, owned or ownerless, the streets of Carhaix. Then there was one grandee among the lot, a double-nosed Spanish pointer, with a skin fine as satin, a stump tail, and a magnificent head: he looked like

Endymion among the satyrs, and, if he had known it, would doubtless have felt thoroughly ashamed of the low company into which he had fallen.

The *ouvriers* and peasants, with three or four small shopkeepers who joined the party, amounted, all told, to fourteen men, but of these not more than eight carried their guns openly; the remainder, not possessing the qualification of a *permis de chasse*, were nevertheless equally well provided with a gun apiece necessary for that purpose. These were the braconniers, or poachers, who, in defiance of the law, followed the chase, early and late, far more keenly than their licensed neighbours; but, till fairly afield and clear of the gendarmes, each man carried his gun snugly doubled up within the folds of his outside wrapper, a skin garment one could scarcely dignify with the name of coat. The appearance of the men was wild and picturesque in the extreme; but, though clad for the most part in sheep and goats' skins of various colours, it would be a libel on Defoe's hero to say their accoutrements were equally well-fashioned with those of the castaway sailor, manufactured by his own hands. He, at least, was dressed *en suite* in goat-skin from head to foot, and, as his biographer represents him, must have looked, as he was, the king of that desert isle; whereas the ragged, parti-coloured attire of these men, torn as it was by the brambles, and patched with the coarsest sackcloth, gave them the appearance of a set of brigands, whose trade had been unproductive for many a long day. Then their heavy broad-brimmed hats and long curly hair, depending over both shoulders, added not a little to their savage aspect, though, to give them their due, a race generally less savage in nature than those Breton peasants it would be difficult to find in many countries boasting more culture and a higher civilisation.

But enough of the men; and now for their mode of chase. On turning from the high road into the broomy waste about a mile beyond Kergloff, the carpenter, who acted as commandant of the party, gave the **signal to** separate and form line abreast, **directing us, at the same** time, **to** preserve a distance of at least twenty paces **between one gunner** and another, and, above **all, to be careful how we** fired when game was afoot—a word **of caution especially** needful on the present occasion. Within a **league or so of** the town, on every side, the country is habitually so well combed by these artists that game of every description is provokingly rare; but as the radius is extended, partridge, red-leg **and** grey, woodcock and snipe, rabbit, hare, and roe-deer are found in sufficient numbers to warrant a good bag; while farther afield still, the fox, the wolf, and the boar are, **one or the other,** to be met with in all the great forests around.

Consequently, for the first hour, although hundreds of acres of gorse, broom, and heather were steadily **drawn at a** slow walk, **the men treading out the lower** growth with minute **care, and the dogs searching the higher and less** accessible cover equally close, **scarcely a dozen shots were fired** by the whole party, and those chiefly at **rabbits and a** woodcock here and there. While we were thus advancing slowly towards better ground, and a covey of red-legs, six in number, had fallen, every bird of them, to the peasants' guns, a low suppressed **whistle,** like that of a steam engine indicating danger ahead, passed rapidly along our line, and created intense alarm among the braconniers, some of whom instantly thrust their guns, muzzle forward, into the densest furze bushes, while others doubled them up, consigning the barrel into one pocket and the stock into another, within the folds of their capacious vests. Immediately after the last volley at the red-legs, **a** man's bare head had been seen peering, stealthily as it were, between two hillocks at some distance in front of us, as if it **was his o**bject to make **out the men who were** carrying guns and had just fired at the feathered game.

That the head could belong to no one but a gendarme, lying

in ambush to catch them, was at once inferred by the braconniers, and the dread they seemed to feel at the chance of being trapped by this law official would have been simply ridiculous if it had not led shortly afterwards to a serious assault on a poor peasant who had been the innocent cause of this panic. The man had been at work grubbing up stumps of furze and heather for firewood, and clearing the ground for future tillage, when, hearing the slugs whistling through the air in his direction, he had prudently placed himself behind some earth-mounds lying between him and the advancing party, and thence taking a survey of the proceedings, his head being unfortunately uncovered, he was at once mistaken for a gendarme, who had laid his helmet aside to avoid discovery—a ruse not unfrequently adopted by the gendarmes when stalking a suspected braconnier.

On coming up to the spot where the peasant lay extended on the ground, the indignation of the braconniers knew no bounds, swearing furiously, notwithstanding the man's protestations to the contrary, that he had intentionally played this trick on them, or "why," it was asked, "had his hat been laid aside when he showed his ass's head over and between the earth-mounds?" One of the braconniers, a well-known wrestler, being more excited than the rest, dashed savagely at the poor fellow as he was rising from the ground, and kicked him down again with his heavy sabot, till he fairly groaned with pain. When this assault, however, took place, those of the party who still carried their guns had gone on with the chase; nor, till we heard the man's cry for help, were we aware that the wrath of the braconnier had broken out into blows. "This is too bad," said Keryfan, who was the first to discover what had happened; "and that luckless peasant will be seriously maltreated, I fear, if we do not return at once to his aid." To the infinite disgust of the carpenter-commandant, St. Prix and Keryfan, facing about, proceeded forthwith to execute this errand of mercy; but before they could reach the spot the man had jumped on his legs, and, starting off like a tail-piped cur, disappeared, amid the shouts and laughter of the braconniers, in an adjoining thicket. He had been more frightened than hurt by the kick, which the bystanders averred was a mere touch of the toe—a wrestling exploit, designed to give the fellow a back fall, and nothing more. But the most provoking part of this affair was the delay occasioned in recovering the hidden guns; and as the braconniers not only possessed by far the best dogs, but knew best where game was to be found, Marseillier, who had always an eye to the pot, insisted on the advisability of going back, all hands, to aid them in the search, and then, with an unbroken line and all the dogs, to go to work again.

This arrangement, after some parley, was acceded to; but the time and trouble expended in finding the guns, shoved, as they were during the short panic, into the densest furze bushes, was a worry not to be described. At length, all being found, we managed to get once more under weigh together, and again the beat was resumed in right earnest. The space of country swept by the extended line could not have been less than four hundred yards, from St. Prix on our right to the pugnacious braconnier on the extreme left; so that, searched and trodden out as the ground was, it would have been almost impossible for a cock-mouse to have escaped detection within the limits of that doomed area. So regular and so systematic was the operation, and so expert the marksmen, that it seemed to me quite wonderful, not that game should be scarce, but that there should be any game at all within two leagues at least of the town of Carhaix, when battues like these were carried on hebdomadally throughout the season.

When a hare, the shiest of animals in this district, was found, and by sheer luck had escaped the shower of slugs that whizzed in her wake, the whole pack, including even the stately Sancho, scurried off in the wildest pursuit, and frequently were not seen again for ten, fifteen, or even twenty minutes. Bawling after them, as their masters did, was of no use whatever, and it was only when the five hounds came to a dead check that they gave the slightest heed to the signal that proved most effective for their recall. The first hare that succeeded in running the gauntlet securely got away, with every dog in full cry at her heels, and, as she had apparently been unhit, I made up my mind the pack were gone for just so long as that hare could stand on her legs before them. "You'll never see them again," I said, somewhat cynically, to the carpenter, "till they have either lost or killed that hare."

"Oh, yes, we shall," he answered, confidently. "The moment they come to a check the hounds will always return on hearing the report of my gun, and when their noses are up the mongrels soon follow."

In a few minutes afterwards the cry suddenly ceased, and the carpenter, who had all the while been straining his listening powers to the utmost, proceeded to exemplify the virtue of his novel signal by firing off both barrels into the air, the shot having been previously drawn, to save the ammunition. Jem Hill's famous *too-too*, when he rattled the old Heythrop back to their hunted fox, never did its work more promptly nor more effectively; for, exactly as the carpenter had represented it, almost immediately the hounds could be seen coming back, followed by the tag-rags soon after, until all had returned to their respective masters. On two or three other occasions, when a hare got away, this process was repeated, and always with the like success.

The habit of the hare, as we all know, is to run in circles, and to return to the ground from which she was first started; and doubtless the knowledge of this habit had been frequently turned to account by the carpenter, who, lying in wait for poor puss on her homeward journey, would rarely draw his trigger in vain at such a time. Then the hounds, with their half-reasoning powers, would quickly put two and two together, and discover that this shot, fired by their master, usually betokened the death of the hare ; and this inference probably led them to fly to the carpenter's signal so readily, whenever a check made it doubtful whether the scent could be recovered again or not.

As we advanced farther into the wilderness—for such, in the absence of all traces of cultivation, it certainly was—we came to a broad plateau in the direction of Huelgoet, so matted with heather, knee-deep and luxuriant on every side, that whenever old Sancho, carrying his head aloft in the air, and indicating by his earnest expression the immediate presence of game, came to a dead point, I almost made up my mind that a grouse must rise from such likely ground. But no ; the inevitable red-leg dominates here, and the grouse and blackcock are as unknown as the dodo in this land of ling. Yet anyone comparing these moors—producing as they do the whortleberry heather, the cranberry, and black fir—with the moors of Great Britain, would be puzzled to explain why grouse are not indigenous here as they are in our own favoured country ; for certainly the means of subsistence for them appear to be as abundant in this as in that land. The great landed proprietors of Lower Brittany might possibly take a leaf with advantage from the Highland laird's farm-book, and, by the cultivation of grouse, hither imported, convert tens of thousands of acres, now lying waste and unprofitable, into valuable shooting ground. Capital would, of course, be required even for such a stock; but here that commodity is rare indeed, and until it is supplied, these vast tracts of waste land must remain, we fear, as desolate to the sportsman's eye as they are profitless to the owner's pocket.

The red-legs, too, were not so plentiful as Marseillier seemed to expect them in such favourable ground, three coveys, numbering not more than six or seven birds in each, being all we sprung over a mile of moor. On descending a gentle slope of the hill facing south, and well sheltered from the westerly wind, which here cuts the tops of the trees exposed to it as with a shears, we came on as fine a patch of gorse, about an acre in extent, as ever grew in our midland shires. The very look of it would have made Osbaldeston's mouth water with expectation, for it was thick as a holly hedge, and would have tried the mettle of even a Furrier hound to face its long and close-matted spines. I heard the word "louarn" passed among the peasants, as three or four of them, breaking line, rapidly advanced to the opposite side of the cover; and as I knew that word to signify "fox" in the Breton tongue, it was clear they were making preparations to give him, if at home, a warm reception at the far end.

Thick and spiky, however, as the cover was, half-a-dozen men forced their way boldly into it, while the dogs, even the satin-coated Sancho, exhibited like courage, and seemed to take as little heed of the spines as if they had been cased in coats-of-mail, like armadilloes. One of the curs first opened, throwing his tongue with a defiant growl, as if half-terrified by the game he had found; then another and another squeaked in; and when the hounds joined cry, the peasants raised a yell that would have done credit to the wild hunters of the Black Forest. "He's up, for a thousand!" shouted Shafto to me, quoting Lord Kintore's favourite expression; "but with those mute peasants posted at the down-wind point of the far side, it will be a miracle if he gets clear away."

Nevertheless the miracle took place. In the heat of the uproar the fox, which was the game afoot, squatted down, and, throwing the yelping pack over the scent, doubled back and broke cover within five yards of my old smooth-bore. He was a fine fellow, yellow as a guinea, and carried his long, white-tagged brush level with his back, as he flashed ahead, like a comet over the arch of heaven.

"Give it him, Frank!" shouted Keryfan, who, although some forty yards off, was my nearest neighbour. "A fair broadside as I ever saw: give him both barrels."

But the *veteris vestigia flammæ* made my pulse tingle at the sight of him, and I felt as if my right arm would have been paralysed at the socket if I had struck down that noble fellow.

"No," I said, "I couldn't do it. Old memories would never forgive the deed; nor could I ever look Jack Russell in the face again if I once shot a fox——"

"Diable!" retorted he, with a look of surprise. "Not shoot a fox, Frank, in this wilderness? Why, here he is really a noxious animal—does a deal of mischief, and shows no sport. Depend upon it, the carpenter, who estimates the value of his skin at three francs, will set you down as a veritable Quixote for the rest of your life."

"Can't help that," I replied; and as I gave him a rattling cheer, his brush swung round, as if saying adieu and waving his gratitude for the clemency I had shown him. A little vicky, however, doubtless his co-partner in the patch of gorse, was less fortunate in her tactics, for, breaking at the point guarded by the peasants, three of whom fired at her one after the other, she fell dead to the last shot. Nevertheless, all three claimed a share in the spoil, swearing, each one of them, that his shot had dealt the fatal *coup*. As a sharp wrangle was the result, the carpenter, on being appealed to as arbitrator, pronounced at once in favour of all three claimants—that being the customary practice on such occasions.

Their eagerness for the skin, considering the grim poverty of these men, was scarcely to be wondered at, seeing it was valued at three francs; whereas a hare, skin and body, could be purchased in the market at Carhaix for fourteen sous, about two-thirds of a franc; a brace of birds or a couple of woodcock for sixteen sous, and a couple of wild-duck for one franc. The best beef, too, was only four sous, or twopence, a pound; and, in fact, at that period, before railways had equalised the prices of Europe, all the ordinary articles of food were equally low at Carhaix and the other inland towns of Lower Brittany. While on this subject let me add that the charge for board and lodging, both as liberal and good as a bachelor could wish, at the Hôtel la Tour d'Auvergne, was on a scale quite commensurate with the above prices, namely, seventy-five francs per head per month! For this sum, just three pounds, a comfortable bed-room, with linen, lights, and firewood, two bountiful meals a-day, including a variety of dishes as well cooked as they would have been at a first-class Paris restaurant, with vin ordinaire *ad libitum*, was supplied to the guest *en pension par mois*; and after a long experience and a somewhat extensive acquaintance with European hotels, I can with truth say I never fared better in my life than at the Hôtel la Tour d'Auvergne. But at the present time, if anyone ventured to ask for the like accommodation at the like price, Marseillier—if he, or rather Madame, still rules the roast of that "festive place"—would stare with astonishment, and probably return for answer, "*Nous avons changé tout-cela*."

But to proceed with the *chasse*. Descending now from the heathery plain, we drew a long scrubby cover, occupying both sides of a narrow valley, and filled with alders, sedge, and slush, the very ground, it might be imagined, to which woodcock would resort both for food and shelter. But after struggling for a mile "through bog, bush, and briar," we scarcely flushed above a dozen cock, and out of these bagged but seven along the whole line. The grass under this copsewood was far too long and thick to allow a free passage for the bird in his gait for food, and hence the paucity of that game in apparently so likely a spot. Farther on, however, the ground improved; the alders were higher, in fact, forest trees, and the bogs, generally bare, carried spare and broken patches of short grass over their quivering crusts; and here the cock were far more plentiful. But, with the trees above their heads, no temptation would induce the *ouvriers* or the braconniers to draw the cover, because, as they averred, it was of no use flushing the cock when it was impossible to shoot them in such a place. The dogs, too, only cared for flax, and would scarcely stoop on the haunt of a cock, much less quest when the bird rose. So there was nothing for it but to go in and tackle them ourselves. Accordingly, Keryfan, Shafto, and myself plunged into the thickest of it; and, with old Sancho for our chief aide-de-camp, we must have had twenty snap-shots in about so many minutes. Of course a great number were missed, every bird of which brought down such a cross-fire upon us that, unless some protecting angel had especially watched over our exposed bodies, the peasants must have bagged other and heavier game than mere woodcock. In vain we shouted for mercy or threatened reprisals; still every cock that escaped our guns brought a volley of slugs whizzing about our ears and cutting off alder-twigs on every side. At length, most unexpectedly, a hare jumped up out of a rushy bog, and, getting instantly beyond our ken, carried back all the dogs in full cry. The peasants, too, believing it to be a fox, darted off in pursuit, hoping to intercept the wily beast at the far end; and thus relieved, we enjoyed, without further annoyance, some very pretty shooting for a good hour or more.

But our danger was not yet quite over. On rejoining us in more open ground, the carpenter directed the whole party again to form line and to beat abreast as heretofore; and scarcely had this order been obeyed, when a rabbit, found by a cur, dodged back, and, coming straight towards me, endeavoured to force the line under my very legs. At that moment two slugs passed through a fold of my leather leggings, and the rabbit fell dead at my feet. The perpetrator, however, an *ouvrier* standing not twenty yards off on my left, did not go unpunished for his reckless temerity. The carpenter-commandant rebuked him fiercely, and told him he should be excluded evermore from joining the town *chasse*. This, too, as I afterwards found, was no idle threat; for over and over again the *ouvrier* came to beg my pardon most pathetically (though he would have done it again the next instant if a rabbit had given him the chance), praying that I would intercede with the carpenter and get him restored to his lost rank. But the carpenter was firm, saying he was a dangerous fellow, and would one day shoot one of his hounds if he allowed him to join them again.

What the total amount of the bag was at the end of the day nobody seemed to know; and, as every man carried the game he killed in his own *carnassiere*, and showed a strong repugnance to disclose its contents, the quantity and variety of the game gathered could not be accurately ascertained. It must have been a considerable lot, to judge from the *carnassieres*, most of which were filled to repletion, and must have heavily burdened the backs of the bearers. Nevertheless, the sturdy little fellows stood up well under them, and fagged and shot as if unconscious of the weighty load. The number of woodcock killed exceeded probably all the rest of the game, flax and wing, put together; but that number might have been doubled if the Bretons had gone manfully into cover and followed up their dogs *per crassum et per rarum*, instead of waiting for the birds to come to them on the outside, and only getting an occasional shot in open ground. But, excellent game-shots as many of them are in the open, they do not seem to understand the business of shooting in cover, provided the growth is at all thick, and higher than their own heads.

The approach of night now brought our *chasse* to an end; and as we had been continually drawing farther and farther afield, we could not have been less than three leagues from Carhaix when, for want of daylight, our steps were homeward turned: the dogs, indeed, had struck work long before, and, with the exception of old Sancho, followed each one his master's heels with a forlorn and spiritless air. This return journey was by far the most disagreeable part of the day's work; for, in order to avoid the slushy lanes, it was necessary to travel in Indian file on the tops of the banks, which, hollowed out by the peasants' sabots, and elevated some ten feet above the level of the land, presented to a stranger, at least, a most awkward and dangerous footpath on a dark night. How the peasants, so often returning in a state of intoxication to their homes in the country, travel over them without breaking their necks, is quite marvellous, when, from the holes and root-snags so often crossing the trough, a sober man finds it difficult enough to keep his legs with all his wits about him.

CHAPTER XXIV.

THE departure of St. Prix and his hounds from Carhaix cast a gloom not only on our little circle, now reduced to a trio, but also on the whole town. His yearly visits, in the execution of his duty as Louvetier, being productive of so much benefit to the community, both by the wolves he killed, as well as by the coin which he and the followers of his hunt so liberally expended, were the chief subject of interest and conversation for weeks before his arrival. But not for the foregoing reasons only was the Louvetier regarded as king of men in that district, nor because he was a Breton, noble by birth and lineage, and the proprietor of vast territorial possessions, extending from Callac, near the Black Mountains, to Morlaix, on the shores of the Atlantic, but rather because he was the most generous of human beings, kind and courteous to all classes alike—a nobleman, in every sense of the word, to the backbone. It is, however, as a chasseur that we have chiefly to speak of him in these pages. As such, whether as horseman or houndsman, thoroughly understanding the nature and habits of the wild game he hunted and the best mode of hunting it with success, he was second to none, either in Brittany or any other country. "In breeding my hounds," he said to me as we were one day jogging together to cover, " I don't go in so much for clean throats and straight legs as you do in England ; but if a hound will hit and drive, and throw his tongue when he hits—for those are the cardinal points in a hound's character—I'll never draft him for his uncomely looks."

"Quite right, too," I replied. "The chase of the present day, however, in your country and ours is so very different, that a hound in every respect qualified for your work would probably very soon find himself 'out of the game' in an English fox chase. Pace is the first consideration with us; and a hound must need be straight in his limbs and clean in his growth, or he could never blow his fox in forty minutes, and, above all, keep clear of the horses pressing on his very stern. These, with condition, are the indispensable points required in a modern English fox-hound; and if, on a flag-inspection, the puppy lack them, he is never given the chance of showing what merits he may possess as a chase-hound: he is drafted at once, and either goes to some inferior pack or to the colonies. So, as I scarcely need add, many a good hound, throaty and out-at-elbow—faults supposed to be incompatible with speed—is parted with in this way."

"No doubt about that," said the Louvetier. "A throaty hound almost invariably possesses a good nose, and, as I have often proved, a hound, though crooked in his legs as a *dachshund*, may be a rare one to drive for all that. But if you are so particular in your selection of hounds, the breeding and rearing of them must be a heavy item in the cost of producing a first-rate pack."

"Very true. Forty or even fifty couple of puppies are annually sent to walk to replenish the wants of a single grand pack, out of which number, after due trial and examination, both in kennel and afield, when they come up, perhaps not more than twelve or fifteen couple are admitted as entries into the regular pack; the remainder, as I have before stated, are drafted without a scruple."

"Ah, well," said the Louvetier, as if lost in astonishment at the boundless wealth of the English people, "a master of hounds must have a mine of gold at his command to support such a system."

"Doubtless," I replied, "vast sums have been expended from time to time in bringing the fox-hound to his present perfection; but as a general rule, men even of moderate means, provided they keep off the Turf and do not gamble, are rarely brought to ruin by keeping hounds; on the contrary, the office of M.F.H. is often considered the best safety-valve for a young man on succeeding to his property, as, being at least an innocent and manly occupation, its tendency is to divert him from less enjoyable and more hurtful pursuits."

St. Prix's observation, which I chronicled at the time, respecting the cardinal points required in a hound's work—namely, that he should be quick to hit, a hard driver, and never fail to throw his tongue on making a hit—left an impression on my mind that if it had fallen to his lot to handle a pack of fox instead of a pack of wolf-hounds, he would have earned a distinction in the craft equal to that of Mr. Tom Smith or Anstruther Thomson, and, like the latter, would have taken to " Welsh blood," or any blood, no matter how unfashionable, that possessed in a superior degree the above requirements.

On the following day, after St. Prix's departure for Morlaix, our horses having been already sent forwards, a voiture, drawn by a pair of dun cobs, the property of a M. Dinguff, conveyed Keryfan, Shafto, and myself with great comfort to Gourin—the distance being just five leagues, and the charge for conveyance, including the coachman, only eight francs. Our destination being the Hermitage, still some four leagues farther—access to which had never yet been attempted by a carriage slung upon springs—ourselves and baggage were now consigned to some rough ponies, which a friendly charcoal-burner for a few francs had placed at Shafto's disposal. Unkempt and grimy to the last degree were these poor ill-conditioned beasts; and when Keryfan's

Parisian dressing-case and **grand** portmanteau, ornamented with fancy buckles and brass **studs, were** strapped aloft on the back **of** one of them, it was impossible to forbear a laugh, so strange was the contrast between the sorry beast and the gay burden. But with **this** weight only on his back, the charcoal-burner seemed **to think the** animal insufficiently freighted, for he constantly solicited Keryfan to mount behind his baggage, avowing that, by the additional weight on his rump, the fore-legs of the beast would be less likely to give way. One glance, however, **at the** knees, which had been recently sorely barked, convinced **Keryfan he had** far better trudge any distance on his own legs than trust his neck to so frail a jade.

The Hermitage has already been described in a previous chapter as the residence fitted up by Shafto for the purpose of pursuing the wild, fierce game inhabiting the forests that surrounded **it on** every side; and so far as its out-of-the-world, solitary site **could warrant** it, no human habitation was ever better entitled to that name. The robbers' nest occupied **by the** Doons in **that Exmoor** gorge could scarcely have been more inaccessible—having a rocky waste on one side, ravines and forests **on the** other, with a footpath, only fit for a goat, leading **up to its** rude and massive walls. Yet that rugged approach, **from long** usage, had become as familiar to Shafto as the steps **of his club to a** lounger in Pall Mall; **on** foot or on horseback, **by** night **or by** day, **he** traversed it with equal confidence. His friends, too, remote and roadless as the country was, found their way to the Hermitage with little difficulty; and once there (for, as Keryfan said, was it not **a** temple dedicated conjointly to St. Hubert and Hospitality?) the difficulty was to get away.

While on the subject **of** inaccessible localities, **an** anecdote of **the great** Bishop of Exeter, Henry **Phillpotts,** occurs to my mind, **and** may not be inaptly quoted on the present occasion. In that vast and unwieldy diocese, over which he presided for upwards of thirty-eight years with such signal success, making his presence and his power known from the Phœnician mines of the Cassiterides to the rugged cliffs of Prawle Head, he was for some time baffled in his wish to visit the parish of St. Cuthbert, by the rector, who, to every proposal on the part of his lordship to come and administer the rite of Confirmation to its inhabitants, ever answered that, the road being so steep and impassable, he doubted the possibility of his being able to reach St. Cuthbert on wheels, but that he (the rector) would bring his candidates to meet his lordship in some adjoining and more accessible parish. Now the rector, a man of fair means, had yet conceived a reasonable dread of the expense attendant on entertaining the bishop and his retinue even for one night; and hence, in reality, the plea of bad roads, by which he hoped to scare the prelate from taxing his hospitality. In every country house, however, for miles around, wherever the bishop dined, there he invariably met the rector of St. Cuthbert; and at length, on hearing the old plea again repeated, he could restrain himself no longer. "Well, Mr. K——," said he, in his measured, caustic, yet most courteous style, "if the *access* to St. Cuthbert be so difficult, the *egress* from it appears to be easy enough, for I have had the pleasure of meeting you every night at dinner for the last week." It need scarcely be added that after such a rebuke a Confirmation was held at St. Cuthbert the first time the bishop visited that neighbourhood again.

It is said of Julius Cæsar that he felt greater pride in making a good road than in gaining a battle; and we know for a certainty that, wherever his conquering legions marched, his roads paved the way for future civilisation, and left a mark behind them ineffaceable to this day. Yet he, the "Victor hostium et sui," was content to describe one of his grandest achievements in that line by the following curt but most comprehensive inscription:

"Hanc viam, inviam, rotabilem fecit.—J. C."

From the condition of the roads, however, within many miles of the Hermitage, it must be considered very doubtful if Julius Cæsar, after conquering the various tribes of Armorica, ever penetrated the rugged region of Celtic Gaul which is known as the backbone of Brittany.. Nor did the Romans occupy that country permanently till the year A.D. 383, when a Roman officer called Maximus, resident in Great Britain, revolting against the Emperor Gratian, withdrew to Brittany, and, carrying with him two Roman legions and a vast number of Celtic islanders, conferred the government of Armorica on Meriadec, a warlike Celt and a chief among his followers. This, the first great emigration of Britons into that province, was soon succeeded by many others, the immigrants finding peace and protection under the rule of the Celtic chief.

Shafto, who had preceded our party by an hour or more, came out to meet and welcome us as we hove in sight of his *porte-cochère*, and the loud greeting he gave us at a distance of some hundred yards, reminded me of that given to Ben Jonson when he was approaching the country mansion of his supposed friend, Drummond of Hawthornden.

"Welcome, welcome, honest Ben!"

shouted the host, as he spied the poet wending his way on foot up a stately avenue leading to the house.

"Thank'ee, thank'ee, Hawthornden!"

responded the expected guest, with that readiness in rhyming for which he was so remarkable. But the poet laureate would have eaten his chop at the Mermaid Club with his friends Raleigh, Shakspeare, Beaumont, and Fletcher with a thankful heart, could he have foreseen the cruel terms in which Drummond described his character, after a three-weeks' visit, from notes taken at the time, and at a subsequent period published to the world. In this respect, however, Shafto's welcome was a very different one;

he would have gone to the stake rather than treated the man to whom he had given the right hand of fellowship with such disloyalty.

Amid a chorus of music, too, from hounds, setters, and spaniels, every one of which had come out from his *barrique* far as the chain would permit, we were welcomed to the Hermitage; while Owen Mawr and his busy little wife proceeded at once to relieve the ponies of their baggage, and to express in the strongest terms their delight at the return of their master and the cessation of the solitude to which of late they had been so frequently condemned. It did one's heart good to witness the honest, homely fashion in which these uncontaminated rustics sought to serve us in every possible way; nor, from their downright refusal to accept a single franc on our departure, could the imputation of mercenary motives be attributed to their service, but, on the contrary, it was all given, beyond a shadow of doubt, as a veritable labour of love and a homage due to their master's guests. "Heu pietas! heu prisca fides!" may we well say in this independent age of education and communism.

Flakes of snow had been falling intermittently during the day, and before we had fairly settled into our nooks at the Hermitage, the leaden aspect of the world around gave token of more to come. The rocky slopes of the hill-side had already changed their hue, and the dark forests below, unruffled by the wind, were gradually growing whiter and whiter under the soft feathery flakes now gathering densely upon them.

"I don't like the look of the weather at all," said Shafto, as he led Keryfan and myself across the courtyard to a kind of outhouse which he called his larder, "for should it continue snowing thus steadily for the next twenty-four hours, it will go hard with us if Owen Mawr has not made ample provision for the impending siege."

So saying, he flung open the door of the outhouse, which,

from the contents it revealed, looked far more like a butcher's shop than an ordinary larder; for there, suspended by hooks to a cross-beam, hung a calf and two little sheep newly flayed, the hind quarters of a bullock, and a couple of heads of wild boar recently killed in the forest of Kilvern by Kergoorlas' and St. Prix's hounds.

"Provision for a month at least," observed Keryfan, "and no fear of short allowance even for a longer period, provided the garrison counts, as it now does, but five heads."

"Add five-and-twenty to that number, and you will be nearer the mark," said Shafto; "for every hound will have his black bread moistened with good broth out of that stock. Annette is a rare kennel-feeder, and would help a favourite hound to the first cut out of a leg of mutton sooner than see him stinted in his food."

During this time a lively conversation was going on between Owen Mawr, Annette, and the charcoal-burner, whose ponies, already well fed, stood with their heads close to the *porte-cochère*, as if eager to be off on their homeward route. But there was a hitch somewhere; and, from the ominous expression of the charcoal-burner's face, who ever and anon looked upwards with alarm, shaking, as he did so, an avalanche of snow from his broad-brimmed hat, it was evident that he was not so ready as his beasts were to turn his back on the hospitality and safe shelter afforded by the Hermitage. "It's only three leagues off, I tell thee; not a mètre more," said Owen Mawr and Annette in the same breath, bent, as they had welcomed him, to "speed the parting guest" to the utmost of their power. But the guest, like the Squire of the pad in the old ballad, who

"Often took leave, but was loth to depart,"

still lingered on the threshold, urging that night was at hand, and that wolves would beset his path ere he could possibly gain the walls of Gourin.

"Here, then," said Owen, impatiently thrusting a box of lucifer matches into the man's hand, "take that for thy protection. Thou hast enough there, with the aid of St. Francis, to scare all the wolves in Brittany."

"I would rather trust to these walls than to all the saints in the calendar," said the charcoal-burner; "and as for the matches, let me but listen to the crackling faggots on thy hearth-stone, and I'll give thee all I have earned by my day's labour with a thankful heart."

Vain, however, were the poor fellow's entreaties for further hospitality. As well might he have hoped to move the mercy of Pluto and the Eumenides as that of Owen Mawr and his wife, who, seeing it was but the commencement of a snow-storm, apprehended no danger whatever from the attack of wolves, and attributed the man's disinclination to quit the Hermitage to his appreciation of the good fare he had found therein. His fears, they believed, were a mere sham; and accordingly, as Owen all but thrust him from the gate, Annette bid him, with a pitiless grin, tell his beads every yard of the way, or the Loup-garou would have him as well as his horses before he reached Gourin.

But the joke was a grim and a cruel one for the charcoal-burner's ears. His beasts, indeed, trotted merrily out the moment the gates were opened, but he himself went forth to the lonesome hill-side with the dread of a man driven to his doom. That very night the wail of a wolf startled Annette in her dreams, and quicker than lightning to her thoughts came the visage of the charcoal-burner pleading for protection at the gates of the Hermitage; and as, again and again, the dismal howling was answered by other wolves near and around the circuit of the walls, she could not help fearing the poor fellow's forebodings would be realised to the bitterest end. Yet, though safe as within the walls of a fortress, in listening to the weird cry of the brutes, a chill of awe penetrated to her very marrow, and she could no more have slept during that hideous concert, broken as it was at intervals by the savage uproar of the hounds, than if the walls of the Hermitage had been assaulted by a band of brigands. At length the sharp report of a gun, that rang through the building, brought the serenade abruptly to a close, and effectually scared the brutes, at least for that night, away from the premises.

It was Annette who had fired the gun, her husband having point-blank refused to rise from his bed, declaring, as she roused him to do so, that the howling of the wolves was music to his soul, and that he was right glad to find there were still a few left for their sport another season. The window of their sleeping apartment, however, formed in the outer wall, and looking out on the forest, happened to be in close proximity to the larder, in which the newly-slaughtered meat was hung, and this attraction for the wolves' noses caused them to make frantic efforts to clamber in at that recess; and it was not until Annette had twice seen the pricked ears of a wolf, as he clung by his claws to the sill of the window, that she could summon courage to seize her husband's gun, and fire it in the face of the assaulting foe.

The next morning, on examining the ground, not a trace of the wolves, beyond the indentation of their claws on the mossy wall, could be anywhere seen, so steadily had the snow fallen even till break of day. The layer could scarcely have been less than two feet deep; and, as there had been no wind to cause it to drift and accumulate in particular spots, an uniform depth of snow had enamelled the whole country, and transformed its withered, haggish old face into one of exceeding fairness and dazzling beauty.

"Have you any idea how many they were?" said Shafto, interrogating Owen Mawr as to the night attack.

"By their tongues, I should say not more than three or four—probably an old bitch-wolf and a brace of young ones."

Annette, however, who, head and shoulders out of window, was supervising the examination of the ground and wall, was of a different opinion. "How can he know their number when, the more the wolves howled, the louder he snored in answer? I'll be sworn there were a dozen at least knocking hard for admission at this window."

That, of course, was an exaggerated estimate, suggested by the fear and imagination of the woman, as there had been no snow previously, nor weather bitter enough to cause the wolves to pack for mutual help and more aggressive depredation. But Shafto, pretending to accept Annette's view of the number, shook his head ominously, and said, with a solemn air, "Then, I fear me, that poor fellow and his ponies made a grand meal for the brutes when they found themselves baulked by our walls."

"God forbid!" said the woman, now stung to the quick at the recollection of the merciless manner in which she and her husband had treated the man. "If indeed such a fate has befallen him, the Loup-garou will terrify my thoughts, awake or asleep, to my dying day."

About an hour afterwards Owen Mawr was despatched to Gourin, with instructions to inquire if the charcoal-burner had arrived safely at that town, and if, as Shafto himself much doubted, the ponies had been equally fortunate; for, if the wolves had attacked them, the man would have been utterly powerless to protect all his four little beasts with a box of lucifer matches only, although, by standing over one, he might possibly save its life from the cowardly brutes. Not a scrap of intelligence, however, could Owen gain of the man and his ponies at Gourin; neither he nor they had been seen in the town since they had quitted it on the previous day; nor could any tidings be gleaned from the gendarmes, who were at once started in search of the man, by order of the chief officer commanding that force.

A whole week had elapsed with a similar result—no news of the charcoal-burner—during which time the conscience-smitten alarm of Annette and the misgivings of her husband would have been painful to witness, if Shafto's faith and argument had not assured us that in all probability neither the man nor his ponies had been attacked at all. "For," said he, "I looked at my watch when Annette fired off the gun—it was then three o'clock; and as the wolves of the neighbouring forest, attracted by the fresh meat, certainly passed the livelong night under our walls, it is quite clear that they, at least, could have had nothing to do with the charcoal-burner's disappearance after he quitted our gates. To my mind, the long serenade they gave us is a sufficient *alibi* in their favour to acquit them of this charge."

On the seventh day after that memorable night Shafto, by St. Prix's especial request, had taken his hounds to the forest of Glomel, to kill, if possible, a wolf that had been doing great damage to the cattle of the Count de Saisy's tenants. This forest lay due east of the Hermitage, near Rostrenen, on the northern slope of the Black Mountains; and although, from one point to the other, the distance could not have been less than four leagues, we found ourselves—men, horses, and hounds—at the cover-side at half-past eight o'clock, soon after the break of day. There was still a thin layer of snow covering the earth, so the piqueurs did their work with little difficulty, bringing back a goodly list of the rough game that had gone into lair during the night, namely, badger, fox, chevreuil, and one old wolf—the latter, from his broad splay fleet and long claws, being, without a doubt, the culprit on whose doom we were bent. Accordingly, by the help of the snow and a couple of rare tufters, we soon roused him from his slumber, and in less than half an hour six couple more were hard at him, waking up the old woods with a roar of melody. Before, however, the sharpest of the peasants could reach the far end of the forest, the wily brute had broken cover, and like an arrow had gone straight away for Pontargoned and the great forests beyond Huelgoet.

The scent was too good to stop them, so there was nothing for it but to follow the hounds as we best could to that vast woodland; and luckily, the roads, proving more favourable than usual, enabled us to catch an occasional view of them as they broke into open ground or topped a hill on their onward course. But now arose a difficulty with which, in that labyrinth of cover, it was hopeless to contend. No sooner had the hounds reached the dense portion of it that lies on the Monts d'Arrée side, than a brace of fresh wolves were roused, and from that moment Shafto, Keryfan, and I did our utmost to stop the hounds. This, however, was no easy task, and but for the accidental help of some peasants engaged in felling timber and clearing the brushwood, it would probably have been more than our jaded horses would have enabled us to accomplish.

While thus engaged, an unexpected but a very welcome object, in the form of a man, emerged from a turf cabin hard by. This was no other than the lost charcoal-burner, who, little aware of the intense anxiety occasioned by his disappearance, was somewhat surprised at the warm greeting he met with from our party. His story was soon told. On quitting the Hermitage, he had travelled but a short distance before he fell in with a company of woodmen proceeding to Pontargoned; and, being persuaded by them to take a share of the labour in which they were engaged, he had struck in, and from that day followed the vocation at which we had found him. On hearing the glad tidings of the man's safety, Annette's relief can scarcely be described, and the following night—the first for a whole week, as she declared—were her dreams undisturbed by the terrible Loup-garou.

CHAPTER XXV.

It was a terrible dusting the old **wolf** gave us that day at Pontargoned ! So beaten **were some of the** leading hounds that getting them home to their kennel **at all** that night was a **business** of no little patience and labour. Indeed, but for the help of our hunting-thongs, attached **to their couples, by which we were able** to lift them along through the miry lanes, many **a time** would they have curled themselves **up by the wayside, and abandoned the painful journey in despair.** When **the Hermitage was at** length reached, it must have been forty-eight hours **afterwards** ere a single hound ventured to stretch his limbs or show a nose outside his *barrique;* Annette, however, taking care to supply each one with food as he lay, too weary to rise, recruiting his lost power and indulging in the warmth and comfort of his ferny couch. The horses, too, were even more beaten than the hounds, Shafto's stout old hunter, Mirabeau, refusing his corn for a week afterwards, and my cob being miserably tucked up in the flank, and looking more like a " garran " **than** the compact, light-stepping steed he was when I first brought him wolf-hunting into these parts. **Bad** grooming, cold stables, and long distances home after the sport of the day was over, were of course the **chief** causes of this change ; for **I took especial** pains myself to see that his daily rations of corn and hay were regularly supplied, the oats being **very dry and of the best** quality, although, from their being thrashed on the bare ground where they grew, the dirt and grit intermixed with them detracted considerably from their weight, and rendered the use of the sieve an absolute necessity. My groom, a trusty Breton, knew more about milking a cow than strapping and feeding a horse; but if he had been skilled as one of Scott's stable-boys, the usually wretched accommodation, in the form of draughty, undrained hovels, in which a bar only separates one horse from another, and through which the winds career as through a windmill, would have defied his utmost efforts to keep a horse, doing hard work, in good form and condition. I allude, however, to the stables of the country inns, not to those of private houses, and to a time when the interior of Brittany was almost as little known by foreigners as Namaqua Land is at the present day.

A wolf, unless crippled, will rarely go to ground, however pressed by hounds, or however tempted by the hollow character of the country: he keeps going so long as he can stand; and, although shier and wilier than most beasts of the forest, he is up to none of the dodges in chase practised by the hare, the fox, and the sinking stag. That day at Pontargoned and Huelgoet he might have gone to ground a hundred times into one of the numerous lead-mines, shafts, and caves with which that district abounds. So frequent and so deceptive were some of the old shafts, being covered with wood long perished and utterly unsafe, that it was only by a sharp look-out we were able to steer clear and avoid those hidden pitfalls scattered around us on every side. Keryfan, indeed, had a very narrow escape, his horse scrambling over one, as the whole fabric of the woodwork gave way and fell with a crash into the abyss below; and sunk as some of these pits are to a depth of several hundred feet into the silurian rocks, it must have proved a fatal fall to both, if the steed, with wondrous activity, had not gained a secure footing on the opposite bank. There are instances on record, however, which indicate that such accidents have happened with impunity both to man and horse; and as two of these have occurred to gentlemen in the West of England, and can be authenticated by witnesses alive at the present day, they are well worthy of being chronicled in these pages, and rescued from the oblivion to which otherwise they would soon be inevitably consigned.

The first accident took place with Mr. George Templer's hounds, the famous "Let-'em-alones," which kept the South of Devon alive for so many years, before a regular pack of foxhounds was established in that division of the county. A fox had been found in Bovey Heathfield—a district in which coal-pits had been sunk in former days, but which, being long abandoned, were covered over with boughs of trees to prevent the farm-stock from breaking their necks. The scent was first-rate, and the hounds trimming him at a rattling pace, when the Rev. Henry Taylor, one of the finest horsemen ever known in that or any other country, in landing over a fence, found his horse's hind-quarters giving way, and only able to save himself from falling backwards by a tremendous effort with his fore-legs. He was riding his celebrated "Nunky" at the time; and instantly being aware that Mr. William Ley was coming at the fence close on his heels, he shouted wildly at him to hold hard, and avoid the coal-pit into which he had himself well-nigh fallen. But the warning came too late, and either was not heard or was disregarded: over they shot and down they went, horse and rider, head foremost into the pit, the whole frame of the woodwork giving way under the weight, and falling before them into the gulf below. This probably saved their lives; the mass of soft, decayed wood acting as a buffer, and easing the force of the final concussion. However that may be, neither the man nor the horse were even bruised seriously by the fall; for, unlike Marcus Curtius of old, by the help of a few ropes they not only reappeared speedily in the land of the living, but did not quit the hunting-field till the hounds went home to their kennel. This anecdote was told to the present narrator by the Rev. Henry Taylor himself—alas! long since summoned to the "Land o' the leal"—a man who would have gone to the stake, aye, and fired it with his own hand, rather than have told a lie.

The other casualty is still more remarkable. In 1848 two gentlemen, meeting by appointment on Roborough Down, soon came to terms in dealing for a clever little bay mare called "Jingalina," the one buying her, as she stood, with saddle and bridle on, and the other walking back, a distance of eight miles, to his home and heronry on the blue Tamar. The latter was Mr. Walter C. Radcliffe of Warleigh, the other the Rev. Richard Sleeman, vicar of Whitchurch, in that neighbourhood. Jingalina's previous history, however, claims a few words ere we proceed to the details of her marvellous escape, the account of which shall be given in the written and expressive language of her quondam owner, Mr. Radcliffe. She had carried him for two seasons with admirable safety and endurance, chiefly with Mr. Russell's hounds, in the north of Devon, and occasionally with those of the Duke of Beaufort. In a brilliant run with the latter from Hullavington to Cirencester, poor John Baily and Mr. Radcliffe on Jingalina had far and away the best of it from first to last; the little mare going home as merrily as if she had been only doing her morning exercise. Notwithstanding her merits, however, Mr. Radcliffe, being about to travel abroad, found it expedient to part with her, and she then passed into Mr. Sleeman's hands.

One morning, not long after this event, that gentleman's groom, a man called John Cowell, who had been exercising Jingalina and another horse on Whitchurch Down, returned with a rueful countenance to his master, saying, "Plaize, sir, I've a-lost the mare:" and all he could explain was that she had suddenly gone down into the earth, clean out of sight. Mr. Sleeman hurried at once to the spot; and, finding the mare was alive, proceeded to a neighbouring mine, and procured the help of several men with shears, pulleys, and ropes. A man then volunteered to go down, stuck a candle in his hat with a lump of clay, and was lowered to a considerable depth; but, his heart failing him, he shouted out to be pulled up again, declaring, as he came to grass (a miner's term), that the air was so foul he could not live below.

Another man, however, whose heart was in a better place, enquired if the mare was alive; and, on being told she was, said confidently: "Then, if she can live, I can; so lower away, my lads:" and down he went fourteen fathoms—eighty-four feet. He was down some time, and at length the signal came to "Pull up;" and up he came. "The mare," said the man, "is resting on her tail, with her fore-legs reared against the side of the shaft. There is a deal of slush and water, but I managed to fix the rope with a timber-hitch round some part of her body. So, all hands, haul away!" Eighteen stalwart men then set to work; and, in a minute or two, up she came to the grass-bank, whinnied and neighed when she saw the light, and was on the point of being released from the rope, when suddenly, either from curiosity to see the mare, or some other cause, the men let go their hold; and, not being fairly landed, down she went again with the running rope to the very bottom of the pit.

Sleeman was now in despair. Indeed, from the first he had given up the mare as lost; but he was now certain she must be dead. However, the men were for making one more trial; and finding the rope fast to something, they hauled away, and up came the mare for the second time, the running noose being firmly fixed round her fore-pastern joint. Safely landed this time, she got up, shook herself, and walked home to her stable, *without a serious scratch.* After this event Mr. Sleeman rode the mare with hounds for fifteen seasons; and then, when done for hunting, drove her on easy journeys, and bred from her; one of her foals, by Nutshell, who was by Nutwith, being ridden at the present time by a lady, a very pretty one too, in the neighbourhood of Plymouth. Jingalina must have been over thirty years old when she died; and oftentimes during Mr. Sleeman's possession of her the sum of £100 offered for the mare would not tempt him to sell her. "No," he would say; "she and I have seen so many adventures together, I can't part with Jingalina."

At the time of the accident a very young lady, the cousin of Mrs. Sleeman, was riding a pony on one side of the groom, while Jingalina disappeared on the other. That lady is now the wife of a clergyman residing just three miles from Folkestone, and from her own lips, in the summer of 1873, imprinted as all the circumstances are, ineffaceably on her memory, I heard Mr. Radcliffe's written account corroborated to the very letter; he having had it "from his dear, staunch, true old friend, Dick Sleeman, a matter-of-fact man, too fearless to prevaricate, too honest to lie."

Of all sports of the field known to a Breton, that of wolf-hunting is by far the most engrossing; to St. Prix it was the grand passion of his life; and, consequently, the preservation of a sufficient stock of game for hunting being ever uppermost in his thoughts, he spared neither expense nor trouble in quietly promoting that object among the landowners he could trust throughout the vast district over which his authority as Louvetier extended. But, owing to the serious depredations so often committed by the wolves, it required no little tact, and sometimes no trifling expenditure, on his part to keep the community in good humour on this point; nevertheless, having no keepers to deal with, he managed the matter admirably. Among the peasantry not a shadow of suspicion ever crossed their minds that his hounds were kept for any other purpose than that of destroying the noxious brutes infesting the land; and this impression was most natural, seeing that **no sufferer** appealed to him in vain, and that in pursuing a wolf he meant killing him, and rarely failed in doing so, **if he** had been guilty of **any daring outrage** or had acquired an especial ill-fame among the country-folk. This being the rule **of the** Louvetier, it was impossible to question the *bonâ fide* manner **in which** he fulfilled the duties of his office, which, if it **provided him** and his friends with a wild and attractive **sport,** contributed in no small degree to the public good. Yet he looked on a she-wolf late in the season as a master of hounds in this country looks on a vixen in February; and no rat-catcher, professing to clear a barn of its rats, but somehow or other allowing the heavy-with-young to escape his clutches, could do his work more adroitly than St. Prix when a she-wolf in a similar condition was roused by his hounds.

Under these circumstances, Shafto, who had been brought **up with a full** knowledge of the conventional laws that govern **fox-hunting in** England—laws which for moral force might laugh **to scorn those of Draco—was scrupulously** particular in deferring to the **Louvetier's wishes** in all matters relating to the chase of the wolf **and the boar;** and as already, by the help of Kergoorlas' and Shafto's hounds, a larger number of heads and hides had been accounted for than in any previous season since the appointment **of St. Prix** to that office, our forest bill of fare was restricted to **the pursuit of** smaller game, of which there was certainly no lack in the immediate neighbourhood.

The woodcock, which before the commencement of the snow had been **scattered** broadcast **over the** vast covers, whether stretching upwards **to** the highest ridge of the Black Mountains **or down** into the hollow and sheltered valleys below, were now **driven** to a limited area **kept** open in well-known spots by warm springs **and** running water—a concentration that enabled us to find **every cock in** the country with one old setter, belled for the purpose, **and** taught to break point and flush his game at the command of the gunner. As is usual, however, with woodcock on the occasion of hard frost or a heavy fall of snow, great numbers of them, impelled by the strong instinct of self-preservation, migrate at once into lower latitudes, winging their way in the gloom of night to the islands and southern shores of the Mediterranean Sea, where, as many a British soldier knows, they are to be found in great abundance at certain times. While the snow lasted, our bag averaged twelve couple a day, with a few teal and duck to vary the sport. But every day the cock grew scarcer and scarcer; and at the end of ten days many a mile of boggy ground might be traversed without flushing a single cock, "the whole fabric of them," as old Cleave, a famous keeper at Tetcott, used to say, "having been destroyed by guns and springles, or gone to a happier land."

But, as the cock fell off, the wildfowl, duck and teal especially, harassed by the cold blustering winds that followed the snow and gave no rest on the sea-coast, dropped in plentifully—insomuch that, unlike a cover, a brook supplying capital sport on one day proved equally productive on the next, every evening and morning bringing in a succession of fresh arrivals from the adjoining sea-shore. Nothing in the way of gunnery, to my mind, could surpass this sport—not even cock-shooting, which, to the gunner, is held to be what fox-hunting is to the hunter—so attractive were the running streams, and so varying the incidents connected with knocking down and recovering the wounded game.

About the tenth day after our arrival at the Hermitage, the snow having entirely disappeared, a sharp frost set in; the wind, from N.E., being "forbiddingly keen" and cutting, and the hill-tops a mass of ice. "This is the very weather for the Scaër brook," said Shafto, as he drew up the blinds of my bedroom window, and in vain tried to clear away the fretwork of frost that was encrusted on every pane; "the upper branch of the stream will be alive with fowl, and Keryfan thinks with me that we should be off at once, while the wind is so favourable."

"So do I," said I; and not unmindful of the good old motto, "*Carpe diem*," in a few seconds I was shaking the dewdrops in a copious shower back into my tub; and long before Keryfan had finished curling his whiskers, both Shafto and I were hard at the coffee and savoury dishes provided by the "neat-handed" Annette for our morning repast.

Although, from the old town of Scaër, the river Elle flows in a southerly direction towards Quimperlé and the broad Atlantic, the main tributary of that stream, springing in the *Montagnes Noires*, and locally called the Scaër brook, trends rather in a westerly course; and as it meanders for miles amid high banks and lonely woods, and is verdant with aquatic weeds at all seasons of the year, it not only supplies ample food to the fowl that frequent it, but affords them a secluded shelter during the prevalence of cold winds and nipping frost on the adjoining coast. Thither, then, for our day's sport we were preparing to proceed with all despatch. But Keryfan was not to be hurried either at his toilet or breakfast-table; and though I chaffed him with being more like the skid of a coach than either of its fore-wheels, no badinage had the slightest effect either in stirring him into quicker action or (I am bound to add) in ruffling his easy temper.

"If he has taken an hour to dress, give him time to feed, do," said Shafto, interposing as the host on Keryfan's behalf; "for however late we may be, the chances are we shall not see a human being nor hear a shot fired for the day, except from our own guns, in that secluded valley."

"Then," said Keryfan, "under those circumstances it would simply be insane to quit this table in a hurry and go half-fed into such a desolate wilderness;" and as Annette had just brought in a fresh dish of *Côtelettes de chevreuil* piping hot, he grasped his knife and fork with renewed vigour, and never dropped them again till he had finished the last cutlet. Dear old Keryfan—but old only in the language of love—he was certainly difficult to move when his head was in the manger, and engaged in the important business of taking in his complement of stock when a day's work was before him, but still more difficult to stir if he was sacrificing to the Graces, by paying tribute (which he held to be the first duty of man) to his sacred person. Yet, once afield and in pursuit of game, who could beat him, no matter how rough the work nor how long the day? His dawdling, luxurious, and even lazy habits at home presented, in truth, a strange contrast to those he exhibited in the forest or on the mountain side, where, keen as a sparrow-hawk after his prey, his energy and perseverance seemed never to flag, his passion for the chase never to grow cold.

We then started for the stream; and, although we stepped along briskly, it took an hour and a half ere we hit the nearest bend of it—our course over the pathless wilds being impeded by rock and heather, copse and broom, throughout the whole distance; and yet that distance, to judge by the eye, could not have been more than a league and a half at most. We then divided forces, Shafto taking downstream with Owen Mawr, who carried a *carnassière* over his shoulder big enough to bag a wolf, while Keryfan and I turned upwards, with my Breton servant, Noel Postollec, in attendance on us.

Duck and teal were more plentiful than I ever saw them on fresh-water before; and the only precaution necessary for getting at them was to keep clear of the banks on the straight reaches, and come in suddenly upon the pools in the bends of the river, where they were too busy in nozzling for their food to hear the sound of our approaching footsteps. The first pool we drew produced a couple of duck which rose under the muzzle of Keryfan's gun; up went the piece deliberately to his shoulder, and giving the game, as he was wont, fair law, he drew first one trigger, then the other. Both caps exploded, but failed to ignite the powder, and instantly the duck, with a quack of delight at their escape, were winging their way in wild flight beyond the range of **my two** barrels. **An** ejaculation not usual with Keryfan, and certainly not fit for **ears** polite, burst from his lips, as he followed the birds with his eye, marvelling at their luck, and reprobating his own in no measured tones. "It's the old story," he went on—"trusting **to** another what I suppose I ought to do myself—namely, clean my own gun: it's what you, Frank, always do for yourself, and I am coming to the conclusion that, with all the dirt, it is the right thing to do in the end."

"No doubt about that," I replied. "**No less** than three personal friends of my own have had their forefingers and thumbs **shattered** by the explosion **of their powder** flasks, owing entirely to the careless way in which their **guns** had been cleaned. A bit of tow remains behind in the breech, and either the gun misses fire, **or worse consequences ensue on** reloading the discharged barrel."

A good hour **was lost** ere we could get Keryfan's gun **into** shooting order again; and I think it will teach him a lesson of self-dependence which **he** will **not readily forget**. The Faucheux breech-loaders were then only known to **a** few, even in France—a great **boon** as regards **time** saved in cleaning, safety, **and** rapidity in loading, **and other advantages.** For the first **half-hour or so** we could hear the **roar of** Shafto's heavy gun ringing **constantly** through the woods; **but either he killed** what he shot at, **or the fowl** winged seawards, **for** not **a** head came up to **enliven** the dull hour wasted **over** Keryfan's gun. At length **we** were off again; **and** from that **time till the shades of** night **made** it a hard matter **to see** even a duck **on the** wing between your gun-barrel and the **dark** woods in the background, we scarcely passed a bend in the brook without springing duck or teal, the latter numbering as many as five or six in a cluster, the former rarely exceeding a couple or a leash at a time.

It often happens that in shooting, "the first blow is half the battle," and if a man begins badly, he is very apt to go on so throughout the day. But, happily, Keryfan's *contretemps* at starting in no wise affected his nerves afterwards. We had arranged to shoot the bends alternately first, and four times in succession he killed his right and left at duck, without giving me a chance to help him in the matter; though, when a leash rose, the crumb necessarily fell to my lot. In the midst of our sport, a mallard I had shot at and wounded made the best of his way, high in the air, direct for the sea. Suddenly, however, a pirate hove in sight in the form of a peregrine falcon, and, darting after the mallard, like a fleet greyhound after a beaten deer, struck it so fierce a blow in the nape of the neck, that the quarry was instantly paralysed, and fell like a rag to the earth, literally

"Decidit exanimis, vitamque reliquit in astris
   Aëriis——"

Noel, who picked up the bird stone-dead, baulked the pirate of his prey; yet, after the closest examination, no marks of violence could be detected about the head or neck; and if we had not witnessed the *coup* with our open eyes, our little jury must have pronounced an open verdict as to the cause of death.

Although on several occasions we managed to floor more than a brace of teal at a rising, the duck, so generally found in couples only, afforded by far the prettiest shooting; they certainly did not slip away so rapidly as the smaller bird; and, presenting from their larger size an easier mark, Keryfan missed but one for the day; that, however, with one of Eley's green cartridges in my left barrel, I was lucky enough to kill after him at a distance of nearly seventy yards. On rejoining Shafto at a small auberge on the road between Scaër and Gourin, our two Bretons compared notes

—the *carnassière* of Owen Mawr being full to repletion, while Noel, who had slung the game over his shoulders and around his waist, fairly staggered under the weight, and looked, enveloped as he was in feathers, more like a mythological harpy, with a man's face and the body of a vulture, than like a human being. However, we soon adjusted the load more equally among the whole party; and leaving enough to maintain the poor aubergiste and his family for a whole week, with two couple of duck and teal for the Curé, whom the aubergiste described as *un brave garçon*, we struggled back through heather and broom; and if, as we gained the gates of the Hermitage, the leg-labour had been somewhat wearisome, we had, at least, nothing to complain of in the fine day's sport we had so thoroughly enjoyed.

CHAPTER XXVI.

MEANING to stay only ten days or a fortnight at the Hermitage, Keryfan and myself were one morning busily preparing for our departure as the latter period drew near, when, Shafto catching sight of the grand portmanteau mounted on a couple of chairs, and Keryfan superintending Annette in the arrangement of its internal compartments—numerous as those of pea-green Hayne's dressing-case—pressed us so earnestly not yet to desert him, that we gladly consented to hold on for another fortnight; and accordingly the portmanteau, with its fancy buckles and brass studs, was shunted forthwith to a position less suggestive of departure than that of the supporting chairs; namely, to the vacant space underneath its proprietor's own bed.

But the fortnight too soon came to an end, and towards the last day or two of our stay at these hospitable quarters we were looking for redlegs in some broomy ground on the south side of the mountain, when, just as we had sprung a covey of eight birds, out of shot, a French chasseur, with a Breton servant, hove in sight, and, coming directly towards us, indicated that he had marked in the whole covey, and would have great pleasure in conducting us to the *remise*, which lay in a hollow valley at least half-a-mile away. This most polite, and, as we thought at the time, most disinterested offer was of course thankfully accepted; and trudging on in company together we discovered that the stranger was an officer, whom we had met at Concarneau, and that he had wandered thus far in search of game, which, owing to the garrison and braconniers, had become lamentably scarce in the neighbourhood of that seaport. The *remise* proved to be a patch of close, stubby gorse, in which the birds would be quite certain to lie dead as stones; for it was impossible they could run a yard in such a cover, wont, as their habit is, to give leg-bail when there is a chance of doing so; and as even the setters found it a difficult matter to force their way through the prickly mass, Shafto suggested that we should form line and tread it out piecemeal, as the only mode of getting the birds to rise from so strong a place.

Accordingly we proceeded at once to adopt this plan; and the strange chasseur, whom we afterwards discovered to be a Capitaine Rainault, was offered, as a point of etiquette, his choice of position, right or left wing, or centre, whichever he preferred. To our great surprise, however, he stoutly refused to use his gun; but, at the same time volunteered to help in beating up the game, insisting that, as we had found the covey in the first place, the privilege of shooting it belonged exclusively to us. But Keryfan, whose good-nature would not permit him to take advantage of the stranger's scruples, planted himself in the old palaver attitude, and proceeded deliberately to argue the point on the very edge of the gorse. "Good," said he; "we certainly were the first to find the birds, but, in all probability, we should never have seen them again if you had not kindly interposed and given us this information; so pray consider that you are fairly entitled to share the sport with us."

His rhetoric, however, was of little use; for the Captain, handing his gun to the Breton servant, and taking possession of his staff, jumped into the gorse, saying jauntily, as he did so, that he wished to take a lesson in shooting from the English chasseurs, of whose exploits such marvellous accounts had reached the Concarneau garrison. The cover was then drawn carefully, and seven out of the eight birds bagged in so many shots; the eighth would probably have shared the same fate had he not risen wildly at a long distance, and so escaped. An outburst of applause from the Captain, followed the success of every shot; and so enthusiastic was the spirit in which he entered into the sport, that if the setters had not been too quick for him, he would have saved them the trouble of retrieving the game as it fell dead or fluttering into the prickly gorse. No schoolboy out for a holiday, or on a poaching excursion, could have been more eager to handle his birds than he was; then he arranged their feathers, admired the beautiful plumage on the breasts of the cock-birds, and finally, ere depositing them in the *carnassière*, which Owen Mawr pointedly held wide open, he declared they were the finest red-legs he had ever seen in Brittany.

All the while there was so much simplicity in his manner that it was impossible to suspect he had any ulterior object in view beyond the mere admiration of the birds and the love of sport; added to which, although he continued to work like a day labourer in beating for us, he steadily still refused to use his gun for the rest of the day. So, altogether, we were not a little puzzled to account for the unusual, and, in the matter of shooting, the disinterested part he took during the time he remained in our company. But the secret came out in five minutes after he had quitted us for Concarneau. Shafto, having insisted on his carrying back with him a good portion of the game, proceeded forthwith to pack the modest and empty *carnassière* borne by the Breton attendant full to the very brim; and not only did the Captain offer no objection to this measure, but his eyes sparkled with delight as he stood by and watched Shafto cramming bird after bird into the bag, till it positively could not have held another head. He then, after many protestations of gratitude and kindly feeling, bid us adieu, and went on his way rejoicing.

In the meantime the Breton had revealed to Owen Mawr that

x

long as he had followed him, he had never seen the Captain kill a single head of game; that, day after day, he fired away more powder and shot than any officer at Concarneau, but all in vain; and that his very dogs had forsaken him, disgusted with his malpractice. "And I, too," added the Breton, "would have done the same long since, if I had not been well paid for enduring the tantalising sight." This inability, then, on his part, was the sole ground on which he declined to use his gun in our company; and intensely as he enjoyed the sport of seeing the birds knocked down, his consciousness of being unable himself to add to the bag impelled him altogether to abstain from shooting rather than run the risk of exposing himself to our ridicule.

On returning towards the Hermitage, as we clambered over a piece of rocky ground forming a kind of crest to an old oak forest that stretched away for miles in the vale below, the setters suddenly came on a wild cat, which, quick as lightning, managed to dodge in and out of the rocks, and finally to take refuge in the trunk of a hollow tree before we could get even a snap-shot at it. Shafto alone had viewed the animal; and, as it was evidently on a marauding expedition among the conies that frequented these rocks, he did his utmost to induce one of the dogs to enter the tree and bolt the beast from his stronghold. But the dog knew too well the danger of putting his nose into such hot quarters, and prudently kept it outside. Shafto, however, determined not to be beaten, commenced rolling some large stones against the butt of the tree, till he had fairly blocked up every cranny by which the brute could escape. "Now then," said he, puffing and panting under his labour, "methinks he'll keep till morning, when we'll smoke him out or cut down the tree if that won't stir him."

"And of course you'll shoot him as he bolts," said Keryfan, who was seated on a boulder hard by, quietly smoking his pipe, and marvelling at the strength and adroitness which Shafto had displayed in completing the blockade. "When Ajax, the son of Telamon, hurled the ponderous rock at Hector that crushed his buckler and brought the hero to his knees, I doubt much," continued Keryfan, "if it was half as heavy as that last millstone you have just added to the cairn."

"Safe bind, safe find," said Shafto; "and now it would puzzle, I think, his big Bengal brother to break out of that prison in anything less than twenty-four hours. But we won't shoot the varmint—no, with a few minutes' law he'll give the hounds some trouble to catch him in the rocky cover below; and, as the brute will probably make the best of his way back to his old haunts, he may show us some more of his family ere we have quite done with him."

So the next morning we were at him again, and this time with three couple of hounds, a hatchet, a crowbar, and a bundle of crackers, manufactured by Keryfan expressly for the work. But these last, as it happened, were not required; for no sooner were the rocks removed by the application of the crowbar, and the aperture fairly laid bare, than, with one stroke of the hatchet, out dashed the cat almost in Shafto's face, its eyes flashing fire, and every hair on its short tail bristling up like the crest on a boar's neck. Nothing so wild and scared in its look and action had ever been seen by me before or since; but so rapid were its movements, that it was impossible to catch more than a glimpse of the brute as it shot, like a meteor, into the scrub below. Shafto then looked at his watch, and when five minutes had elapsed, sounded the signal to let go the hounds; but in consequence of their eagerness to be quit of the couples, and Owen's delay in liberating them, a good ten minutes' law was obtained by the cat ere they were clapped upon the scent. This, however, proved rather to be a help than an impediment to the sport, for, in consequence of the cat's incarceration, the scent emitted by the brute was tenfold stronger than it would otherwise have been had it been found at large; and thus, from the impetuous dash with which the hounds pursued it, the cat, with less law, would have probably taken to tree immediately. As it was, a rattling good run for an hour or more, from Pen-kerrig Hill to the lowest point of the Kilvern covers, was the fortunate result. The cat then, being apparently beaten, sought refuge under the roots of a gigantic alder-tree which, half-uprooted, fairly bridged over the brook that fretted and foamed 'neath its shade. From the worn condition of its upper bark, the tree had evidently been long used as a crossing-place during the prevalence of floods, not only by the peasantry, but probably by the wild animals frequenting the adjoining forests; and the cat, in seeking refuge under its roots, could scarcely have chosen a stronger holt.

The hounds turned to and marked uproariously, working with teeth and claws as if they would tear up the tree. But while they are thus engaged, let me relate an anecdote which, in the matter of securing the cat for the night and turning it out before the hounds in the morning, comes freshly to mind on the present occasion. Peter Horsall, a well-known squire and justice of the peace, living within a short distance of the wildest coast of the south of Devon, was on a winter's evening entertaining a party of friends at dinner, when the cry of "A wreck!" rung through his hall, and a man rushed breathlessly into the dining-room to announce, with the exception of one living creature, the total loss of a foreign ship and its crew.

"And what creature is it?" inquired the justice, whose interest as lord of the manor was naturally roused by these tidings.

"Plaize your worship," said the countryman, "'tis a Jesuit. Us have a caught 'un, and want to know what us be to do with 'un?"

"A Jesuit! a Jesuit!" repeated the puzzled squire, looking round for imformation in vain to his equally puzzled guests; and at last, coming to the conclusion that it was some wild animal from beyond the seas, he resolved on having a day's sport with it, and thus gave his orders—" Shut 'un up in the barn, John, for the night, and then," said he, " us'll turn him out before the hounds in the morning."

The schoolmaster at this period had evidently not penetrated into that district. But to return to the sport. In the absence of a terrier it was found impossible for some time to bolt the cat, till at length Keryfan hit upon a plan which, with a few strokes of the hatchet, did the work most effectually. The alder being supported on the opposite bank by one of its limbs only, and that not a very bulky one, it was evident, if this prop was cut away, that the weight of the tree would bring it bodily to the ground, and, by tearing up the roots, would expose the cat to the open attack of the hounds. Accordingly, a few vigorous strokes severed the propping limb, and, instantly following, down came the mighty tree level with the waters; at the same moment out shot the cat, like a scared fiend, and, plunging into the brook, attempted to gain the opposite bank. But its efforts were vain: the hounds were on it, and in the space of two minutes the stripy wild beast, than which I scarcely ever saw a handsomer, was torn into "a hundred tatters of brown."

That night we had the company of a French gentleman at the Hermitage, who loudly deplored the waste committed by the loss of the skin and body of the cat. " I can understand your regretting the loss of the skin," I said, " because you turn all skins so adroitly to account in your country, but am puzzled to know what use you would have made of the body."

" Puzzled ? " he replied, as if wondering at my simplicity. " Well, sir, it would have made a delicious *ragoût*, and with far more flavour than that of the finest wild rabbit."

" What ! eat a cat ? " I ejaculated, with an air of disgust which, I fear, I took no pains to conceal.

" Yes," he said ; " I have shot and eaten many, and would

strongly recommend you to try the next you kill; but, of course, you should cut off the head first, and then hang up the carcase in a fig-tree to mellow and make it tender."

Here, then, was the very trite motto, "*Chacun a son goût*," exemplified to the letter; and although at first I thought he was hoaxing me, I had afterwards ample proof that his statement was nothing more nor less than the naked truth.

Shafto, by his long residence among the French, had himself become an accomplished cook, and, with Annette for his scullery-maid, could manufacture various dishes, and especially soups, with consummate art and proficiency. The latter, so far as I am able to judge, is usually a less generous mixture among our neighbours on that side of the channel, probably because our meat is better, and less water is used in its composition. Shafto, however, had a method in the concoction of soup which rendered it unrivalled in strength and flavour by any I have ever tasted at home or abroad. His plan was simply this for the week round: A vast earthenware *pot-au-feu* stood simmering among the embers of his wood-fire from morning to night and night to morning, and was thus supplied, day after day, with the stock and materials needful for producing and replenishing its contents. On Monday, a shin of beef, say 10lbs., simmered gently all day in a gallon and a-half of water, Annette taking care to keep it well skimmed, and about an hour before dinner adding the usual vegetables.

On Tuesday, the vegetables being carefully extracted by means of a colander, a brace of uncooked partridge and a little fresh water were popped in to the beef, and the whole left to simmer and amalgamate as on the day before.

On Wednesday, another brace of birds, roasted brown, with water if required, were added to the *pot-au-feu*. On Thursday, the character of the mixture was altogether changed by the addition of a couple of woodcock or half-a-dozen snipe, which, after simmering all day, imparted a most delicious gamy flavour to the whole concoction. On Friday, what remained of the shin of beef at the bottom was fished out, and a couple of rabbits substituted for stock, water added if required: this, too, was a soup than which no better was ever set before a London alderman. Then on Saturday, the concoction assumed again a totally changed colour and flavour: a fresh hare, with a handful of peppercorns, was added to the ingredients, which, as they now nearly filled the *pot-au-feu* with a variety of game, produced a hare soup of the finest and most delicate character. The amalgamation of the whole on Sunday was positively perfect; but as the *débris* of bone and meat accumulated upwards, Annette at the last found some difficulty in expressing the liquor from the mass below, although, as the palmer of old was wont to use his scallop-shell when expressing water from the bibulous sand, she managed with an iron ladle to squeeze up enough—the very essence of game—to supply our wants. This ended the week. The *pot-au-feu* was then emptied, and its contents fetched every Monday morning by some poor peasant women occupying a hamlet about a league from the Hermitage, to whom, doubtless, the food must have proved little less than a God-send.

Having now given a long list of the most stirring events connected with forest life in Brittany, I dare not inflict on the reader a more minute detail of our daily adventures; although, among ourselves, sundry incidents were never wanting to mark one day's sport from another, and to create an ever-varying interest in the wild scenes by which we were surrounded in that primitive country. But as there is one description of sport to which hitherto no allusion has been made, namely, that of wrestling—a sport ancient and popular among the Bretons of Cornouaille—I propose in the next chapter to describe a meeting that took place at Pleyben, where the athletes had assembled in great force to compete for prizes and establish their prowess in the wrestling ring. This non-forestal **event,** however, was summer affair, and occurred many a long day after we had taken **leave of our self-exiled host** and his strange isolated home at the Hermitage.

CHAPTER XXVII.

The people inhabiting Pleyben and the surrounding district are probably as purely Breton as any in Lower Brittany; for there the old Celtic ballads of the sixth century may still be heard at their festive meetings, and there many a legend and many a quaint custom, half pagan and half Christian, traceable even to an earlier period, is still retained by the descendants of the ancient race with singular tenacity and devotion. The manly game of wrestling, too, of long standing in the country, is still to the fore; and although they have had no Homer to chronicle the achievements of their antique heroes, long passed away, the names of many such are still handed down from generation to generation, and their prowess in the ring recorded with just pride throughout the region of Cornouaille.

The very name of *Ar Gourren*, which is the Breton term for a wrestling-match, indicates its classic origin, that being also the Breton for the crown or prize awarded to the successful wrestler. In the "Testamant Nevez," however, the word, as used by St. Paul in reference to the Isthmian Games so well-known to the Corinthians, is spelt *Gurunen*, which of course is a corruption of *corona*, the crown bestowed on the victor in the athletic sports of old Rome at a subsequent period, the translation being doubtless made from a Latin rather than the Greek text into the Breton language.

From the adoption of the word *ar gourren*, then, it may fairly be inferred that the game of wrestling was derived from the Romans who, in the time of Cæsar, occupied in great numbers the country of Armorica, when it was constituted a province and called "Lugdunensis Secunda;" but, from the still earlier visits of the Phœnicians to that country, it may have had even an older origin, though, as it has been already remarked, the Bretons have had no ancient chronicler to record the fact. A comparatively modern one, however, has informed us how, on the Field of the Cloth of Gold, in the time of Francis I., a grand wrestling-match took place between the French and English athletes; and how, when England gained the mastery, the greatest regret was expressed that the Bretons had not been sent for to oppose the English, as they were deemed unconquerable champions in this manly game. The accounts, too, of the treasurers to the Dukes of Brittany constantly make mention of sums of money given to their wrestlers; it being the object of the Government to cultivate the muscle and bodily strength of the people by such gymnastics.

Having so far referred to the antiquity of the sport in that country, let me endeavour to describe a wrestling-match, such as every summer may be seen at Pleyben, a small town in Finisterre, nearly midway between Châteaulin and Châteauneuf-du-Faou. To him, however, who has ever witnessed a gathering for the like purpose in Cornwall or Devon, I cannot, I fear, hope to contribute information either of a novel or startling character; still, although the game may be somewhat similar, a strange difference exists in the picturesque and mediæval appearance of a Breton assemblage from that of our Western counties.

On a favourable grass-plat, and under the shade of a clump of chestnut-trees, the spectators were compelled to form a vast ring, which, although unroped, was admirably kept by a staff of men appointed for that purpose. These, answering in some degree to our sticklers, twirled their whips and sticks with wondrous effect in the face of the crowd; and, besides maintaining the circle, performed the further office of seeing fair play enacted between the combatants. Then, the hubbub of the crowd as some favourite champion stepped manfully into the ring, the shrill squeal of the bagpipes and the rattle of the kettle-drums, created a din equalled only for its discord by our betting-ring and race-course previous to a grand event.

It is impossible to overstate the picturesque appearance of the whole assembly, dressed, as the peasants were, men and women, in the holiday costume peculiar to their own Communes. That of the men, although varying in shape and colour, resembled the fashion of dress worn in the sixteenth century rather than that of the present or any previous age. There was the trunk-hose; the round, short blue or claret-coloured jacket and vest, studded with buttons; the broad garnished leathern belt, encircling the waist and secured by a metal buckle, often of silver, and huge dimensions; and, lastly, the broad-brimmed hat and flowing hair, to finish the quaint picture. But how shall I describe the wonderful caps of the women, especially those from Rosporden, Elliant, and Pont l'Abbé, in the neighbourhood of Quimper, some of which were decorated with straw plaits and some with point lace, very dingy and apparently very precious? They must be seen to be understood; and that can best be done by a visit to Quimper on a fête or a fair-day, when the Bretonnes from the neighbouring Communes throng into the town in all the variety of their gay *coiffures*, voluminous petticoats, and tight-fitting bodices. But, strange to say, that chief ornament of a woman, the hair, is carefully hidden under the cap, and is only revealed to the Paris perruquier, who pays periodical visits to that country, and for a small sum, often nothing more than a cotton pocket-handkerchief, secures a tress of golden hair that shortly after probably adorns the head of some proud duchess, and puts a handsome per-centage into the pocket of the wily trader. At Lanvollon, near Port Rieux, an annual fair is held, to which the peasant-maidens of Côtes-du-Nord and Finisterre resort in swarms; and there come too the Paris perruquiers, or their agents, to bargain with them and carry away, for an old song, grand crops of hair that have been growing, probably without much cultivation, for many a previous year. With a sharp scissors and a practised hand, three snips are sufficient to render the head a bare pole in an instant. Expedition in the matter is important, as not unfrequently after a bargain has been made, the lasses are wont to repent and altogether decline the proposed operation.

But now to the ring. The Greek wrestlers went naked to the fight, their bodies being well lubricated with oil, and sanded afterwards to assist the grip of the hand; but among the Bretons, the combatants were at least decently attired, a close-fitting canvas shirt enveloping the body, with the continuation of the bragon-hose from the waist to the knee, and strong leggings thence to the ankle. The head, however, presented a most grotesque appearance: the long hair, having been carefully drawn back, was plaited with coarse straw into a pig-tail, being less likely in this form to become troublesome to its owner during the ups and downs of the exciting struggle. This process, which is the finishing touch to his toilet, a bystander performs for the combatant, who, on his knees, is receiving at the same time sage counsel from a Nestor interested in his favour. He then springs on his legs, and having selected the prize for which he is prepared to contend, he stalks bare-footed round the ring, and with defiant air challenges a rival to come forth and enter the lists against him. Three times is he bound to repeat this ceremony; and if at the last round no one is found valiant and strong enough to oppose him, it is pronounced a "walk over," and he pockets the prize. If, on the other hand, some daring competitor steps like Ulysses into the arena, and touches the shoulder of this son of

Telamon, a ringing cheer bursts from the crowd, and both heroes prepare forthwith for the encounter.

"Certain preliminaries, however, are still necessary before the struggle actually begins. In order to give proof that no enmity exists between them, the two combatants advance to the centre of the ring, and, shaking hands cordially, swear that as they commence the contest in a friendly spirit, so will they continue to regard each other after the struggle is over. They then make the sign of the cross, to indicate that they are Christians, and have neither had recourse to witchcraft, enchanted herbs, nor made compact with the devil, who, at the expense of their eternal damnation, might give them superhuman strength for the battle. This ceremony over, they and the crowd feel satisfied that so far no foul play has been imported into the match, and that the combatants go to work on equal terms."

They then seize each other, shoulder and hip, deliberately and firmly; and, with legs apart and foreheads fixed against each other, like two rafters of a house, "each propping each," the beams of their backs fairly creak, and the sweat runs down like rain, as, interlocked and with a lively use of the heel on the hollow of the knee, they tug, they strain, till at length one, more breathless and exhausted than the other, is uplifted bodily in the air and thrown on the flat of his back heavily to the ground.

The prize is then awarded to the victor; not such, however, as Achilles offered when Ajax and Ulysses strove in vain for the mastery—not a fireproof tripod, valued at twelve oxen, to the champion; nor a damsel, valued at four oxen, to the vanquished; no, the first prize at Pleyben is simply a hat—fluffy, broad-brimmed, and heavy as the helmet of a dragoon; but yet contended for with as much earnestness and honesty as if it had been a crown of gold.

The wrestlers being barefooted, there was none of that savage shin-kicking which, in the days of Cann and Polkinghorn, often inflicted severe punishment on the legs of our West-country heroes; still, the back kick of the Breton, horny and hardened as the heel is by its contact with the sabot, was no child's play, and served frequently to help the man most adroit in its use to bring his adversary to his knees and weaken the hold that seemed to root him to the ground. Barring the hubbub of the bagpipes and kettledrums, it was in every respect a quiet and orderly meeting; no drunkenness, no foul play, and no savage wrangling. Two or three priests were present, and by their influence on the peasant mind served, doubtless, to keep the crowd under salutary restraint with respect to drink and licentious behaviour. I could not but infer, too, from the little interest they took in the "play," that the object of their attendance was rather to act as *Censores morum* than from any wish to view the *spectacle*, or indicate partizanship with any particular wrestler in his struggle for victory; still, there was a kind, pleasant-faced priest looking on whose eyes twinkled luminously as one of his parishioners stepped out of the ring, prize in hand, and followed by the plaudits of the admiring crowd.

This intermixing of the clerical with the lay population, the shepherds with the sheep of their flocks, in such innocent and manly games, might be extended, I venture to think, with the utmost advantage to both parties in other countries besides that of Lower Brittany; for, where excesses and bad language are checked by the presence of a clergyman, there he cannot be out of place, either in behalf of his own work or for the good of the company in which he is found mixing. My old friend Bob Buckstone thought so too, or, honest and conscientious as he was in all that appertained to his duty as a curate, he never would have devoted two days a week to the mere pastime of fox-hunting, if he had not been convinced that his little parish, numbering but thirty inhabitants, suffered no neglect from this practice; that in the field his presence, so far from giving offence to any, was welcomed by all, and, moreover, had the quiet and unobtrusive effect of checking the utterance of many a coarse word as it rose to the lips of those around him. This was Bob's conviction, and, with his love for the chase, hereditary and inborn as it was, well might he say that "he only wished his whole life had been spent as innocently and happily as in the hunting-field or on the riverside."

Still, his bishop—a man who, by his zeal, industry, and untiring activity did the work of ten ordinary men, and whose eloquence, now, alas! silent for ever, was wont to charm every ear, patrician or proletarian—strongly objected to Bob's hunting tendencies; and, with the hope of persuading or compelling him to renounce them, he summoned him to his palace, where accordingly on a stated day Bob made his appearance.

"I am told, Mr. Buckstone," said his lordship, very gravely, "that you are in the habit of regularly joining a pack of fox-hounds in your neighbourhood; and such a practice being inconsistent with the sacred character of your office, I must beg you to give me a distinct promise that you will renounce it at once so long as you continue to be a curate in my diocese."

"My Lord," said Bob, with an air of remonstrance, but at the same time with the utmost deference, "I neglect no duty; and my health, which is not strong, is greatly benefited by the exercise. I have, too, but a cob pony to ride; so I trust your Lordship will not bind me to give a promise which some day I may be tempted to break."

"And is your nature so weak and your passion for the chase so strong," said the Bishop, somewhat sarcastically, "that not only your word, but interests even of the highest import must needs be sacrificed to such indulgence? What was your reason given you for, but to control your passion? No, Mr. Buckstone, let me have your promise, and be a man and keep it."

Now, Bob's spirit was a very independent one; and to be lectured as if he were a mere schoolboy was not exactly the most judicious mode of dealing with him on this or any other subject. But when he perceived the Bishop's temper was getting the better of his reason, that sense of awe with which he had been inspired, and which, at the commencement of the interview, had brought an icicle to his nose, now vanished like a vapour; and Bob, writhing under the taunt, firmly refused to give the demanded promise.

But the colloquy did not end there. It so happened that a short time previously the newspapers had commented sharply on the appearance of his Lordship at a grand ball given by the Duchess of ———; and the Bishop had written a letter to explain that he had never entered the ball-room at all, but had remained in the ante-room, with the sole object of enjoying the fine music performed by the band on the occasion. This circumstance being fresh in Bob's memory, some imp of mischief must have possessed his tongue when that "unruly member" proceeded to say that, "if there was any moral turpitude in the matter, there was at least as much in going to a dance as in going to hounds."

The cap fitted at once; and the Bishop, taken aback by this counter-hit, instead of continuing to attack Bob's position, was compelled to defend his own. "I know, of course, what you allude to, Mr. Buckstone; but I have already explained, and again repeat, that I never entered the dancing-room, but remained in another apartment enjoying the music."

"My Lord," said Bob, "your position and mine are precisely similar: I delight in the music of the hounds, but am very seldom in the same field with them."

The Bishop's gravity fairly gave way; and feeling the parallel was too accurate to be questioned, he dropped the subject, insisting only that Bob should stay to luncheon with him ere he turned on his homeward route. Before that meal was over Bob became so charmed by the Bishop's good company that he begged his Lordship's acceptance of his cob, an offer, however, which, it need scarcely be added, was most graciously declined. Those two men, the one a poor but honest curate, the other a magnate of unrivalled ability, since that event have both been brought by one sickle to the same level; but who shall say which of the twain is now the more exalted?

When the wrestling at Pleyben had been brought to a close, the bagpipes seemed suddenly inflated with fresh wind and renewed vigour as they struck up a lively air, the prelude to a wonderful dance called the "Jabadao." It is the Breton Fandango; and though most popular among the Bretons *pur sang*, it is utterly unknown beyond the region of Cornouaille. No pen but that of a Frenchman, and he need be a master of the art, could describe intelligibly the saltatory action, the pirouettes, the jigging and figures of the dancers engaged in the "Jabadao." From the name, which so nearly resembles the Spanish word "Zapateo," or the knocking of sabots, the dance probably owes its origin to that country, formerly and in better days the land of song and dance; but, if it does, the grace and elegance said to distinguish the old Asturian "measure" have certainly not descended to the "Jabadao," as at present danced by the Breton peasantry.

The priests, it should be added, were now no longer visible; the wild turn of the music and the passionate delight with which the young men and maidens dashed into the dance had put them to flight; and, although there was nothing bordering on indecency in the exhibition, the close contact of the couples and the pirouettes performed by the lady, when her hand was passed over her head, were enough to disturb the virtue of an anchorite. So, perhaps, it was quite as well on their own account that they did not stay to witness the "Jabadao."

This dance, which is held in high contempt by the French bourgeoisie, is not altogether confined to the peasant class of Lower Brittany; for it has been my lot to meet more than one member of the old Breton noblesse, whose proficiency in footing it was the talk of the country, and who, whenever the tunes of the bagpipe invited them to a caper, never missed an opportunity of mingling with the peasants, and indulging their fancy in this provincial amusement. It was said of a fine young fellow, who frequently joined our wolf-hunting expeditions, a cadet of the ancient house of de Morlaix, that his passion for dancing the "Jabadao" had been the ruin of his life. He was engaged to be married to a lady, who, in addition to great personal charms, was reputed to be the wealthiest heiress in all Brittany; the day had been fixed, the trousseau provided, and wedding guests bidden to the ceremony, from the storm-beaten cliffs of Penmarch to the château of Larochejaquelin on the distant Loire. A week or so before the event was to have taken place, his presence was required at Quimper to meet the father of the bride elect, the Baron St. Pol-de-Leon, between whom and himself certain legal documents, relating to the lady's settlements, were to be signed and attested by both parties. St. Pol, one of the few specimens left of the Grand Monarque School, punctilious, proud, and treating the slightest liberty taken with himself as an affront to his dignity, was duly in attendance at the appointed time. Not so, however, young de Morlaix, who, in passing through a village between Le Faou and Quimper, unfortunately heard the strains of a bagpipe playing the "Jabadao" tune, and, unable to resist the attraction, had fastened his horse to a tree and flung himself into the circle with the spirit of a Spaniard dancing the Bolero.

While he was thus engaged, amusing himself and fascinating a peasant girl, who was the belle of the district and his partner in the dance, the horse broke his bridle, and, turning his head in the direction of his own stable, trotted off unseen by a human being. Still the wild notes of the bagpipes **kept** the revellers going ; and not until de Morlaix, looking at his watch, discovered that already he had overstayed his time, and could only by hard riding keep his appointment at Quimper, did he hurry away from the attractive ring. His dismay, on finding his steed **gone, no** one knew whither, and himself stranded at least three **leagues** short of his destination, may be better imagined than described. However, after tracking the animal a long distance without being able to overtake him, he gave up the chase, and started at once on foot for Quimper, hoping still to catch St. Pol in the town, **and** explain the cause of his delay. But he was too late. The haughty old baron, after waiting two weary hours in the Avocat's office, ordered out his carriage, in an ungovernable rage, declaring his daughter was slighted and himself insulted by this **cool** conduct of de Morlaix. Nor did **the** matter end there. The next day came a challenge, worded in fierce language, and demanding immediate satisfaction for the offence offered. To this, however, de Morlaix returned a mild apologetic answer, explaining his brief **enjoyment of** the " Jabadao" *en route*, and the misadventure with **his horse ;** but **the fiery baron was not to be** appeased, **and,** although no **duel ensued, the match** was broken off, **and de Morlaix never saw the lady afterwards.** The **result, however, made** little or no impression **on his** spirits, for **only a** week after the **event he was the** life **and soul of a party** hunting **with St. Prix's wolf-hounds in his** father's forest ; neithe **was his fancy for** the " **Jabadao"** impaired a whit by the loss of the heiress, but, on the contrary, he never failed to take a turn in it whenever a peasant girl and the bagpipes gave him the chance of doing so ; and he was wont, moreover, to say that, had he been connected with St. Pol, the scruples of the haughty old peer would **probably have** compelled him to give **up** that exhilarating and delightful dance—a sacrifice too painful to be contemplated.

After that day at Pleyben no particular incident worthy of record, with respect to the wild sport of the forest or the social amusements of the people, occurs to my recollection during the remainder of my stay in Brittany. Carhaix being my headquarters, the centre of the roughest and wildest country between St. Brieuc and Douarnenez, the point of divergence from which the best hunting and shooting could be obtained, and the town of all others the least frequented by strangers, I returned thither to pack up my goods and bid adieu to the many Breton friends, gentle and simple, who had shown me no little kindness during my long and pleasant sojourn amongst them. To M. de Leseleuc, a grand specimen of a native gentleman, I was especially indebted for his never-failing courtesy and counsel with respect to the customs of the people, for his hospitality, and, above all, for his good company on many a shooting excursion in the surrounding forests. On shaking him by the hand for the last time, and thanking him for all the favour he had shown me—" It is nothing," he said; " nothing at all: nor can I ever repay the kindness my father received from your countrymen when he was a prisoner of war so long at Wincanton."

Great was my regret on parting with these primitive people, among whom I do not remember to have passed a single unhappy hour; for, wander where I would in search of game, I was never once given to understand that I was an intruder on the soil, nor, with one exception, and that most justifiably, was my *permis de chasse* ever demanded either by a gendarme or a peasant proprietor. I had just shot a woodcock which rose from a spring close to a peasant's homestead; and, as my faithful old Rover brought me the bird, a wild-looking Breton rushed out upon me, exclaiming with great excitement, "That's my fowl; I have been feeding it daily for the last fortnight; there are my traps (*da lindag*) by which I hoped to have caught it."

I looked down, and saw the bog round the spring pegged all

over with horse-hair springles, and the marvel was how the cock managed to evade them even for a single hour. "By what authority are you here," he continued, in an angry strain, "destroying and carrying off the produce of my own property?"

"By the authority of this document," I said confidently, pulling out my *permis de chasse*, and handing it to him for inspection. While he was examining it, literally upside down, I took the woodcock alive out of the old dog's mouth and begged his acceptance of the bird; while, at the same time, opening my tobacco-pouch, always well stocked with *caporal*, I insisted on his filling his own *plaque* with that fragrant and much-coveted tobacco. Had we, like Tam o' Shanter and Souter Johnny, been

"———————— fou' for weeks thegither,"

we could not have become better friends than we did in two minutes. The offerings, especially the latter, acted like magic upon him; and I left with a pressing invitation on his part that I would soon come again and shoot woodcocks in that locality.

The two good hounds I brought with me into Brittany, one of which was bred at Lanharran and the other at Ty-isha, both possessing the same blood with the Welsh hounds now so famous in the Chepstow and Langibby kennels, I left as a legacy to my kind friend M. de St. Prix. The Lanharran hound, however, going astray, was soon after eaten by wolves; but the other, the black and tan "Warrior," took to the rough game at once, and became one of the best hounds for wolf and boar in the Louvetier's pack.

A fair passage in a spanking bullock-craft, called the "Eclipse,' conveyed me in four hours from Port Rieux to Jersey, and thence, taking the mail-steamer on the following morning, I was landed at Southampton comfortably that same evening.

THE END.